Abiding Mission

Abiding Mission

Missionary Spirituality and Disciple-Making
Among the Muslim Peoples of Egypt
and Northern Sudan

DICK BROGDEN
Foreword by David W. Shenk

WIPF & STOCK · Eugene, Oregon

ABIDING MISSION
Missionary Spirituality and Disciple-Making Among the Muslim Peoples of Egypt
and Northern Sudan

Wipf & Stock
An Imprint of Wipf and Stock Publishers
199 W. 8th Ave., Suite 3
Eugene, OR 97401

www.wipfandstock.com

PAPERBACK ISBN: 978-1-4982-9330-3
HARDCOVER ISBN: 978-1-4982-9332-7
EBOOK ISBN: 978-1-4982-9331-0

Manufactured in the U.S.A.   07/06/16

To my father and mother, Richard and Soula Brogden, for teaching me to love Jesus and enjoy abiding in him.

Contents

Tables

Foreword

By David W. Shenk

THIS BOOK IS BOTH disturbing and immensely encouraging. Dick Brogden acclaims the forthright statement of Jesus, "Without me, you can do nothing!" This is coupled with the promise of Jesus: "If you abide in me, and I in you, you will bear much fruit."

Brogden writes within the context of predominantly Muslim Egypt and northern Sudan where the church faces enormous challenges. He serves from within the lands of the ancient Christian desert fathers who invested lifetimes in prayer. However, Brogden is not advocating the retreatist spirituality of the desert monks; rather he calls for a lively and sacrificial engagement that emulates the lives of 7 noteworthy leaders of the western missionary movement within Egypt and Sudan a century ago. Brogden's observation is that the missionary quest for fruitfulness among Muslims is most often focused on strategic programming; however, the command of Jesus is to abide in Jesus extravagantly. Obeying that command is the essence of this book.

I was renewed spiritually reading Brogden's exegetical study of the teachings of Jesus in regard to the vine and the branches (John 15:1–17). I was immensely encouraged reading the biographical sketches of seven missionaries of a century ago who abided in Jesus and whose ministries were extraordinarily fruitful; I was refreshed reading the brief biographies of these missionaries. I was encouraged, reading descriptions of twenty-three contemporary missionaries who abide in Jesus and whose lives bear much fruit. I was surprised and grateful, reading accounts of contemporary missionary leaders who are abiding Christians serving fruitfully.

I was intrigued reading the sociological data with the variety of empirical tools that Brogden used in garnering his findings. I was amazed by the way he wove together the scriptural study with sociological data. He garnered the data and then applied his 76 findings to the contemporary realities of teams serving in Muslim societies in Sudan and Egypt. This book is a feat of scholarly information and insight.

This book merits lively discussion among all Christians serving among Muslims. In fact, missiologists as well as pastors will benefit from Brogden's provocative insights. It will be on my ready-reference shelf for a long time. I expect this book will be read and discussed in the missions' circles with whom I am the most closely associated. I commend this book for all missions' leaders who are positioned to effectuate changes in their organizations!

The essence I shall carry in my soul is that abiding Christians continually commune with Jesus. The most effective approach to abiding is daily immersion in the Word of God and prayer. My impression reading Richard Brogden's tome is that missionaries who abide in Jesus are extraordinarily joyful people. Apparently abiding Christians bear fruit joyfully!

David W. Shenk
Global Consultant with EMM (Eastern Mennonite Mission)

Preface

THIS RESEARCH BEGINS WITH an exegesis of John 15:1–17 to establish what Jesus taught about abiding and bearing fruit in this specific biblical text. Next, it examines the abiding praxis of seven fruitful missionaries to Muslims in North Africa between the years 1880 to 1920: Daniel Comboni (Catholic), Samuel Zwemer (Presbyterian), Oswald Chambers (YMCA/ Pentecostal League), Lillian Trasher (Assemblies of God), Lilias Trotter (Algerian Missions Band), Douglas Thornton (Anglican–CMS), and Temple Gairdner (Anglican–CMS).

The social science portion draws from the exegetical and historical findings to design questions about abiding. These questions were addressed to twenty-three multinational leaders of current church planting teams in Muslim North East Africa representing nine different mission agencies (Assemblies of God World Missions, Frontiers, Africa Inland Missions, Youth With A Mission, Global Missions Service, International Mission Board, Stay On The Spot Ministries, Operation Mobilization, and Pioneers) and eight different nationalities (American, Dutch, Canadian, Korean, Egyptian, Brazilian, Swiss, and Sudanese). These questions probed both the corporate and individual abiding praxis of team leaders. The findings were cross-referenced by a self-administered electronic survey of team members. The findings of each research method were triangulated with one another and with participants' demographic information. The synthesized findings form the data on which the theory of a spirituality that leads to disciple making is based.

This research is based in an epistemological sequence of biblical exegesis, historical reference, social science research, and theory development from the synthesized findings.

The result of this research is a theory of spirituality that posits missionaries who serve among the Muslim peoples of Egypt and northern Sudan and abide by continually communing with Jesus and by lavishing extravagant daily time on Jesus make disciples. The state of abiding requires missionaries to continually commune with Jesus. The discipline of abiding requires missionaries to spend daily blocks of time with Jesus. Neither the state of abiding nor the discipline of abiding is fruitful without the other. If this theory is true, then abiding should be both the first priority of the missionary and the base methodology for mission.

Acknowledgments

I EXPRESS MY THANKS to Dr. DeLonn Rance for believing in me and guiding me through the program as the chair of my committee. He showed me how education can be worship and his passion is an inspiration. I honor Dr. Debbie Gill, Dr. Marvin Gilbert, Dr. Bob Braswell, and Dr. Alan Johnson for guiding me through the dissertation process with such patience and grace. They all are heroes to me: Dr. Gill for her joy; Dr. Gilbert for his gift of encouragement; Dr. Braswell for his quiet brilliance; and Dr. Johnson for his humility and grace. I am grateful to all AGTS faculty and staff for the advice, love, encouragement, and inspiration they have provided along the way. I owe Jackie Chapman at least half my meager kingdom for her tireless editing efforts at every step.

I am indebted to AGWM for their blessing and empowerment to pursue further education. I have been blessed with peerless leaders throughout my mission service. Don Corbin, Jerry Spain, Brian Correll, Greg Beggs, Mike McClaflin, Omar Beiler, and Mark Renfroe are men to whom I have been proud to submit. I bless and honor them.

In ministry and mission all are replaceable—but not in family. My wife Jennifer is the center of my affection and the love of my life. A million PhDs could not equal one moment in her presence. My sons, Luke and Zack, are the light of my eyes and the joy of my heart. I acknowledge nothing on earth is as valuable to me as my family.

I finally and most importantly acknowledge Jesus as my Lord and Savior. He is all I want, and for his glory and his mission I live and breathe and have my being.

Abbreviations

AD	Anno Dominus (Year of our Lord)
AGTS	ssemblies of God Theological Seminary
AGWM	Assemblies of God World Mission
AIM	African Inland Mission
AMI	Antioch Mission International
BA	Bachelor of Arts
BAM	Business as Mission
BMB	Believer from a Muslim Background
BS	Bachelor of Science
CD	Compact Disc
CMS	Church Missionary Society
DF	Degree of Freedom
ESV	English Standard Version
GMS	Global Missions Service
IMB	International Mission Board
LXX	Septuagint
MBB	Muslim Background Believer
NASB	New American Standard Bible
NKJV	New King James Version
NRSV	New Revised Standard Version
OM	Operation Mobilization
P	Population Set

PQ Method	Piles of Statement Numbers in a Q Study
Q	A form of Factor Analysis used in Data Analysis
QS1	Q-sort, Practice
QS2	Q-sort, Values
QSP-F1	Q-sort Factor on "Practice" Research
SA	Self Administrated Electronic Survey
SST	Semi-Structured Interview
STAY	Stay on the Spot Ministries
TL	Team Leader
UPG	Unreached People Group
WWI	World War One
X2	Chi Square Test for Statistical Variance
YMCA	Young Men's Christian Association
YWAM	Youth With A Mission

Introduction

IN A 2007 INTERNATIONAL conference in Pattaya, Thailand, over 500 practitioners from the Muslim world gathered to discuss fruitful practices in
ministry to Muslims. I sat with a group that included veteran missionary/
author David Shenk. Shenk, a Mennonite with years of experience among
Somalis, led the discussion with grace and truth. At the end, he closed the
time with one quiet statement: "My greatest concern in all this is that no one
is thinking or talking about abiding."

A question rose in my mind: "What if the key to reaching Muslims
is not a method but simply abiding in Jesus?" That question led directly
to this research and the resulting theory of spirituality: missionaries who
serve among the Muslim peoples of Egypt and Northern Sudan and abide
by continually communing with Jesus and by lavishing extravagant daily
time on Jesus make disciples. The state of abiding requires missionaries (and
all followers of Christ) to continually commune with Jesus. The discipline
of abiding requires missionaries to daily spend blocks of time with Jesus.
Neither the state of abiding nor the discipline of abiding is fruitful without
the other.

BACKGROUND

Billy Burr, Area Director for Assemblies of God World Missions—Southern
Africa first proposed the concept of a time tithe to Africa Regional Director
Don Corbin in the 1990s.[1] The concept parallels the financial tithe. Christians believe that all resources belong to God and they return ten percent
of his money as a sign of his overarching Lordship. He then, in turn, blesses
what is less, stretching it to meet all needs and the occasional want. A tithe
of a day equals two hours and 24 minutes. The essence of Burr's concept

1. Conversation with Don Corbin, July 10, 2009, in Springfield, MO, and with Billy
Burr, August 6, 2009, in Orlando, FL.

theorizes extravagant daily time spent in the presence of Christ, primarily in prayer and reading the Word, leads to fruitful missiology and missionary praxis—namely making disciples.

This research examines the concept of abiding as found in John 15:1–17. Second, it examines the lives of fruitful missionary leaders in the Muslim context of Egypt and Northern Sudan (1880–1920) to see their abiding praxis. Third, it examines and analyzes the abiding praxis (personal and corporate) of current team leaders of church-planting teams among the Muslim peoples of Egypt and Sudan. Finally, it attempts to integrate research findings into a theory of spirituality in which abiding in Jesus empowers missionaries among the Muslim peoples of Northeast Africa to make disciples.

My qualifications for study include nineteen years of service in the Muslim world. I worked with Muslims in Northern Sudan for fifteen years and was an active team leader in Sudan for ten of those years. I currently serve as an overseer for team leaders in North Africa and the Middle East, and am active in mobilizing and training team leaders for the Muslim peoples of the Arab world. In September 2012, my wife and I opened a church-planting team training center in Cairo, Egypt, which prepares teams and team leaders for service across the Arab Muslim world.

PURPOSE STATEMENT

The purpose of the study is to develop a theory of spirituality that leads to fruitful disciple making in the Muslim contexts of North East Africa.

PROBLEM STATEMENT

The study problem is to discover the impact abiding has on the disciple making of fruitful missionaries—particularly those making disciples planting churches in Muslim contexts.

RESEARCH QUESTIONS

To achieve the purpose of this study, these research questions will be considered:

1. What does Jesus teach about abiding and fruitfulness in John 15:1–17?

2. How did fruitful missionaries to Muslim peoples in Egypt and Northern Sudan (1880–1920) abide in Jesus?

3. How do contemporary disciple-making and church-planting missionaries (particularly team leaders) in Egypt and Northern Sudan (2012–2013) abide in Jesus, both personally and corporately?

The answers to these questions provide the basis for a formulation of a spiritual theory of discipleship.

RESEARCH LOGIC

The research logic is: (1) an exegesis of John 15:1–17 to review what Jesus taught about abiding and bearing fruit; (2) a review of exemplary fruitful missionaries in North East Africa between 1880 and 1920 to examine their abiding praxis; and (3) the use of social science tools to examine the abiding praxis of current leaders of church-planting teams among Muslims in Egypt and northern Sudan. These reviews and research will examine the lives of those who have been fruitful to discern what their abiding looked like and how their abiding impacted fruitfulness.

SIGNIFICANCE OF STUDY

This study is significant on three levels. Personally, I desire to bear lasting fruit among Muslim peoples. I want to arrive at the end of my missionary service sweeter, humbler, kinder, and more passionate for Muslim souls and more in love with Jesus than at the beginning, but I also want to make disciples. Organizationally, I want Assemblies of God World Mission (AGWM) team leaders with whom I collaborate and train to last in the Muslim world, to give lives to their teams, to be used in making disciples and planting churches among Muslims, and to bear lasting fruit.

Globally, the greatest challenge and opportunity in missions is the Islamic block. Much attention is directed to the practical/missiological aspects of mission to Muslims, but equal research and attention must be given to the spiritual formation aspects. If a theory of spirituality in which abiding in Christ empowers church-planting team leaders among the Muslim peoples of Egypt and northern Sudan to make disciples can be proposed, examined, clarified, and implemented, it will become the backbone of praxis in the efforts to see credible church planting efforts among every Muslim people. This will be a great leap forward in hastening the return of the Lord and the fulfillment of Revelation 5:9—Muslims of every tongue and tribe around the throne of heaven.

LIMITATIONS AND DELIMITATIONS

Theological research in this study will be limited to the Johannine use of abiding in John 15:5. This is not a study on all fruitfulness, but on the specific fruit of making disciples. The assumption of John 15:5 is that fruitfulness is guaranteed if missionaries will abide in Christ. Historically, this study will be limited to seven fruitful (disciple-making) missionaries to Muslims who served in Egypt and northern Sudan between 1880 until the end of World War I in 1920.[2] This specific period was chosen as it begins with the end of the Great Century of Christian mission (late 1800s) and ends with the beginning of the Pentecostal Century of Christian mission in the early 1900s. Many contemporary missiological issues are a repetition of what greater souls and greater minds resolved in that time period.

I intentionally did not try to falsify my theory by looking for missionaries who made disciples without abiding in Jesus. I acknowledge that the sovereign God can do whatever he wants with whomever he wants. There are multiple examples of strange and sinful missionaries making disciples. This research is limited to identifying missionaries of sterling reputation who were or are fruitful and examine their abiding praxis to look for commonalities. My contemporary research is limited to the leaders of evangelical church-planting teams among Muslims in Egypt and Northern Sudan.[3] Both spouses from a team will be interviewed, however, one will be randomly selected to answer a unique research question.

DEFINITIONS OF KEY TERMS

The following terms are used in this dissertation. I created these definitions to fit the context of the discussion.

Abiding: This research will present a broad and flexible definition of abiding sourced in John 15:1–17, recognizing that abiding is both a discipline of abiding and a state of abiding, which have components of obedience and time.

---

2. While the Armistice that ended fighting was signed in 1918, it was not until the peace conference of 1920 that the war officially ended with terms settled.

3. While this study focuses on Egypt and northern Sudan, there are a few interviews of missionaries working among Somalis and one interview of a team leader who now resides in the Comoros islands but used to live and minister in Sudan.

Baptism of the Holy Spirit: This is understood to be an ongoing experience with the Holy Spirit subsequent to salvation, which empowers the supplicant for witness according to Acts 1:8.

Disciple: A convert to Christ or a follower of Christ[4] who is growing in obedience to Christ.

Fruit: A continuum of meanings that include everything from Christ-like character (Gal 2:22–23) to souls saved (Rom 16:5). John, however, in chapters 14–17, uses "fruit" to refer to "disciples" (see section 2).

Fruitful: This refers to making disciples, but disciples are neither limited to converts, nor those influenced while the missionary is alive. A disciple may be a young missionary who is mentored, or it may be a missionary or national believer who studies the life of the deceased missionary and is impacted (posthumous discipleship).

Longevity: Residential missional presence in Muslim contexts for longer than ten years.

Missions: The work of making disciples and planting the church among unreached peoples.[5]

Spirituality: Refers to how an individual relates to and interacts with both the triune God and the spirit world of demons and angels. Particular attention is given to Scripture, interceding, fasting, meditating, praying in the Spirit, worshipping, and waging spiritual warfare.

ASSUMPTIONS

This research assumes while every missionary is saved and has some measure of a devotional life, a cursory walk with Christ cannot empower fruitful longevity (disciple making) in Muslim contexts. A basic assumption in John 15:1–17 is one can be in the vine (in Christ), but not abiding. Abiding is not assumed to be the same as faith or a perfunctory devotional life. This research also assumes the Baptism of the Holy Spirit is intended for

---

4. As will be repeated in this dissertation, disciples are not necessarily converts. Samuel Zwemer did not lead Muslims to the Lord according to the historical record, but he discipled a whole generation of missionaries who lived in the Islamic world. Disciples are not necessarily made while the disciple maker is living. Oswald Chambers made more disciples posthumously through his writings than he did while alive.

5. Orthodox evangelical thinking has restricted "missions" to mean evangelism and church planting (Robert Hall Glover, C. Gordon Olson, George Peters, and Harvey Hoekstra) as opposed to what C. Peter Wagner denounces as "mission"—a broadening of the definition to include the social gospel and a shift from making disciples to doing good works in the world.

everyone,[6] and if a missionary is filled with the Spirit, he or she will be more effective than otherwise. Both Pentecostal (in praxis[7]) and non-Pentecostal leaders will be interviewed and their theological stances recorded in order to compare responses between Pentecostal and non-Pentecostal team leaders. This research assumes what Jesus said in John 15:5 is true: "He who abides in me, and I in him, bears much fruit." This research assumes that most missionaries are not abiding in Christ to the level he intends and that if missionaries learn to abide deeper in Jesus, they will be more fruitful and will make disciples that abide.

6. The implied assumption is that a missionary filled with the Spirit will be more effective in making disciples than themselves unfilled. Increased fruitfulness is in reference to themselves, not to another. This assumption is not examined or analyzed in this research of seven historic missionaries but warrants further investigation.

7. Pentecostal "in praxis" means that not only do these team leaders believe in subsequent experiences and empowerments of the Holy Spirit post-conversion, but they also lead their teams in the operation of the spiritual gifts and ecstatic prayer.

SECTION 1

Exegetical Foundations

THIS SECTION CONTAINS THE exegesis of John 15:1–17 with particular attention given to John's use of the terms abiding and fruit.

1

Exegetical Background of John 15:1–17

HERMENEUTICAL BACKGROUND

The Bible is a missiological document. Missions—unveiled in Genesis, expounded by every contributing author of Scripture, and celebrated in Revelation—centers on the God who desires worship from every tribe, tongue, people, and nation. Everyone who bears Christ's name must direct energy toward this passion of God.

John 15:1–17 highlights the harvest goal of God—many disciples made. It also reveals the means by which this goal shall be obtained—abiding in Christ. This passage describes three categories: (1) The disciples who abide in Christ will, in turn, make lasting disciples; (2) not all who are in Christ are abiding; not all who abide produce the disciples they should (John reveals remedial measures for both those categories); (3) those who refuse Christ's mission and face removal from the vine and utter destruction.

The hermeneutical background of John 15:1–17 is summarized in this chapter.

JOHN'S MISSIOLOGICAL GOSPEL

The Gospel of John is a missiological gospel.[1] "Since John wrote his gospel in order to fulfill a mission task, it is logical to assume that mission is a fairly

1. Martin Erdman in his chapter "Mission in John's Gospel and Letters" in *Mission in the New Testament: An Evangelical Approach* lists in a footnote on page 208–209

prominent theme in John's writings."[2] John conveys a Christological missiology in John 20:31. Though essentially a theologian,[3] his missionary status enhanced his theological reflection. In Johannine writings, God's mission and Christians' mission interconnect.

> For John, then, the mission of Jesus, the mission of the Paraclete, and the mission of the community are tightly stitched together . . . These missions are interrelated. All . . . are accomplished in the arena of the "world" and, ultimately have the salvation of the world as their goal . . . [The Gospel of John] distinctive as it is, shares with the rest of the Gospels a universal outlook and a missionary orientation . . . The Gospel is "mission" in orientation because its final word to the community is that authentic disciples of Jesus are "sent" as he was sent, to the whole world, to bring it life.[4]

E. Ridley Lewis says that John "has an eye to the whole world of his time as it stands in need of salvation, Jews and Greeks, slaves and free, men and women, educated and uneducated, and to all alike he offered then, as his gospel book still offers, the gift of the knowledge of God, perfectly manifested in Jesus."[5] John's purpose is broader than conversion; he also intends to equip those who believe for mission.

> The conviction itself which the Evangelist aims at producing is twofold . . . The whole narrative must therefore be interpreted with a continuous reference to these two ruling truths . . . Each element in the fundamental conviction is set forth as of equal moment. The one (Jesus is the Christ) bears witness to the special preparation which God had made; the other (Jesus is the Son of God) bears witness to the inherent universality of Christ's mission.[6]

In John's gospel, the evangelist not only establishes the deity of Christ, he also elucidates the need for this Christ to be preached to all people everywhere and details the means by which this is to be done. John uses the

other scholars who support a missiological premise for the Gospel of John. They include W. C. van Unnik, John A. T. Robinson, Leon Morris, D. A. Carson, Miguel Rodriguez Ruiz, Teresa Okure, J. C. B. Mohr, Andreas Köstenberger, Philip H. Towner, David Bosch, and A. Wind.

2. Larkin and Williams, *Mission in the New Testament*, 209.

3. Eckman, *Studies in the Gospel of John*, 20.

4. Senior and Stuhlmueller, *The Biblical Foundations of Mission*, 292.

5. Lewis, *Johannine Writings and Other Epistles*, 23.

6. Cook, *The Holy Bible According to the Authorized Version*, xl.

word ποστέλλω (I send with a commission) more than any other writer, with forty-one references to the sending of the Son.[7] John's Gospel, then, is missiological in intent and pedagogy.[8]

PURPOSE OF JOHN'S GOSPEL

John explicitly reveals his purpose in writing: "And truly Jesus did many other signs in the presence of his disciples which are not written in this book; but these are written that you may believe that Jesus is the Christ, the Son of God, and that believing you may have life in His name" (John 20:30–31).[9] He reveals that to believe in Jesus is to elevate him, and he concentrates on the divinity of Jesus and the universal mission of Jesus to save all people from every ethnicity to himself. "It is a book about Jesus. This is underlined by the fact that John uses the name 'Jesus' 237 times, far and away the most in any New Testament book . . . John is absorbed in Jesus."[10] Martin Erdman writes in *Mission in the New Testament: An Evangelical Approach*:

> This purpose clause in John 20:31 strongly suggests that John's intention was propagandistic in nature . . . The purpose statement of John 20:30–31 appears to be aimed at unbelievers who need to make a decision about the identity of Jesus. Viewed in this light, John is primarily pursuing a missions objective in writing his gospel.[11]

Not all agree with the evangelistic interpretation of John's purpose. Some consider John's purpose missiological.

> In current New Testament research, there is great disagreement over the exact missionary nature of the Gospel. The primary point of disagreement concerns the missionary purpose of the Gospel. Is this a document which is intended primarily to convert people to Christianity? Or is a missionary document something that encourages the Church to missionary activity?[12]

7. Morris, *New Testament Theology*, 251.

8. Andreas Kostenberger lists Karl Bornhäuser, Wilhelm Oehler, Albrecht Oepke, John Bowman, Edwin D. Freed, Wayne A. Meeks, W. C. van Unnik, John A. T. Robinson, and C. H. Dodd all as scholars who understand John's Gospel to be missionary (*missionsschrift*) in purpose (*The Missions of Jesus*, 201–202).

9. All Scripture citations, unless otherwise noted, are from the New King James Version.

10. Morris, *New Testament Theology*, 225.

11. Larkin and Williams, *Mission in the New Testament*, 208.

12. Prescott-Erickson, "The Sending Motif in the Gospel of John," 139.

Within John's purpose statement (20:30–31), the interpretation of belief crucially influences the determination of the author's intention.

> A significant question revolves around the verb, "by believing" in [John] 20:31. The two textual variants are present subjunctive and aorist subjunctive. The aorist subjunctive would imply, "that you may believe here and now." This would make the purpose to convert unbelievers to belief. The present subjunctive would be translated, "that you may continue to believe." This would make the purpose lean to encouraging Christians to continue in their faith commitment . . . Some scholars say that [John] 20:31 is a statement of missionary purpose in terms of conversion, and therefore addressed to unbelievers. The major commentators favor the interpretation of continuing in belief, and insist that it is addressed to Christians.[13]

The majority opinion, therefore, leans toward the Gospel of John being a missionary treatise that exhorts Christians to make disciples among every ethnic group in the world. According to Sean Kealy, John's purpose is pastoral: "It is to strengthen, illuminate, defend, and think deeply about the faith. This pastoral aim includes elements of polemic, apologetic, and missionary, unifying them under the pastoral aim, dealing with many practical problems which John's audience was encountering."[14] John's pastoral heart comes through in his gospel as he encourages those he loves to be about the business of making disciples among every people group.

CONCENTRIC CIRCLES OF CONTEXT

John 15:1–17 is a portion of Jesus' concluding instructions to his disciples during the last week of his life. John records what Jesus believed was of primary importance for those who would receive his transferred apostolate. In the context of the gospel as a whole, John's missionary teaching and exposition is in harmony with his focus on God's missionary focus, Jesus' missionary task, and his followers' missionary inheritance.

With regard to the entire Johannine corpus, similar themes may be found in both the epistles and the Apocalypse. The connection with Revelation is more explicit, as John continues to unpack the supremacy and deity of Christ and the ultimate triumph of God's majestic plan—men and women from every tribe, tongue, people, and nation worshiping around his

---

13. Ibid., 141–42.
14. Kealy, *That You May Believe*, 18–19.

eternal throne. John 15:1–17 prefigures the language and centrality of love found in the Johannine epistles. Of all gospel writers, John is most clear on Jesus' divinity and missionary ambition. In the broader scope of the New Testament, John contributes to the diachronic revelation of God's passionate pursuit of worship from every ethnic group. In reference to the whole of Scripture, John's unique and complementary contribution is to unveil the eternal word, the God with us, the God lauded by every tongue, and the missionary Son of God who sends his people as missionaries, even as he was sent.

PURPOSE OF JOHN 15:1–17

The purpose of John 15:1–17 is to reveal Jesus' methodology for disciple making. In this passage, John records Jesus affirming his desire for disciples to make disciples. Jesus reminds his followers that the way to reproduce is to abide in him. He warns of the dire consequences for those who do not abide in him as well as for those who do not reproduce disciples. He organizes his instructions around harvesting souls, which can be analyzed as in the following exegetical outline:

I. Responsibility of harvest (vv. 1–2a)

    A. Jesus is the vine (v. 1a).

    B. The Father is the vinedresser (v. 1b).

    C. Disciples are the branches (v. 2a).

II. Bearers of harvest (v. 2)

    A. Fruitless branches in Christ (v. 2a)

    B. Fruitful branches in Christ (v. 2b)

III. Conditions of harvest (vv. 3–4)

    A. Cleansing by Christ (v. 3)

    B. Abiding in Christ (v. 4a)

    C. Depending on Christ (v. 4b)

IV. Promise of harvest (vv. 5–7)

    A. The one who abides bears fruit (v. 5a).

    B. The one who does not abide bears nothing (v. 5b).

    C. The one who does not abide is withered and burned (v. 6).

    D. The one who abides has prayer answered (v. 7).

V. Glory of harvest (v. 8)

    A. God is honored by bearing fruit (v. 8a).

   B. Disciples bear much fruit (v. 8b).

 VI. Spirit of harvest (vv. 9–15)

   A. Love (vv. 9–10)

   B. Joy (v. 11)

   C. Sacrifice (vv. 12–13)

   D. Obedience (v. 14)

   E. Friendship (v. 15)

 VII. Participation of harvest (vv. 16–17)

   A. Jesus chooses the workers (v. 16a).

   B. Jesus appoints workers to raise new workers (v. 16b).

   C. Jesus desires new workers to abide (v. 16c).

   D. Jesus commands workers to love one another (v. 17).

A Study of the Word μένω (abide)

The word μένω is key to this passage. This study will show its significance from the Scriptures and other literature.

Classical Literature

"Found already in Homer, [μένω] is related to Lat[in] *Maneo*: intrans[itive]. It means to remain in one place, at a given time, with someone . . . In religious language, [the word] is used for the gods or inspired by them . . . as having continuous existence. It is only seldom used trans[itively], with the force of waiting for, or expecting someone or something."[15]

Septuagint

"In the LXX [μένω] translates some 16 Hebrew words . . . Generally it is concerned with the existence or continuing validity of something . . . It is therefore particularly used of God . . . always in the living context of the worship and praise of God."[16] According to Kittel and Friedrich:

> The LXX uses μένειν mostly for עמד ("to stand," "to last," "to remain," "to endure," "to remain alive"), commonly for קום ("to

---

15. Brown, *The Gospel According to John*, 224.

16. Ibid., 224.

stand up," "to stand," "to take place," Isa 7:7, "to be lasting," Job 15:29, "to stand on something," Is. 32:8, "to be in force," Nu. 30:5), more rarely for ישב ("to remain sitting," Gn. 24:55, "to dwell," "to remain undisturbed," Zech. 14:10), חכה ("to delay," 2 K. 7:9; Is. 8:17), קוה ("to wait," Is. 5:2, 4, 7) etc.[17]

Koine Papyri and Inscriptions

"[μένω] always involves a negation: *not to give way*. It does not . . . respond to the question 'where?' but rather to the question 'how long?' In the earliest Greek usage it concerned *continuing* at an objectively fixed place for an objectively determined time, and then later it involved continuation in a personal bond."[18]

Patristic Literature

Mark Edwards quotes Alcuin, "To abide . . . is to believe, obey, and persevere."[19] Joel Elowsky quotes various church fathers, including Clement of Alexandria, Cyril of Alexandria, and Augustine on the topic of abiding: "Abide in the Word and then ask since the Word is a possession that lacks nothing"; "The confession of piety towards God should accompany faith"; and "When someone abides in this way, is there anything he or she can wish for besides what will be agreeable to Christ?"[20] Basil the Great thought that love is the underlying basis for a life of abiding that glorifies God. Irenaeus said disciples become like Christ as they abide in him. Chrysostom thought that disciples abide by obeying his call to love through obedience to his commands. Cyril expressed that abiding in Christ leads to joy in trial.[21]

New Testament

The New Testament uses the Greek word μένω 118 times with sixty-four uses in Johannine literature alone (forty in John and twenty-four in Johannine epistles). New King James Version (NKJV), English Standard Version (ESV), New American Standard Bible (NASB), New Revised Standard

17. Kittel and Friedrich, *Theological Dictionary*, 575.
18. Balz and Schneider, *Exegetical Dictionary of the New Testament*, 407.
19. Edwards, *John*, 148.
20. Elowsky, *Ancient Christian Commentary on Scripture*, 165, 169.
21. Ibid., 165.

Version (NRSV), and most other translations translate μένω as "I abide." The use of μένω takes "different forms according to the different relations and antonyms in view. The intransitive form μένειν means 'remain in a place,' 'tarry,' or 'dwell.'"[22]

There are several compounds of μένω in the New Testament. These include ἐμμένω (stay, Acts 10:48; remain, Gal. 1:18; persist/persevere, Phil. 1:24); παραμένω (remain, Heb. 7:23; stay on/continue in, James 2:22); προσμένω (remain, Matt. 15:32; stay with/stay longer, Mark 8:2); περιμένω (expect/wait, Acts 1:4; Luke 24:49); and ὑπομένω (endurance). The Vulgate uses the Latin term *mansio*, or "resting place on a journey."[23]

Johannine Literature

In John 15, μένω is used twelve times (vv. 4, 5, 6, 7, 9, 10). Ten times NKJV translates μένω as "I abide." Twice it translates μένω as "I remain" (vv. 11, 16). The translations of μένω as "remain" refer to joy and fruit (inanimate), while the previous ten references refer to the person who is to abide in Christ. From a linguistic perspective, the uses are indistinguishable. Disciples are to abide/remain in Jesus (vv. 4, 5, 6) as the branch must abide/remain on the grapevine (v. 4). Jesus' words must abide/remain in disciples (v. 7), even as they must abide/remain in his love (vv. 9, 10) and as he abides/remains in the love of the Father (v. 10). As a result, his joy is to abide/remain in disciples (v. 11), and the fruit that disciples bear will abide/remain (v. 6). By simple definition, "to remain" involves time—elongated time.

In the epistles of John, μένω is used the following ways:

Use of μένω	Scripture Reference
Believers abiding in God	1 John 2:6, 24, 27; 3:6, 24; 4:13, 16
God abiding in believers	1 John 3:24; 4:12, 13, 15, 16
Believers abiding in the light	1 John 2:10
Believers abiding forever	1 John 2:17
The word of God and the truth about Jesus abiding in believers	1 John 2:14, 24; 2 John 2, 9
God's anointing abiding on believers	1 John 2:27
The possibility of abiding life and death	1 John 3:14, 15
God's love abiding in believers	1 John 3:17
Believers abiding in love	1 John 4:16

22. Kittel and Friedrich, *Theological Dictionary*, 575.
23. See Brown, *The Gospel According to John*, 227–29.

In Johannine epistles, μένω is also translated as "remain" when referring to the seed of God that helps the believer to resist sin (1 John 3:9).

Consistently, the Johannine usage of μένω refers to extended time in one place or with one person as that person is staying/dwelling/remaining/lingering in a state or condition—usually in obedient submission. When John uses μένω, there is a sense of dependence and obedience, endurance, continuance, tarrying, and waiting with expectancy over time. "In Jn. [John] the secular Gk. μένω ἐν gained a meaning parallel to the Pauline conception of Christ's dwelling in the believer (Rom 8:9ff.) and his dwelling in Christ. It is even expanded and strengthened."[24]

John gives examples of what abiding means. In John 6:56, Jesus declares, "He who eats my flesh and drinks my blood abides in Me, and I in him." Abiding includes repeated feeding on Jesus. Those who abide in his word are true disciples (8:31). Disciples know they are abiding when they bear fruit (15:5). John 15:10 connects obedience to abiding as does 1 John 3:24. In 1 John 2:6, John writes, "He who says he abides in Him [Christ] ought himself to walk just as He [Christ] walked." By inference, abiding is walking as Jesus walked. Abiding precludes habitual sin (1 John 3:6). First John 4:12 states, "If we love one another, God abides in us." An abiding state (reciprocal by definition of John 15:4) is indicated by love for one another. Christians can be certain of their abiding state by the Spirit (1 John 4:13). First John 4:15 links abiding with confession: "Whoever confesses that Jesus is the Son of God, God abides in him, and he in God." First John 4:16 reveals that "he who abides in love abides in God, and God in him." Second John 9 says, "He who abides in the doctrine of Christ has both Father and Son." Christology, then, is also part and parcel of abiding.

According to John, those who abide are those who draw their daily life from Jesus (John 6:54), obey his word (John 8:31; 15:10; 1 John 3:24), bear fruit (John 15:5), behave as Jesus behaved (1 John 2:6), live a holy life (1 John 3:6), are loving (1 John 4:12, 16), are empowered by the Spirit (1 John 4:13), and publicly testify to the biblical nature of Jesus, including his divinity (1 John 4:15; 2 John 2:9). John defines those who do not abide as unbelieving (John 3:36; 5:38), cast out, withered and consumed (John 15:6), hateful (1 John 3:15), selfish (1 John 3:17), sinful and unable to continue in biblical praxis (2 John 1:9).

24. Ibid., 225.

Abide in John 15:1–17

John 15:7 reveals two principles in regard to abiding in Jesus. One is that Jesus' words abide (remain/stay) in his disciples. The second is that the disciples may ask what they desire and have it done for them. John seems to indicate that the central disciplines of abiding are linked to the word of God and prayer. Prayer, according to Jesus, is inescapably linked to mission (John 15:16). John Piper says, "Notice the amazing logic of this verse. He gave them a mission 'in order that' the Father would have prayers to answer. This means that prayer is for mission. It is designed to advance the kingdom."[25]

John is consistent in his use of *abide*. He uses the word μένω to mean a continuance in obedience over time. This time is usually characterized by submission, waiting, endurance, continuance, expectation, and intimacy. According to the Johannine literature, outcomes of those who abide include intimacy with Jesus, obedience, fruitfulness, holiness, empowerment, and public testimony. Those who do not abide are described by their unbelief, dryness, hate, selfishness, and inconsistency.

A Study of the Word καρπός (fruit)

The word καρπός is another key word in this passage. This study will show its significance from the Scriptures and other literature.

Classical Literature

"In secular Greek . . . [καρπός] is used *especially* of the fruit of the ground (Homer), but also often of the offspring of animals (Xenophon). It is also found in an extended sense for the result of an undertaking, whether good or ill: the outcome, consequence (Philo, Marcus Aurelius)."[26] "Plutarch reports that Socrates wanted to cultivate Alcibiades as a plant so that his 'fruit' would not be destroyed."[27]

---

25. Piper, *A Holy Ambition*, 155.

26. See Hensel, "καρπός," 721.

27. Keener, *The Gospel of John*, 997.

Septuagint

"In the LXX [Septuagint], [καρπός] stands chiefly for the [Hebrew word] which in the Old Testament (OT) is used for the fruit of plants (e.g., Deut. 7:13; Mic. 6:7; Ps. 21:11). καρπός is also used metaphorically for the fruit of an action (e.g., Hos. 10:13; Jer. 6:10; 17:10)."[28]

Patristic Literature

"Theophylact writes that the fruits of the apostles in v. 8 are the Gentiles."[29]

New Testament

The New Testament uses καρπός a variety of ways: one time as the adjective καρποφόρος ("fruitful"); seven times as ἄκαρπος ("unfruitful"); eight times as the verb καρποφορέω ("to bear fruit" or "produce crops"); and fifty-one times as the noun καρπός—twenty-seven of which include the definite article ὁ καρπός—meaning "benefit," "crop," "descendant," "harvest," "profit."

Fruit is understood as literal (James 5:7, 18; Matt 21:19; Mark 4:29; Rev 22:2); children (Luke 1:42; Acts 2:30; Heb 13:15); consequence of the acts of people (Matt 21:43); good works (Matt 3:8); results of missionary labor (Rom 1:13; Phil 1:22); offerings (Rom 15:28); character of the Spirit (Gal 5:22–23); and righteousness (Heb 12:11; James 3:18).[30] John, however, has a very distinct and focused use of *fruit*.

Johannine Literature

Of the eleven uses of καρπός in John (ten in John 15 and one in John 4), all can be understood in the context of harvest. In John 4:36, John uses the word καρπός (which NKJV translates "fruit") in the context of harvest. The word καρπός literally means "that which is harvested—'harvest, crop, fruit, grain.'"[31] The sense is an external yield that can be gathered. Andreas Kostenberger, C. K. Barrett, and Adolf Schlatter all argue that καρπός indicates converts.[32]

---

28. See Hensel, "καρπός," 721.

29. Edwards, *John*, 149.

30. Kittel and Friedrich, "καρπός," in *Theological Dictionary*, 416–17.

31. Louw and Nida, "καρπός," in *Greek-English Lexicon*, 517.

32. Kostenberger, *The Missions of Jesus*, 184.

John 4:35–37 (NKJV) reads, "Do you not say, 'There are still four months and *then* comes the harvest'? Behold, I say to you, lift up your eyes and look at the fields, for they are already white for harvest! And he who reaps receives wages, and gathers fruit for eternal life, that both he who sows and he who reaps may rejoice together." The word translated "fruit" in verse 36 is καρπός, and the context explicitly identifies this fruit as harvested souls. John 15:2 states, "Every branch in me that does not bear fruit He takes away." The word translated "fruit" in this verse is also καρπός and in this context is linked to the secular Greek usage meaning the fruit of trees or earth.[33]

There are four references to fruit in Revelation. Revelation 18:14 uses the word πώρα (late summer, ripe fruits) in the context of Babylon no longer being able to provide bodies and the souls of humans (Rev 18:13) to the merchants of the earth. Verse 14 distinguishes the "fruit your soul longed for" from the "rich and splendid things," indicating that the fruit could refer to people but could possibly also refer to nice things. The other three references in Revelation (all found in chapter 22) directly refer to the natural fruit of a tree.

The Johannine use of καρπός centers heavily on harvest. While not unique in the New Testament in this regard (see Rom 1:13; Phil 1:22), John—especially in chapters 4 and 15—emphasizes that the fruit of abiding is a harvest of people. When John links the word καρπός (fruit) with the verb φέρω (I bear), this focus on a harvest of people is even more pronounced. The word φέρω is used many different ways in the New Testament. It can mean "I carry," "I bring," "I drive along," "I guide," I lead into," "I bring about," "I put," "I experience," "I sustain," "I demonstrate reality," "I accept," "I endure," or "I bear fruit."[34] When φέρω is used referring to bearing fruit—

> the term has the special sense of bearing fruit in the metaphors of the tree which bears good or bad fruit (Mt. 7:18), the field which bears varying degrees of fruit (Mk. 4:8) and the vine with branches that bear fruit (Jn. 15:2, 4). Materially the term denotes in Mt. and Jn. the following of the words and commandments of Jesus, abiding in fellowship with Him, and hence doing God's will in the life and work of the disciples, while in the parable of the sower (Mk. 4 and par.) the primary reference is to the power with which, in defiance of all resistance, the rule of God achieves fulfillment.[35]

---

33. Kittel and Friedrich, "καρπός," in *Theological Dictionary*, 416–17.

34. Louw and Nida, *Greek-English Lexicon*, 256.

35. Kittel and Friedrich, *Theological Dictionary*, 58.

John, however, uses the term φέρω (I bear) to specifically refer to the fruit of disciples. "In [John] 12:24 Jesus uses the image of the grain of wheat that falls into the ground, dies, and bears much fruit, to describe the fruit of his own death. What is meant is the winning of disciples out of the world and the gathering of the community."[36] John intentionally connects fruit-bearing in the life of Jesus with winning disciples and gathering them into churches.

Fruit in John 15:1–17

John 15:5 continues this same sense of fruit as the harvest of souls. Kostenberger quotes D. A. Carson: "The fruit primarily in this verse [15:16] is the fruit that emerges from mission, from specific ministry to which the disciples have been sent. The fruit, in short, is new converts."[37] Kostenberger points out that Marie-Joseph Lagrange, Brooke Foss Westcott, John H. Bernard, and C. K. Barrett all agree with fruit being understood as converts or disciples.[38] "Jesus chose us to be ambassadors . . . first to come to Him, and then to go out to the world and that must be the daily pattern and rhythm of our lives . . . Jesus sends us out . . . to attract men into Christianity."[39] Christians go into the world as Christ's friends, "but the idea of being the friend of God has also a background. Abraham was the *friend* of God (Isaiah 41:8)."[40] Abraham's friendship with God intertwined with God's missionary purposes. God blessed Abraham to be a blessing to all nations. Friendship with God is inseparably linked with passion for God's glory among all peoples. Abiding in Jesus leads to friendship with him, which must result in sharing his heart for all peoples to glorify his name.

REVIEW OF THE WORDS ἈΊΡΩ (RAISE) AND ΚΑΘΑΊΡΩ (PRUNE, CLEANSE)

αἴρω

John 15:2 (NKJV) states, "Every branch in Me that does not bear fruit He takes away; and every branch that bears fruit He prunes, that it may bear

---

36. Ibid., 59.
37. Kostenberger, *The Missions of Jesus*, 185.
38. Ibid.
39. Barclay, *The Gospel of John*, 209.
40. Ibid., 208.

more fruit." NKJV translates αἴρω "I take away" while the literal meaning is "I raise" or "I lift up." Other meanings include:

> bear (4), carried (1), carry (1), get (4), hoisted (1), keep (1), lifted
> (2), pick (9), picked (11), pulls away (2), put away (1), raised (2),
> remove (1), removed (3), suspense (1), take (13), take away (5),
> take . . . away (4), taken (3), taken . . . away (1), taken away (12),
> takes away (7), taking (1), took (2), took . . . away (1), took away
> (3), weighed anchor (1).[41]

The major lexicons relegate "I take away" or "I destroy" to secondary or tertiary options. Louw and Nida define αἴρω variously as "carry,"[42] "destroy,"[43] and "execute."[44] *A Dictionary of Bible Languages* also defines αἴρω as "carry, destroy, and execute."[45] The *Greek-English Dictionary of the New Testament* defines αἴρω as "I take, I take up, I take away, I remove, I set aside, I carry, I raise, or I take over."[46] James Swanson in *A Dictionary of Biblical Languages with Semantic Domains* cites possible meanings of αἴρω as "I carry, I take up, I take away, I destroy, I execute, I withdraw, I cause to no longer experience, I remove from, I lift up, and I keep in suspense."[47] In John 10:24, αἴρω is used in the sense of "lift up the soul of someone" (ὁ ψυχή ἐγώ αἴρω), which can be translated "how long will you keep us up in the air?" The *Lexham Analytical Lexicon* defines αἴρω as "I lift / I take up, I raise, or I take along."[48] *Building Your New Testament Greek Vocabulary* defines αἴρω as "I lift up."[49] In all of these lexical definitions, αἴρω is first defined as "I carry," "I take," "I lift up," or "I raise." *Thayer's New Testament Greek-English Lexicon* lists three primary definitions for αἴρω: (1) I raise up, elevate, lift up from the ground; (2) I take upon myself and carry what has been raised up, I bear; and (3) I bear what has been raised, I carry off. This is consistent with the wider use of αἴρω across the New Testament.[50]

The following references use some form of the verb αἴρω, "I bear": In Matthew 27:32 and Mark 15:21, Simon is compelled to bear Christ's cross. In Matthew 4:6 and Luke 4:11, the devil taunts Jesus by telling him angels

41. Thomas, "αἴρω," in *Hebrew-Aramaic and Greek Dictionaries*, 1,628.

42. Louw and Nida, *Greek-English Lexicon*, 207.

43. Ibid., 233.

44. Ibid., 236.

45. Swanson, *A Dictionary of Bible Languages: Greek New Testament*, 149.

46. Newman, "αἴρω," in *Greek-English Dictionary of the New Testament*, 5.

47. Swanson, "αἴρω," in *A Dictionary of Biblical Languages w/ Semantic Domains*.

48. *Lexham Analytical Lexicon*, "αἴρω."

49. Van Voorst, "αἴρω," in *Building Your New Testament Greek Vocabulary*, 30.

50. Thayer, "αἴρω," in *Thayer's Greek-English Lexicon*, 16.

can bear him up. In Matthew 9:16 and Mark 2:21, αἴρω is used to mean "I detach, I pull away." In Mark 2:3 and John 5:10, a paralytic and his bed are borne to the one who can care for him. In Luke 9:17 and Acts 20:9, αἴρω is translated "taken up," again in a conserving or restorative way. In Mark 10:21, the rich young ruler is told to bear his cross. In Luke 17:13, those in distress bear/lift their voices to Jesus for help. In John 11:41, Jesus bears or lifts his eyes to thank the Father. Consistently, in the New Testament, αἴρω is used to mean I lift up or bear. Often that lifting is to preserve, help, or take toward help. The verb αἴρω is often used to mean a lift toward restoration or help. The primary meaning is "I lift up." The Gospel of John in NKJV translates αἴρω thirteen times as some form of I take, I take away, I take up, I take out, and I take him. Once in John αἴρω is translated "I lift" (John 11:41).

In light of the New Testament use of αἴρω to mean "I lift," the one reference in John 15:2 to αἴρω has as much possibility of meaning "I lift" as it does "I take away." When the circumstantial evidence of the verse is examined (the branches in question are "in" Christ), then it becomes probable that the branches are being lifted up off the ground with the intention that they concentrate on gaining life from the vine. Many scholars view the original branch as being the Jews. "The original branches in God's vine were the Jews; these being unfruitful (unbelieving), God removed . . . [John's] primary thought [concerning unfruitful branches] was of apostate Christians."[51] This view seems limited, as "even the unfruitful branches are true branches. They are also 'in Christ', though they draw their life from Him only to bear leaves."[52] It is difficult to conclude that the Jews are "in Christ" as a national entity.

καθαίρω

The verb καθαίρω in John 15:2 (NKJV) is translated "I prune" even though its literal meaning is "I clean." This is the only use of "pruning" as a translation of καθαίρω in the Johannine literature. Elsewhere in John (13:10, 11; 15:3), the same root word (in adjective form) καθαρός is translated "I clean." John's intention was "cleaning" or "purifying," a cleansing not necessarily exclusive of "pruning." The text of John 15:2 can best be understood to say, "and every branch that bears fruit he *cleans*, that it may bear more fruit." Ernest Colewell and Eric Titus observe that "it is important to note that in

---

51. Barrett, *The Gospel According to St. John*, 395.
52. Cook, *The Holy Bible According to the Authorized Version*, 217.

verse three the idea of pruning is conveyed by the same word which is used in the story of washing the disciples' feet."[53]

Cleaning is not to be understood as "ritual washing" in John's use. It has the implication of purification through suffering, difficulty, and loss, which is why translators chose the word "prune" instead of "clean" as they wanted to indicate the purifying process of washing that occurs through suffering. Evidence for this alternate translation is given by John's account of tribulation in Revelation 6 and 7. In Revelation 6:9–11, those slain for the word of God and the testimony they held were each given a white robe. Then in Revelation 7:14, John explains that those who have suffered through great tribulation "have washed their robes and made them white in the blood of the Lamb." John implies that suffering purifies or washes, even though he uses the verb ἔπλυναν (I wash) in Revelation instead of καθαίρω (I clean). J. H. Bernard writes:

> [The] Great Husbandman does "cleanse" the fruitful branches by pruning off useless shoots, so that they may bear fruit more abundantly. It is not as if the branches were foul; on the contrary, they are already clean by virtue of their share in the life of the vine (v. 3). But pruning may be good for them, nonetheless. Such pruning . . . illustrates God's painful discipline for his true servants.[54]

This reading is consistent with the parallel teachings of Paul in 2 Timothy 3:12 and Philippians 1:29. The sense of John's text is that branches will be prepared for greater fruit-bearing by the cleansing of suffering. Cleansing, biblically, often has an element of redemptive suffering.

> Suffering is not only the consequence of completing the Commission, but it is God's appointed means by which he will show the superior worth of his Son to all the peoples. Just as it was "fitting that he . . . should make the founder of [our] salvation perfect through suffering" (Heb. 2:10), so it is fitting that God save a people from all the peoples from eternal suffering through the redemptive suffering of Jesus displayed in the temporal suffering of his missionaries . . . What is lacking in Jesus' sufferings is not their redemptive value but their personal presentation to the peoples he died to save.[55]

---

53. Colewell and Titus, *The Gospel of the Spirit*, 181.

54. See Bernard, "The Gospel According to St. John," 480.

55. Piper, *A Holy Ambition*, 31.

By suffering, disciples of Jesus are purified and prepared for greater effectiveness, just as he was. John's use of "cleansing" implies a suffering that perfects and works toward redemption. The means of cleaning is by Jesus' word (John 15:3). "The word *cleanseth* . . . , which is used of lustrations, appears to be chosen with a view to its spiritual application. Everything is removed from the branch which tends to divert the vital power from the production of fruit."[56] Barclay points out that this pruning is more regular early on for the newer disciple and ongoing for the more mature one: "A young vine was not allowed to fruit for the first three years. Each year it was cut drastically back that it might develop and conserve its life and energy."[57]

56. Cook, *The Holy Bible According to the Authorized Version*, 217.
57. Barclay, *The Gospel of John*, 202.

2

Exegesis of John 15:1–17

RESPONSIBILITY OF HARVEST

The following section asserts Jesus is ultimately responsible for the production of fruit.

Jesus Is the Vine

1 ἐγώ εἰμι ἡ ἄμπελος ἡ ἀληθινὴ

1 I am the true grapevine . . .

Jesus spoke these opening words of the passage to state the parameters for his teaching on abiding and fruit bearing. When Jesus uses ἄμπελος, he draws on a vast reference base of passages relating to vines in the Old Testament. "The barely concealed reference to Israel (cf. Isa 5:1–7; 27:2–6; Ezek 15; 19:10–14; Hosea 10:1; Ps 80:9–16) casts Jesus as the true vine, i.e., the representative of Israel, and his disciples as the branches, participants in Jesus, the new Israel."[1] By declaring himself the true vine, "Jesus displaces Israel as the focus of God's plan of salvation."[2]

The vine in the inter-testamental period also took on national significance. "The emblem on the coins of the Maccabees was the vine . . . It was

---

1. Köstenberger, *The Missions of Jesus*, 164.
2. Köstenberger, *John*, 448.

the very symbol of the nation of Israel."[3] The temple mount also included a graven vine–the Golden Vine—clearly visible to all who approached the temple to worship.[4] Possibly, of the "sight of a local vineyard" on the way from the upper room to Gethsemane also "prompted the discourse."[5] Jesus, knowing the importance of the imagery of the vine (nationally, religiously, historically, and scripturally) and seeing it again (either a literal vineyard, the Golden Vine of the temple mount, or the fruit of the vine at the Last Supper) redefined its symbolic meaning. Jesus declares that he alone is the source and center of life. John quotes Jesus using the nominative singular feminine article and adjective ἡ ἀληθινὴ to imply that all other vines are false or incomplete sources of life and that only Jesus can truly give life.

The nominative singular feminine noun ἄμπελος is best translated "grapevine," rather than "vine," as "vine" may refer equally to a vine that does not bear fruit.[6] John uses ἄμπελος three times in his gospel (John 15) and twice in Revelation to mean "the only source of life." The term directly refers to a vine that produces grapes.[7] John draws on the wisdom literature of Sirach, where Sophia is "pictured as a vine (Sir 1:20; 24:17,19) providing 'sustenance and abundance of life through the fruit of her branches' and seeking faithful disciples who will bear such fruit in contrast to the faithless (Sir 23:25)."[8]

Jesus thus sets the stage for his teaching on abiding and fruit by establishing that he alone is the source of ongoing life.

The Father Is the Vinedresser

1b καὶ ὁ πατήρ μου ὁ γεωργός ἐστιν

1b my Father is the vinedresser.

The nominative singular masculine noun πατήρ, corresponding to the Aramaic word for "father," refers to "one who combines aspects of supernatural

---

3. Barclay, *The Gospel of John*, 201.

4. Mark Edwards cites Tacitus, *Histories* 5.5 to note that some pagans, seeing the Golden Vine at the temple, mistakenly thought that the Jews worshiped Dionysus; *Apocalypse of Baruch* considers the tree in Eden to have been a vine. Bultmann regards the vine as a scion of the "tree of life,"—a ubiquitous motif in the cults and myths of the ancient Mediterranean. See Edwards, *John*, 147.

5. Edwards, *John*, 147.

6. Louw and Nida, "ἄμπελος," in *Greek-English Lexicon*, 32.

7. Thomas, *New American Standard Hebrew-Aramaic and Greek Dictionaries*, 288.

8. Scott, *Sophia and the Johannine Jesus*, 130–31.

authority and care for his people."[9] The noun γεωργός is also nominative singular masculine and refers to one who cultivates the land or engages in agriculture or gardening. The Father gardener takes spiritual and practical responsibility for the grapevine, its branches, and the surrounding environment. Some theologians (including Augustine who thought that Christ was at once grapevine and gardener) have argued that Jesus is the vinedresser, but "Dionysius of Alexandria retorted that the dresser of the vine and the vine itself must be distinct."[10] By distinguishing the role of grapevine (God the Son) and vinedresser (God the Father) in John 15:1b, Jesus implies that hypostatic union allows a distinct role for God the Father as the one who oversees the whole process of fruit bearing. Not all agree on this division of labor. Dunn and Rogerson write, "As always, Jesus undertakes the work of God who is the gardener."[11] The text, however, implies a model union and interdependence of Father and Son (vinedresser and grapevine) that allows for distinct roles in the harvest process. The most likely interpretation of γεωργός linked to πατήρ is literal: Father God is the one who cares for grapevine and vineyard. This interpretation is most consistent with Jesus' simple demarcation in this verse and with the biblical record. "[Old Testament] images of Israel as God's vine imply God or his workers as tenders of that vine; [and] Paul speaks of God's church as [God's] field (1 Cor 3:9)."[12]

Disciples Are the Branches

> 2a πᾶν κλῆμα . . .
>
> 2a Every branch . . .

The word κλῆμα refers to a vine branch, a "shoot / young twig," which is broken off to be replanted[13] or "a more or less tender, flexible branch, as of a vine . . . (principally of grapevines)."[14] "Although it is only later in the speech that the disciples are identified as the 'branches,' already it is clear at the outset that Jesus is addressing the words to that group."[15]

Scholars have divided opinions about the branches. Some think the branches represent the body of Christ. B. K. Rattey states, "[In] the Fourth

9. Louw and Nida, "πατήρ," in Greek-English Lexicon.

10. Edwards, John, 148.

11. Dunn and Rogerson, Eerdmans Commentary on the Bible, 1198.

12. Keener, The Gospel of John, 994.

13. Kittel and Friedrich, Theological Dictionary, 757.

14. Louw and Nida, Greek-English Lexicon, 34.

15. Dunn and Rogerson, Eerdmans Commentary on the Bible, 1198.

Gospel, the vine and the branches together represent the new Israel, the Church."[16] This thinking is linked to the grapevine being Christ, and the Church emanating from him. "The true vine is now brought before the disciples as the new ideal of the spiritual Israel."[17] In John 15:5, however, "Jesus makes it clear that the branches in the present symbolic discourse represent his followers."[18] The most probable intention of Jesus' use of branches is in reference to his disciples.

There are two implications of John's use of κλῆμα: (1) disciples are young (in spirit), moldable, pliable, and flexible, and (2) they are the type of disciple that can be broken off[19] and transplanted. Taken together with John's broader understanding of the passage (15:5) and interpreted with a missiological lens, John uses the word branches to refer to those disciples who are flexible enough to be sent out by the vinedresser to new vineyards in order to bear fruit.

BEARERS OF THE HARVEST

This section examines the different kinds of branches in John 15 and their relationship to the vine. John describes both fruitless and fruitful branches in Christ.

Fruitless Branches in Christ

> 2a πᾶν κλῆμα ἐν ἐμοὶ μὴ φέρον καρπὸν αἴρει αὐτό . . .
>
> 2a every branch in me that does not bear fruit he lifts up . . .

Three distinct types of κλήματα are noted in this passage. The first is the branch ἐν ἐμοὶ ("in me") that does not bear fruit—proving that "[a] branch may be truly in Christ and not bear fruit."[20] ἐν is a preposition and refers to those who have been included in Christ, having been inserted in him or who have sprouted out of him.[21] The second type of κλῆμα is the one ἐν ἐμοὶ

---

16. Rattey, *The Gospel According to Saint John*, 169.

17. See Bernard, "The Gospel According to St. John," 478.

18. Köstenberger, *John*, 452.

19. The phrase "broken off" does not imply separation from the vine. The vinedresser is omnipresent God, and his promise is to be with his sent ones always (Matt 28:20). Sent missionaries/disciples are not disconnected from God. Conversely, there is a special promise of God's presence to those employed in his mission.

20. See Bernard, "The Gospel According to St. John," 479.

21. Webster, *Syntax and Synonyms*, 157.

(in Christ, by implication) that does bear fruit. The third type of κλῆμα in the passage is found in 15:6 and refers to the branch who μή τις μένη ἐν ἐμοὶ (does not abide in Christ).

Bernard says that the unfruitful branch of 15:2 has a specific referent: "The unfruitful branch of 15:2 has an obvious allusion to Judas, who has just gone away to his act of treachery."[22] This may be the case, but there is also the possibility of wider application. Many scholars view the original branch as being the Jews. "The original branches in God's vine were the Jews; these being unfruitful (unbelieving), God removed [them] . . . [John's] primary thought [concerning unfruitful branches] was of apostate Christians."[23] This view also seems limited, as "even the unfruitful branches are true branches. They are also 'in Christ,' though they draw their life from Him only to bear leaves."[24] It is difficult to conclude that the Jews are the unfruitful branches to which John is referring as his gospel is written to believers, and in the narrative, Jesus indicates to his disciples that they are the branches.

The phrase ἐν ἐμοὶ μὴ φέρον καρπὸν reveals that one can be a branch in Jesus and not bear fruit. Yet "those who abide in Christ are assured of bearing much fruit (John 15:5), which shows that those bearing no fruit were not abiding in Christ."[25] Jesus differentiates to his disciples between being ἐν ἐμοί (in me) and μείνατε ἐν ἐμοί (abiding in me). The whole context of the chapter guarantees fruit if one abides in Jesus; therefore, a necessary difference between μένων (abiding) and ἐν ἐμοὶ (in me) exists. It is possible to be in Jesus without μένων (abiding).

The fate of those who are in Jesus, but do not bear fruit (μὴ φέρον καρπὸν) is different than those who do not abide. Those in Jesus who do not bear fruit he lifts up (αἴρει—as in John 15:2) and those who do not abide are burned (καίεται—as in John 15:6).

The word φέρον can be analyzed either as an active verb in the present tense or as a neuter singular participle in the accusative case. It means "producing fruit" or "yielding." It can also mean "I carry."[26] Those who are not bearing fruit (καρπὸν) he (Jesus) lifts up (αἴρει).

In light of the New Testament use of αἴρω meaning "I lift,"[27] the circumstantial evidence of the verse (the branches in question are "in" Christ)

---

22. See Bernard, "The Gospel According to St. John," xxi.

23. Barrett, *The Gospel According to St. John*, 395.

24. Cook, *The Holy Bible According to the Authorized Version*, 217.

25. Guthrie, *New Testament Theology*, 613.

26. Rogers and Rogers, *The New Linguistic and Exegetical Key*, 218.

27. The major lexicons relegate "I take away" or "I destroy" as meanings of αἴρω to secondary or tertiary options.

suggests the branches that are not bearing fruit will be lifted up off the ground. The lifting is intended to aid the branches to concentrate on gaining life from the vine that they may one day bear fruit. This interpretation is consistent with the methods of viticulture, as practiced both in modern times and in Christ's time. Jesus used an example familiar to the disciples.

In a vineyard, there are multiple reasons that the branches of the vine have to be lifted up. One reason is that "vines . . . have rigorous, slender, flexible stems that require support in order to grow upright."[28] If these branches are not lifted up, they tend to grow along the ground. "There are dozens of trellising systems used around the world, each providing a grower with a support suited to his climate and variety. Behind them all is a desire to get the vine up off the ground."[29] If they are not lifted off the ground, they grow quickly, but not in a way that works toward harvest. "Total leaf area and number of shoots on a vine is directly related to vine capacity. A vine with few shoots that elongates rapidly appears vigorous, but another vine which is less active because of numerous shoots of slower growth produces a larger total leaf area capable of greater production."[30] Production is linked to leaf area, and leaf area is linked to being lifted off the ground.[31]

This lifting process is not a one-time effort. "Whether a tree or shrub used as an espalier is placed in a formal or informal design, it needs a firm guiding hand to direct placement of branches . . . Tying is a part of espalier training that must be done constantly through the growing season as required."[32] This continual lifting is necessary as "upright shoots grow more vigorously than horizontal or drooping shoots."[33] Lifting, then, is not only lifting the branch off the ground, but it is also training it to grow upward in order to be strengthened. Once strong, a branch can level out and have the ability to carry heavy fruit. Drooping shoots, which when developed are called canes (branches), are thus lifted up and tied—a process referred to as training. When the canes are trained by being lifted and tied into position, they are better able to bear fruit.

Another reason vinedressers lift the branches off the ground is for inclement weather. "A prediction of frost . . . causes some mental anguish;

28. Harris, *Arboriculture*, 448.

29. Cox, *From Vines to Wines*, 47.

30. Weaver, *Grape Growing*, 177.

31. This "lifting up" refers solely to the need for the natural vine branch to receive sunshine in order to survive. In the same way, the disciple/missionary must abide in order to be able to lift up Christ. John 12:32 makes clear that it is the lifting up of Jesus (the vine) that draws all men to the Father.

32. Perkins, *Espaliers and Vines*, 32.

33. Wagner, *A Wine-Grower's Guide*, 110.

but the vines, being trained on their trellis, are not affected by this ground frost."[34] If they are not lifted up from the ground, the result can be disastrous for the branches.

> When vinifera are grown in a region subject to severe winters, they are frequently killed to the ground, and hence rarely produce crops, unless they are protected. For this purpose conventional training methods must be modified ... [one successful trainer] trains the trunk very low to the ground, with spurs emerging here and there along its length. In the autumn this low horizontal trunk is completely buried. In the spring it is disinterred, lifted, and held clear of the ground with a forked stick or by tying it to a stake ... [Another] method is a modification of cane training. The trunk is left very low, and with the approach of winter the canes to be used ... are bent gently to the ground and buried. In the spring, these are disinterred and pruned, the fruiting canes being tied up to a trellis wire. The bunches of grapes are thus kept fairly clear of the ground—especially if the relatively unfruitful lower buds are rubbed off—and are thus less subject to mold and to spattering by mud.[35]

Sometimes the lifting process is used to straighten a branch or beautify a design. This lifting process is not to be confused with pruning. "Although pruning is the primary method of training young plants, other procedures may be used. Staking may be used to encourage a straight trunk or a more upright growth habit ... Branches may be tied to supports to create special forms, cover a wall, or form a screen."[36] Phillip Wagner affirms that pruning and training (or lifting) are two different processes. "Training gives a certain preconceived form to the permanent and semi-permanent parts of the vine. Pruning regulates the annual growth so as to produce a maximum crop consistent with quality and regularity of production."[37] As Richard Harris points out, there is some crossover between the processes, yet they retain distinct functions: "Lifting the crown, raising the head, raising the canopy, and lift-pruning: All these refer to the removal of lower branches from the trunk or lower limits of a tree ... [When] raising the crown, thin back to a more upright large lateral ... [The] removal of low branches might increase

---

34. Ibid., 88.
35. Ibid., 120–21.
36. Harris, *Arboriculture*, 419.
37. Wagner, *A Wine-Grower's Guide*, 108.

stress on the lower trunk, immediately below the new lowest branch, and on the root system."[38]

This practice of "lifting" or "training" in viticulture verifies John's understanding of the vinedresser's intervention on behalf of unfruitful disciples.[39] The text then indicates an answer to two fundamental exegetical questions. First, it is possible to be in Christ, yet not bear fruit (ἐν ἐμοὶ μὴ φέρον καρπὸν). Jesus addresses this warning to those who believe in him. At this juncture chronologically, Judas has left the community; thus, there is no likelihood for ἐν ἐμοὶ (in me) to refer to non-believers. Second, there is sufficient exegetical justification to understand αἴρει to mean "he lifts up." The implication is that the Father will use means (a lifting of some nature) to help those who are not bearing fruit. The verses that follow detail the result of that lifting and its link to abiding.

Fruitful Branches in Christ

2b καὶ πᾶν τὸ καρπὸν φέρον καθαίρει αὐτὸ ἵνα καρπὸν πλείονα φέρη.

2b and every branch that bears fruit he cleans, that it may bear more fruit.

38. Harris, Arboriculture, 421.

39. This was certainly the case for Hudson Taylor. An intervention (or lifting) was used to teach Taylor to abide, and in abiding, he eventually produced fruit. Hudson Taylor returned to England due to illness after six years of missionary service in China—

> [He] settled with his little family in the east end of London. Outside interests lessened; friends began to forget; and five long hidden years were spent in the dreary street of a poor part of London, where the Taylors were 'shut up to prayer and patience.' From the record of those years it has been written, 'Yet, without those hidden years, with all their growth and testing, how could the vision and enthusiasm of youth been matured for the leadership that was to be?' . . . there is the 'deep, prolonged exercise of a soul that is following hard after God . . . of a man called to walk by faith not by sight; the unutterable confidence of a heart cleaving to God and God alone, which pleases Him as nothing else can' . . . 'Prayer was the only way by which the burdened heart could obtain any relief'; and when the discipline was complete, there emerged the China Inland Mission, at first only a tiny root, but destined of God to fill the land of China with gospel fruit." (Edman, The Disciplines of Life, 82)

The crucial word to be exegeted in this clause is the present active indicative third person singular verb καθαίρει (he cleans).[40] The verb "involves a play on two different meanings. The one meaning involves pruning of a plant, while the other meaning involves a cleansing process."[41]

The verb καθαίρει in John 15:2 is translated "he prunes," even though its literal meaning is "he cleans." This is the only use of "he prunes" as a translation of καθαίρει in the Johannine literature. Elsewhere in John (13:10, 11; 15:3) the same root word (in adjective form) καθαρός is translated "clean." John's intention was cleaning, or a process of purification through suffering, difficulty, and loss. Bernard writes of this discipline:

> The Great Husbandman does "cleanse" the fruitful branches by pruning off useless shoots, so that they may bear fruit more abundantly. It is not as if the branches were foul; on the contrary, they are already clean by virtue of their share in the life of the vine (v. 3). But pruning may be good for them, nonetheless. Such pruning . . . illustrates God's painful discipline for his true servants.[42]

This reading is consistent with the parallel teaching of Paul in 2 Timothy 3:12, "All who desire to live godly in Christ Jesus will suffer persecution," and Philippians 1:29, "For it has been granted on behalf of Christ, not only to believe in Him, but also to suffer for His sake." The sense of John's text is that branches are prepared for greater fruit bearing by the cleansing of discipline, difficulty, and suffering. Craig Keener concedes the possibility: "The image could involve judgment or difficulty; early Jewish texts also could describe the flood as a 'cleansing' of the earth (1 En. 106:17) or speak of the Messiah purging . . . Jerusalem to restore it in holiness."[43] Andrew Murray agrees with the understanding of pruning to mean the cleansing of suffering:

> And so He has prepared His people . . . to hear in each affliction the voice of a messenger that comes to call them to abide still more closely.

Abide in Christ! This is indeed the Father's object in sending the trial . . . So, by suffering, the Father would lead us to enter more deeply into the love of Christ . . . He does it in the hope that, when we have found our rest in Christ in time of trouble, we will learn to choose abiding in him as our

---

40. An interpretation of καρπὸν will be considered in the exegesis of John 15:5.

41. Louw and Nida, "καθαίρω," in *Greek-English Lexicon*, 517.

42. See Bernard, "The Gospel According to St. John," 480.

43. Keener, *The Gospel of John*, 996.

only portion; and so that when the affliction is removed, we will have grown so more firmly into him, that in prosperity He still will be our only joy. So much has He set his heart on this, that though He has indeed no pleasure in afflicting us, He will not keep back even the most painful chastisement; He can thereby guide his beloved child to come home and abide in the beloved Son. Christian, pray for grace to see in every trouble, small or great, the Father's pointing to Jesus, and saying, "Abide in him."

> Abide in Christ; so will you become partaker of all the rich bless-ings God designed for you in the affliction . . . So will your times of affliction become your times of choicest blessing—prepara-tion for the richest fruitfulness.[44]

Cleansing in the wider biblical context often has an element of re-demptive suffering.

> Suffering is not only the consequence of completing the Com-mission, but it is God's appointed means by which he will show the superior worth of his Son to all the peoples. Just as it was "fit-ting that he . . . should make the founder of [our] salvation per-fect through suffering" (Heb 2:10), so it is fitting that God save a people from all the peoples from eternal suffering through the redemptive suffering of Jesus displayed in the temporal suffer-ing of his missionaries . . . What is lacking in Jesus' sufferings is not their redemptive value but their personal presentation to the peoples he died to save.[45]

God leads branches that bear fruit into affliction. The intention of affliction is to teach disciples to abide in Christ. Abiding in Christ leads to bearing more fruit. There is a symbiotic relationship between affliction and abiding; they work together to bear fruit. Suffering cleansed and pre-pared the disciples of Jesus for greater effectiveness, just as it did for Jesus himself. John's use of καθαίρω implies a cleansing through difficulty (prun-ing), working toward the disciple bearing more fruit than he or she had before. "Training gives a certain preconceived form to the permanent and semi-permanent parts of the vine. Pruning regulates the annual growth so as to produce a maximum crop consistent with quality and regularity of production."[46] A primary aspect of discipleship, namely reproduction, is ac-complished through καθαίρω.[47]

---

44. Murray, *Abide in Christ*, 152–53, 156.

45. Mathis, "Missions," 31.

46. Wagner, *A Wine-Grower's Guide*, 108.

47. The other primary aspect of discipleship is training.

Exegetically then, the fruit bearing disciple is promised further discipleship (formation and reproduction) through a cleansing process. This cleansing process often involves suffering and trial, and results in the fruit-bearing disciple being equipped to bear more fruit.

CONDITIONS FOR HARVEST

This section of the exegesis examines the conditions necessary for harvest.

Cleansing by Christ

> 3 ἤδη ὑμεῖς καθαροί ἐστε δλὰ τὸν λόγον ὅν λελάληκα ὑμῖν . . .
>
> 3 You are already clean because of the word which I have spoken to you . . .

The means of cleaning is by λόγον, a noun in the accusative singular masculine. It refers to Jesus' word—"what has been stated or said, with primary focus upon the content of the communication."[48] Jesus' words are the agent of correction, pruning, and cleansing. The fulfilling of the promises of God and the fulfilling of the words of God is what cleans/prunes his disciples. These promises/words of God that cleanse include both pleasant and difficult realities. The word λελάληκα (I have spoken) is an active verb in the perfect tense and indicates that λόγον may remain with the disciples.[49] "The word cleanseth . . . which is used of lustrations, appears to be chosen with a view to its spiritual application. Everything is removed from the branch which tends to divert the vital power from the production of fruit."[50] Francis J. Maloney writes:

> The disciples at the table, listening to the discourse, are fruitful branches, united to the vine and pruned by having the word of the Sent One of the Father. Because they have heard and accepted the word of Jesus, the pruning process is already in place . . . They are told that the cleanliness comes from the words of Jesus. Jesus has established the essential frame of reference for vv. 1–11 in vv. 1–3. Jesus is the vine, the Father is the vinedresser,

---

48. Louw and Nida, "λόγος," in *Greek-English Lexicon*.

49. Rogers and Rogers, *The New Linguistic and Exegetical Key*, 218.

50. Cook, *The Holy Bible According to the Authorized Version*, 217.

and disciples, made clean by the word of Jesus, can be fruitful branches of the vine.[51]

John declares the strategic role of the words of Jesus in the formative and reproductive processes. In light of the promised cleansing, "every branch that bears fruit He cleans" (John 15:2b), Jesus explains this cleansing process as ongoing because of the disciple's exposure to his teaching. Those that heed and apply the words of Jesus will continually be prepared and used to bear fruit. Jesus will expound on the relationship of his word to prayer in 15:7 (See page 45).

Abiding in Christ

4 μείνατε ἐν ἐμοί, κἀγὼ ἐν ὑμῖν.

4 Abide in me, and I in you.

The verb μείνατε in the aorist, active, imperative, second person plural sense means, according to Louw and Nida, "remain in the same place over a period of time . . . stay."[52] Buist M. Fanning says, "The constative aorist [is] used to heighten the urgency of the command and [calls] for customary or general occurrence."[53] Cleon Rogers Jr. and Cleon Rogers III describe μείνατε as an ingressive aorist.[54] Those being addressed should "begin to stay in Christ." According to Kittel and Freidrich, the intransitive use (μένειν) means "remain in a place," "tarry," or "dwell."[55] Regarding μείνατε ἐν ἐμοί, Maxmilian Zerwick points out that the preposition ἐν according to John denotes that "the dwelling of God (Christ) in us and our dwelling in God (Christ) are two correlative and inseparable aspects of the same reality."[56] Steven Wakeman considers abiding a reciprocal act, and thus the emphasis of abiding involves developing relationship with God, not in doing things for God.[57] He references Daniel Wallace who espouses the force of the aorist imperative μείνατε to punctuate urgency and priority.[58] Therefore, Jesus effectively commands his disciples to make abiding in him their top priority.

51. Maloney, *The Gospel of John*, 420.

52. Louw and Nida, "μένω," in *Greek-English Lexicon*.

53. Fanning, *Verbal Aspect in New Testament Greek*, 369–70.

54. Rogers and Rogers, *The New Linguistic and Exegetical Key*, 218.

55. Kittel and Friedrich, "μένω," in *Theological Dictionary*.

56. Zerwick, *Biblical Greek*, 39.

57. Wakeman, "The Nature of Fruit," 58–75.

58. Wallace, *Greek Grammar Beyond the Basics*, 720–21.

In classical literature Homer used μένω as "related to Lat[in] *Maneo*: intrans[itive]. It means [I] remain in one place, at a given time, with someone . . . In religious language, it is used for the gods or inspired by them . . . as having continuous existence. It is only seldom used trans[itively], with the force of waiting for, or expecting someone or something."[59] It is from the Latin *maneo*, from which linguists derive the English word mansion. The Septuagint uses μένω quite broadly: "In the LXX [μένω] translates some 16 Hebrew words . . . Generally it is concerned with the existence or continuing validity of something . . . It is therefore particularly used of God . . . always in the living context of the worship and praise of God."[60] In the Koine papyri and inscriptions, Balz and Schneider point out that R. Bultmann thinks "[μένω] always involves a negation: *not to give way*. It does not . . . respond to the question 'where?' but rather to the question 'how long?' In the earliest Greek usage it concerned continuing at an objectively fixed place for an objectively determined time, and then later it involved continuation in a personal bond."[61] "In John the secular Greek [μένω ἐν] gained a meaning parallel to the Pauline conception of Christ's dwelling in the believer (Rom. 8:9ff.) and his dwelling in Christ. It is even expanded and strengthened."[62]

The Patristic literature also allows for continuation. "To abide . . . is to believe, obey, and persevere."[63] (See our discussion above on page 9.) The theme of continuance is explicitly or implicitly connected to the majority of patristic writings on abiding.

Various commentators speak generally about abiding. A master's thesis by Linda Oyer on the Johannine usage of μενείν indicates that abiding means remaining in the new covenant—the person of Christ.[64] She asserts that fruit corresponds to faithful obedience in response to what Christ has done. Andrew Murray writes of the work (or effort) abiding requires.[65] Rattey points out its uninterrupted nature: "Only when the life giving sap flows uninterruptedly through all the branches of the vine can they bear fruit freely."[66] Neal Flanagan likens abiding to love. "Abiding in Jesus through

---

59. Brown, *The Gospel According to John*, 224.

60. Ibid., 224.

61. Balz and Schneider, *Exegetical Dictionary*, 407.

62. Brown, *The Gospel According to John*, 225.

63. Edwards, *John*, 148.

64. Oyer, *Continuing in Covenant*, 79–82.

65. Other works on this topic include Carson, *The Gospel According to John*; Laney, "Abiding Is Believing"; Dillow, "Abiding Is Remaining in Fellowship"; and Segovia, *The Farewell of the Word*.

66. Rattey, *The Gospel According to Saint John*, 169.

love is what this little homily is about."[67] J. H. Bernard points out the volition and discipline of the one abiding: "In the spiritual sphere this 'abiding' is not maintained without the constant and conscious endeavor of the disciple's own will."[68] George Stevens says, "The fundamental thought of the allegory is that of the close, constant, loving fellowship of life between the believer and his Lord."[69] He also points out that "the Johannine conception of religion is especially favorable to devotion. It appeals powerfully to the imagination and the heart; it keeps alive the sense of a real and present Savior; it fills life . . . with a present fullness of joy and richness of experience."[70] F. Dean Lueking writes, "'To abide' has to do with persevering, continuing, lasting, staying with it. No wonder the term is rare. What it means is rare, in this or any time."[71] F. F. Bruce writes of abiding that it is "mutual indwelling, the coinherence, of Christ and his people."[72] Paul Anderson thinks abiding in Jesus is abiding in his love and that abiding finally manifests itself in knowing and doing the will of God in the world—as to love Jesus is to obey him.[73]

The phrase κἀγὼ ἐν ὑμῖν implies that abiding is reciprocal. Ernest Lussier develops the concept of mutual abiding in his thinking on reciprocal abiding.

> The Johannine use of the verb to abide . . . introduces us to the Johannine theology of immanence, that is, a remaining in one another that binds together Father, Son, and the Christian believer . . . [The] concept of reciprocal indwelling . . . is not the exclusive experience of chosen souls within the Christian community; it is the essential constitutive of all Christian life.[74]

As to the nature of what abiding actually consists of, Barclay writes:

> The secret of the life of Jesus was His contact with God. Again and again He withdrew into a solitary place to meet God. Jesus was always abiding in God. It must be so with us and Jesus. We must keep contact with him. We cannot do that unless we deliberately take steps to do it. There must be no day when we never think of Jesus and feel His presence. To take but one example—to

67. Flanagan, *The Gospel According to John*, 72.
68. See Bernard, "The Gospel According to St. John," 481.
69. Stevens, *The Johannine Theology*, 260.
70. Ibid., 264.
71. Lueking, "Abide in Me."
72. Bruce, *The Gospel and the Epistles of John*, 308.
73. Anderson, *The Riddles of the Fourth Gospel*, 224.
74. Lussier, *God Is Love*, 36, 38.

pray in the morning time, if it be for only a few moments, is to
have an antiseptic for the whole day; for we cannot come out of
the presence of Christ to touch the evil things. For some few of
us abiding in Christ will be a mystical experience . . . For most
of us it will mean a constant contact with Jesus Christ. It will
mean arranging life, arranging prayer, arranging silence in such
a way that there is never a day when we give ourselves a chance
to forget him.[75]

Cook writes about the elongated time factor and patient waiting. "For
fruitfulness there is need of 'abiding,' continuance, patient waiting, on the
part of those already 'in Christ.'"[76] Eckman develops the idea of continuance by saying that "the idea of abiding carries with it not only the thought
of continuousness, but also of exclusiveness."[77] The following illustration
shows the result of abiding and maximum nutrition:

There is an orchard on the north side of my orchard. Every week
the orchardists spray minor elements on the trees as leaf feeds.
Those trees have the best of care including the best irrigation
system, and the orchard continues to be manicured. Sometimes
I wonder how he can afford to continue to spend the money
he does. One day I took five minutes to walk through his gala
block. The fruit size was huge and leaf color was of the dark-
est green. I was envious. As I was admiring his fruit, I thought
about how we are to abide in Christ to produce his fruit. My
neighbor's trees are drawing life from the same water and the
same type of soil as mine only a few hundred yards away. My
trees are doing well and our nutrition program is good. But he
has given his trees the maximum levels of needed nutrition and,
as a result, his trees are doing fantastic—not just good.[78]

Consistently, the Johannine use of μένω refers to extended time in one
place or with one person who is staying/dwelling/remaining/lingering in
a state or condition. When John uses μένω, there is a sense of endurance,
continuance, tarrying, and waiting with expectancy over time.

John is clear and consistent in his use of μένω. Particularly in John
15, his use infers continuance, obedience, and extended time. John uses the
word to mean "extravagant time with Jesus." Extravagant time is marked
by both quality and quantity as abiding is both a state and a discipline. The

75. Barclay, *The Gospel of John*, 205.

76. Cook, *The Holy Bible According to the Authorized Version*, 218.

77. Eckman, *Studies in the Gospel of John*, 127.

78. Trask and Goodall, *The Fruit of the Spirit*, 166–67.

state of abiding requires the disciple to continually commune with Jesus. The discipline of abiding requires the disciple to spend daily blocks of time with Jesus.

In summary, the aorist imperative μείνατε lends an urgent priority to this lavishing of extravagant time on Jesus. The exegetical sense is that this time is spent dwelling with someone, continuing in a personal bond, and not giving way to other pressing needs.

Depending on Christ

4b καθὼς τὸ κλῆμα οὐ δύναται καρπὸν φέρειν ἀφ ἑαυτοῦ ἐὰν μὴ μένῃ ἐν τῇ ἀμπέλῳ, οὕτως οὐδὲ ὑμεῖς ἐὰν μὴ ἐν ἐμοὶ μένητε.

4b As the branch cannot bear fruit of itself, unless it abides in the grapevine, neither can you, unless you abide in me.

Jesus continues the metaphor of grapevine and branch by declaring the necessity of the branch to abide on the grapevine if it is to live and be fruitful. The phrase οὐ δύναται καρπὸν φέρειν ἀφ ἑαυτοῦ places negative emphasis, with ἀφ ἑαυτοῦ highlighting that the branch cannot bear fruit from itself. This emphasis points out that life and fruit are not simply "in itself the branch," but also not "from the branch," underlining that vital energy only comes from the grapevine.[79] In other words, "so neither can ye bear fruit of yourselves, or bear fruit at all, except in vital fellowship with me."[80] Rodney Whitacre points out that "people are able to produce much without God, including converts, good deeds and even prophecies, exorcisms, and miracles . . . but the divine life such as we see in Jesus is dependent on God's own character, power and guidance at work in the life of the disciple."[81] Brown writes that abiding is remaining in Jesus and states of the disciples that "if they remain in Jesus through faith, he remains in them through love and fruitfulness."[82] Abiding, for him, is total dependence on Jesus. His commentary on John 15:6 states: "The total dependence of the Christian on Jesus, which is the leitmotif of Johannine thought, is expressed nowhere more eloquently than here."[83] He refers to this abiding as "indwelling." The sense of the verse, in context, is that the only way to produce anything of substance requires intimate connection with divine life. One can produce

79. Westcott, The Gospel According to St. John, 199.
80. Ibid.
81. Whitacre, John, 375.
82. Brown, The Gospel According to John, 678.
83. Ibid.

fruit of oneself, but it will not be life giving.[84] Anderson agrees: "The mutual abiding of the branch and the vine is not only the source of vitality; it is also the only way to fruitfulness."[85] Only by abiding in Jesus does one produce life-giving fruit.

PROMISE OF THE HARVEST

This section of the exegesis studies Jesus' promise of fruit to the disciple that abides in him.

The One Who Abides Bears Fruit

> 5a ἐγώ εἰμι ἡ ἄμπελος, ὑμεῖς τὰ κλήματα. ὁ μένων ἐν ἐμοὶ κἀγὼ ἐν αὐτῷ οὗτος φέρει καρπὸν πολύν . . .
>
> 5a I am the grapevine, you are the branches. The one who abides in me, and I in him, this one bears much fruit . . .

As noted in our discussion of καρπὸν on page 12 above, the noun refers in secular Greek to the fruit of the ground, to the offspring of animals, or, in an extended sense, to the outcome or consequence of an undertaking, whether good or ill. In the Septuagint, "[καρπὸν] stands chiefly for the Hebrew *peri*, which in the OT is used for the fruit of plants (Deut. 7:13; Mic. 6:7). Finally it is used metaphorically for the fruit of an action (Hos. 10:13; Jer. 6:10; 17:10)."[86] The Church fathers tended to view fruit as those discipled. "Theophylact writes that the fruits of the apostles in verse 8 are the Gentiles."[87]

There is a divergence of opinion in modern literature as to what fruit could mean. Rosscup defines fruit as Christ-like character, confession of Christ's name in praise, contribution to those in need, conduct in general, and those converted through one's witness, citing 1 Corinthians 16:15 and Romans 1:13 as proof texts.[88] Rosscup does point out that "fruit" meaning "converts" has long been debated. F. F. Bruce has a polycentric approach to defining fruit, alternatively calling it the fruit of the Spirit or "likeness to

---

84. While it is true that some come to saving faith in Jesus through branches (disciples or pseudo-disciples) that are less than exemplary and that no disciple is perfect, it is also true that (over time) those imperfect disciples that abide in Jesus are used to continually make disciples—with no regrets, remorse, or negative repercussions.

85. Anderson, *The Riddles of the Fourth Gospel*, 224.

86. See Hensel, "καρπὸν," 721.

87. Edwards, *John*, 149.

88. Rosscup, *Abiding in Christ*, 78–84.

Jesus" or the one who "lives in union with the everlasting Christ."[89] John MacArthur seemingly borrows categories directly from Rosscup, listing definitions as Christ-like character, thankful praise, help to those in need, purity in conduct, and converts.[90] A. B. Bruce thinks fruit does refer to souls,[91] and R. C. H. Lenski thinks it refers to Christian character.[92] Rosscup points out that A. C. Gaebelein and John R. W. Stott agree with Lenski, but use the term *Christlikeness*. D. Moody Smith postulates that "the fruit of the branches is, of course, love; the command to love (verse 17) is the command to bear fruit."[93] In a later work he claims that the Synoptic Gospels show "fruit" to be good deeds accomplished through obedience to the words of Jesus, but then claims this text has no direct answer for the question of the nature of fruit.[94] He can only state, "It is therefore a reasonable inference that these fruit are works of love. Yet it may be a mistake to ask about the fruit specifically, as if, in allegorical fashion, it represents one specific thing or even theme."[95] Enough biblical and analytic evidence exists to make a case for both—fruit refers both to internal character issues and souls saved / disciples made. Other definitions of fruitfulness include Andreas Kostenberger's "love, character, and outreach,"[96] G. R. Beasley-Murray's "apostolic preaching,"[97] and Colin G. Kruse's "entire life and ministry."[98]

Many scholars view John's understanding of fruit to refer to making disciples. Andreas Kostenberger cites Birger Olsson's 1974 monograph detailing John's use of καρπός missiologically: "Olsson considers the word καρπός as the keyword of mission in John."[99] Olsson "also draws attention to the fact that Jesus' death is often linked in the Fourth Gospel to statements regarding the gathering of God's children (cf. especially 6:12–13, 17:21; 19:23–24; cf. also 11:52; 12:32; and John 21)."[100] Robert Hensel agrees with Kostenberger. "Paul uses [καρπὸν] in a further sense for the results of his missionary work (Rom. 1:13; Phil. 1:22). It can even be understood in the

---

89. Bruce, *The Gospel and the Epistles of John*, 312.

90. MacArthur, *Abiding in Christ*, 39–45.

91. Bruce, *The Training of the Twelve*, 412–14.

92. Lenski, *The Interpretation of John's Gospel*, 1029–1030.

93. Smith, *New Testament Theology*, 147.

94. Ibid., 283.

95. Ibid.

96. Köstenberger, *The Missions of Jesus*, 454.

97. Beasley-Murray, *Word Biblical Commentary*, 273.

98. Kruse, *John*, 318.

99. Köstenberger, *The Missions of Jesus*, 9.

100. Olsson, *Structure and Meaning*, 9.

sense that the apostles and, in particular, missionaries who are building up the churches by their labors 'live by their fruits.'"[101] Kostenberger continues, "Integrated into the strand of passages which deal with Jesus' calling of others to follow him are also references to these followers 'bearing fruit,' i.e., participating in the Messianic 'harvest.'"[102] In this sense, disciples are the fruit given by the Father to Jesus, so disciples are the fruit Christians are granted by Jesus to bear. Emmanuel Tukasi says, "The Father gives human beings to the Son (John 17:2, 6, 9, 24). The 'giving' is in the sense of 'assigning' or 'selecting' those people for the Son."[103] Both branch and fruit are chosen and guaranteed by election according to Lewis: "In verses 15 and 16, the thought turns to what we may with entire accuracy speak of as a doctrine of election . . . the initiative has been wholly that of Jesus. He has done the choosing, not the disciples."[104] W. F. Howard presses further and argues that "fruitfulness is the test of vitality."[105] He implies that if one is not bearing disciples, one is not performing one's vital work. Martin Luther agreed in his commentary on Galatians. He wrote that "those who follow the Lord bring with them most excellent fruits and maximum usefulness, for they that have them give glory to God, and with the same do allure and provoke others to embrace the doctrine and faith of Christ."[106] Barrett agrees with the general consensus of fruit referring to souls saved and discipled: "The fruits of the apostolic mission will be gathered in, and not be lost."[107] Brown states:

> Bearing fruit is symbolic of possessing divine life . . . and seems to relate to the apostolic ministry. In the agricultural *mashal*[108] involving harvest and fruit, the focus was very much on missionary enterprise. Seemingly, then, the imagery of trimming clean the branches so they bear more fruit involves a growth in love which binds the Christian to Jesus and spreads life to others . . . It may be false to think that the Johannine writer would have been aware of a distinction between a Christian's internal vitality and his apostolic activity directed towards others, for he would not have thought of the "life" of a Christian as something bent in upon itself in an unproductive seclusion. The sense that there were others who had to be brought into the flock (verse

101. See Hensel, "καρπὸν," 723.

102. Köstenberger, *The Missions of Jesus*, 130.

103. Tukasi, *Determinism and Petitionary Prayer*, 89.

104. Lewis, *Johannine Writings*, 59.

105. Howard, *Christianity According to St. John*, 133.

106. Luther, *Commentary on Galatians*, 378.

107. Barrett, *The Gospel According to St. John*, 399.

108. *Mashal* is the Hebrew word for "proverb."

16) was too strong in the first century to have been left out of any understanding of what it meant to be united to Jesus.[109]

Brown also makes a case that John's use of fruit in this passage refers to disciples made by disciples.[110]

Other scholars insist that fruit must have a broader definition. "Fruitfulness is defined in terms of loving relationships."[111] Fruit appears both in service and in character.[112] "In him there is the fruitfulness of true service to God, answered prayer, and of obedience in love."[113] "The bearing of fruit is simply living the life of a Christian disciple (see vv. 5, 8); perhaps especially the practice of mutual love (v. 12)."[114] Whitacre writes:

> Some scholars suggest Jesus is referring to the fruit that comes from bearing witness to Jesus, that is converts, the fruit of evangelism. At least twice in John the image of bearing fruit is used with something like this meaning (4:35–38; 12:24). Other scholars interpret this fruit as being the ethical virtues characteristic of the Christian life . . . But something more basic, something that underlies both missionary work and ethical virtues, seems to be intended. The development of the image in the next section (vv. 7–17) suggests that bearing fruit refers to the possession of the divine life itself and especially the chief characteristics of that life, knowledge of God (cf. 15:15) and love (15:9–14).[115]

This interpretation of fruit as the possession of divine life expressed in the knowledge of God and love for others is helpful but incomplete. The implication of that divine life is the producing of fruit—something tangible resulting from knowledge and love. Johannine expert Craig Keener seems to hold the view that in John's Gospel, fruit refers to gathered disciples.[116]

> Just as John the Baptist functions as a paradigmatic witness in the opening of John's Gospel, so do Jesus' disciples function as

109. Brown, *The Gospel According to John*, 676.

110. Brown notes that Polycarp (literally "much fruit"), a direct disciple of John, received his name because he bore much fruit (ibid., 676). Thus, Polycarp becomes a living example of the principle of fruit meaning disciple as he was the fruit of John's ministry, and he in turn made many disciples.

111. Colewell and Titus, *The Gospel of the Spirit*, 180.

112. See Bernard, "The Gospel According to St. John," 483.

113. Barrett, *The Gospel According to St. John*, 393.

114. Ibid., 395.

115. Whitacre, *John*, 373.

116. Although in Keener's 2003 commentary on John, he seems to indicate that fruit is not disciples but love.

paradigmatic for the community of believers. John is interested in those who believe through their proclamation (17:20). It is not only the first disciples who are fruit-bearing branches on Jesus the vine (15:1–8), who must abide and bear fruit (15:2–5, 8) persevere (15:6), and so forth. In his epistles John does not limit the Spirit to the Twelve (who receive the promise of the advocate in Jn. 14–16); rather, he limits the Spirit to all true believers (1 Jn. 2:20, 27; 3:24; 4:2, 13). Not all believers in the community have the same role as the first disciples, but the community as a whole shares their same mission and purpose: to make Christ known.[117]

Bernard makes provision for fruit to be both disciples and character growth: "Primarily the fruit of success in their apostolic labors, but also indicating the perfecting of personal character."[118]

The New Testament has a variety of understandings for fruit. Fruit is understood as literal fruit (Matt 21:19; Mark 4:29; James 5:7, 18; Rev 22:2), children (Luke 1:42; Acts 2:30; Heb 13:15), consequences of the acts of people (Matt 21:43), good works (Matt 3:8), results of missionary labor (Rom 1:13; Phil 1:22), offerings (Rom 15:28), character of spirit (Gal 5:22–23), and righteousness (Heb 12:11; James 3:18).[119]

John, however, has a very distinct and focused use of fruit. Of the eleven uses of καρπός in John (ten in John 15, one in John 4), all can be understood to be in the context of harvest. καρπός literally means "that which is harvested—'harvest, crop, fruit, grain.'"[120] The sense is of an external yield that can be gathered. While not unique in the New Testament in this regard,[121] John, especially in John 15, seems to emphasize that the fruit of abiding is a harvest of people. When John links the word καρπός (fruit) with the verb φέρω (I bear), this focus on a harvest of people is even more pronounced. John uses the term φέρω to specifically refer to the fruit of disciples. "In John 12:24 Jesus uses the image of the grain of wheat that falls into the ground, dies, and bears much fruit to describe the fruit of his own death. What is meant is the winning of disciples out of the world and the gathering of the community."[122] John intentionally connects fruit bearing in the life of Jesus with winning of disciples and gathering them into churches.

117. Keener, *The Gospel of John*, 41.

118. See Bernard, "The Gospel According to St. John," 489.

119. Kittel and Friedrich, "καρπός," in *Theological Dictionary*, 416–417.

120. Louw and Nida, "καρπός," in *Greek-English Lexicon*, 517.

121. Both Rom 1:13 and Phil 1:22 use the word fruit to refer to the fruit/harvest of souls.

122. Kittel and Friedrich, *Theological Dictionary*, 59.

John 15:5 carries this same sense of fruit being the harvest of souls. Kostenberger quotes D. A. Carson: "The fruit primarily in this verse [15:16] is the fruit that emerges from mission, from specific ministry to which the disciples have been sent. The fruit, in short, is new converts."[123] Kostenberger points out that Brooke Foss Westcott, John H. Bernard, Marie-Joseph Lagrange, and C. K. Barrett all agree with fruit being understood as converts/disciples.[124] Murray in "The True Vine" agrees:

> Just as entirely as Christ became the true Vine with the one object, you have been made a branch too, with the one object of bearing fruit for the salvation of men. The Vine and the branch are equally under the unchangeable law of fruit-bearing as the one reason of their being. Christ and the believer, the heavenly Vine and the branch, have equally their place in the world exclusively for one purpose, to carry God's saving love to men. Hence the solemn word: Every branch that beareth not fruit, He taketh it away.[125]

The weight of the evidence—in light of John's missionary intent—lends itself to "disciples" being the most likely meaning of Jesus when he used καρπὸν. Jesus is saying, "I am divine life; you are my disciples. If you abide on me, with me, in me—you will make disciples." Understanding καρπὸν to refer to disciples suggests an answer to the lingering question from 15:2. When Jesus notes that it is possible to be "in me" (ἐν ἐμοὶ) but not "bear fruit" (φέρον καρπὸν) (v. 2), he means it is possible to be a disciple of Jesus and not be making disciples. Disciples who are not making disciples are not acceptable to Jesus, so he makes provision to help them. God will lift up these non-disciple-making disciples out of the external context or internal conditions that inhibit disciple making. God will also further disciple (through allowed difficulty and active, loving discipline) those disciples who are making disciples so they may make more disciples.

When Jesus promised that the one who abides in him will bear much fruit, he meant "fruit" as disciples. The disciple who abides in Jesus will have divine life and power and will be used by Jesus to make many more disciples.

---

123. Köstenberger, *The Missions of Jesus*, 185.

124. Ibid. For other biblical references showing the link between abiding and fruit with fruit being understood as disciples/followers/converts, see Gen 1:11, 22, 28; 9:1, 7; 17:20; Psa 1:1–3; 91:1–2; 92:10–15; Isa 32:15; Jer 21:14; Hos 12:6; 14:8; Matt 4:19–20; 7:15–23; 10:1–16; 21:33–41, 43; Mark 4:13–20; Luke 8:15; John 5:38; 6:37; 8:28–32, 35; Acts 1:21–22; 2:42–47; Rom 7:4, 5; Eph 5:11; Phil 1:11; Col 1:6, 10; 1 Thess 2:19–20; 2 Tim 3:12; 4:17; Titus 3:14; James 1:3; 1:18; and Rev 14:4, 14–20.

125. Murray, "The True Vine."

The One Who Does Not Abide Bears Nothing

5b ὅτι χωρὶς ἐμοῦ οὐ δύνασθε ποιεῖν οὐδέν.

5b for without me you can do nothing.

The phrase οὐ δύνασθε ποιεῖν οὐδέν is a combination of two verbs. οὐ δύνασθε is the negation of the present indicative second person plural ("you are not able") and ποιεῖν the present tense, active, infinitive ("to do" or "to make") combined with the neuter singular negative pronoun οὐδέν ("nothing," "not one thing," or "not anything"). In the first half of verse five, Jesus promises that the result of abiding is disciples made. The second half of the clause warns that apart from abiding in Jesus, one "accomplishes nothing, there is no permanent result."[126] ποιεῖν means "to make or to do." Jesus/ John is specifically saying that without abiding, disciples cannot produce anything. Nothing—souls or otherwise—not one thing of spiritual, eternal value can be produced apart from abiding in Christ. The one who abides in Jesus bears (produces and carries to maturity) disciples; the one who does not abide in Jesus does not bear (produce and carry to maturity) anything.

The One Who Does Not Abide Is Burned

6 ἐὰν μή τις μένῃ ἐν ἐμοί, ἐβλήθη ἔξω ὡς τὸ κλῆμα καὶ ἐξηράνθη καὶ συνάγουσιν αὐτὰ καὶ εἰς τὸ πῦρ βάλλουσιν καὶ καίεται.

6 If anyone does not abide in me, such a one is let fall outside as a branch and is withered; and they gather them and throw them into the fire, and they are burned.

At this juncture in the text, Jesus introduces a third branch. The first branch introduced (15:2a) is in Christ, but not producing disciples. That branch will be lifted up (nurtured and taught to abide) so divine life will flow and disciples will be made. The second branch (15:2b) is the disciple of Christ who does make disciples. This disciple is disciplined, allowed to pass through difficulty and suffering, so he or she might be even more effective in making disciples. The third branch (15:6) is the disciple (in Christ) who does not abide.

The verb ἐβλήθη (aorist, passive, indicative, third person singular from βάλλω, "I throw / I let fall") indicates the fate of the one who does not abide in Jesus: that person is thrown / let fall. Scholars view the aorist use of ἐβλήθη differently. Some consider it an action predicted: ἐβλήθη is

126. Westcott, *The Gospel According to St. John*, 200.

used in the "prophetic past tense signifying that although the event is still future it is certain, and in the divine foreknowledge and decree is already done."[127] C. F. D. Moule explains that "the Aorist may be similarly explained as dramatically suggesting immediacy: he has forthwith been thrown out."[128] A reconciliation of these two views may be found in what is termed the proleptic aorist. "The proleptic aorist looks like a future, taking place after some actual or implied condition. The timeless aorist is a suitable tense to express this projection of the future into the present as if some event had already occurred."[129] In other words, the consequences of not lavishing extravagant daily time on Jesus are sure and swift. The immediate effect of not abiding is the absence of divine life that quickly leads to a condition "outside or apart from" (ἔξω)[130] the source of life and, thus, to dryness. The word ἐξηράνθη (he dries up) is an aorist passive indicative third person singular verb that suggests "immediacy of result, timeless and futuristic (Gnomic), a timeless tense connected to the past."[131]

The eventual negative result John records for the disciple who does not abide in Jesus is to be collected, thrown into the fire, and burned (καὶ συνάγουσιν αὐτὰ καὶ εἰς τὸ πῦρ βάλλουσιν καὶ καίεται). Because βάλλω can also mean "to let fall,"[132] the text implies that the falling out (ἐβλήθη) is an allowance, not a judgment. The disciple that (volitionally) does not abide withers and is allowed to fall off / outside from the grapevine to the ground. Then, after it dries and detaches from the grapevine, it is to be gathered and cast into the πῦρ (a fire, place of punishment, or shame).[133] The word ξηραίνομαι also means stiff or rigid.[134] Rigid, stiff branches are unable to draw life from the grapevine and, thus, dry up. The vinedresser lets them fall out. Eventually, they are καίεται, meaning ignited and burned until they are consumed.[135] A negative cyclical combination occurs—inflexibility and rigidity hinder abiding and lack of abiding results in inflexibility and rigidity.

These interpretations raise the question of sequence. Does the branch dry up and then fall, or fall and then dry up? ἐβλήθη ἔξω ὡς τὸ κλῆμα καὶ ἐξηράνθη ("that one falls [off] and is withered") suggests withering follows

---

127. Webster, *Syntax and Synonyms*, 91.

128. Moule, *An Idiom Book of New Testament Greek*, 12–13.

129. Moulton and Turner, *A Grammar of New Testament Greek*, 74.

130. Louw and Nida, "ἔξω," in *Greek-English Lexicon*, 715.

131. Moulton and Turner, *A Grammar of New Testament Greek*, 73.

132. Louw and Nida, *Greek-English Lexicon*, 43.

133. Ibid., 215.

134. Swanson, "ξηραίνομαι," in *Dictionary of Biblical Languages*.

135. Newman, *A Concise Greek-English Dictionary*, 91.

falling out. Viticulture offers an alternative option. Some viticulture experts contend, "unwanted growth is most easily removed while it is small, and early removal will have less of a dwarfing effect. Broken, dead, weak, or heavily shaded branches can be removed with little or no effect on a plant, no matter what the timing."[136] Others allow the branches that are unproductive to fall to the ground and dry up, making the separation from the vine easy—without tearing or ripping. Once the unproductive branch has dried, it disconnects easily from the vine and is discarded or burned.

Branches are not forced to abide. "The impartation of Christ's life is conditioned upon the will of the believer to possess it. If he [or she] desires and endeavors to secure attachment to Christ, his [or her] purpose will be met by the favor of the Lord. If this responsibility is neglected, then separation from the vine ensues."[137] According to John, disciples that become stiff and rigid are unable to draw life from the grapevine. The result is that they dry up and the vinedresser allows them to fall to the earth (in contrast to the branches that do not bear fruit and he lifts up in John 15:2). Eventually, these branches are so dry that they separate from the grapevine, are collected, and burned. They are burned (disposed of) as they are not accomplishing their intended purpose (bearing disciples) and so are good for nothing.[138] "The branch 'in Christ' that is eventually cut off from the vine is the man who called himself a Christian on earth even though his life did not manifest the fruits of genuine discipleship."[139]

In Jesus' missiological thinking, disciples are sent to harvest disciples. The power to harvest disciples comes from abiding in Jesus in order to draw life from him. Disciples who do not abide in Jesus will not harvest disciples (i.e., disciples with divine life), and the Father then lifts them up (or nurtures them) so they learn to abide (for the eventual purpose of harvesting disciples). This is the first branch. Disciples who do not respond to this grace period (this invitation to focus on drawing life from Jesus) eventually become hard, stiff, and resistant to God's overtures. He lets them fall to the ground where they wither and disconnect themselves from the vine. This is the third branch. There is nothing left for them but to be gathered and burned. Disciples who abide in Jesus will harvest disciples, and their reward is the joy of participating in the sufferings of Christ with the purpose of being used to bring even more disciples into the kingdom. This is the second

---

136. Harris, *Arboriculture*, 385.

137. Eckman, *Studies in the Gospel of John*, 132.

138. Similar to Matthew 5:13, salt that loses its flavor is good for nothing and is thrown out.

139. Espenhain, "Abiding in the Vine."

branch. In God's great master plan, the harvest cycle continues (John 15:16) as those disciples brought to faith by disciples, in turn, learn to abide in Jesus, which, in turn, grants the promise of their harvest participation.

The interpretation of βλήθη as "he lets fall" satisfies the question of sequence. Branches both begin to wither before falling and continue to do so after falling. Branches that refuse to abide in Jesus cut themselves off from the offered life of the grapevine and, thus, are allowed to fall to the ground where they begin to wither (though still connected to the grapevine). Once the branch is completely withered (ἐξηράνθη), it detaches itself from the grapevine and nothing is left for it but to be gathered and burned (shamed). Jesus candidly exhorts his disciples to abide in him. Abiding positions the disciple for all the other necessary components (dependence, obedience, and empowerment of the Spirit) needed to make disciples. Jesus warns his disciples if they do not abide in him, they will of their own choosing remove themselves from his life. They will wilt, be allowed to fall, and, ultimately, dry up and disconnect from the grapevine altogether. Nothing can be done for them; their lot is fiery shame.

When John related Jesus' command to abide, he used the verb μείνατε in the aorist, active, imperative, second person plural. According to Louw and Nida, when used in this sense, μείνατε means "remain in the same place over a period of time . . . stay."[140] The link to abiding being (customarily) repeated is provided by Buist M. Fanning, who says, "The constative aorist [is] used to heighten the urgency of the command and [calls] for customary or general occurrence."[141]

The One Who Abides Has Prayer Answered

7 ἐὰν μείνητε ἐν ἐμοὶ καὶ τὰ ῥήματά μου ἐν ὑμῖν μείνῃ, ὃ ἐὰν θέλητε αἰτήσασθε, καὶ γενήσεται ὑμῖν

7 If you abide in me, and my words abide in you, you will ask what you desire, and it shall be done for you.

ῥήματά, a neuter plural noun in the nominative case, refers to "a minimal unit of discourse, often a single word."[142] "This is how we remain in Jesus: by receiving and permanently holding . . . his utterances, the ῥήματά that come from his lips. He in us, and we in him, the medium and bond of

---

140. Louw and Nida, "μένω," in Greek-English Lexicon, 729.

141. Fanning, Verbal Aspect in New Testament Greek, 369–70.

142. Louw and Nida, "ῥῆμα," in Greek-English Lexicon, 390.

his spiritual union being his spoken word."[143] When Jesus' ῥήματά (words) abide in his disciples, the disciples ask what they desire and have it done for them—γενήσεται ὑμῖν (literally, "it shall come to pass for you"). αἰτήσασθε is to ask with urgency (second person plural imperative), even to the point of demanding. R. C. H. Lenski writes, "The aorist imperative 'ask for your-selves' is peremptory. We not merely *may* ask, we *must* ask."[144] αἰτήσασθε is also in the middle reflexive, an indicator that asking can be done personally with direct access to the throneroom of God. In other words, those who lav-ish extravagant daily time on Jesus have direct access to him, just as if they were the high priest entering the very presence of God. The asking reflects the will of the disciples, which when disciples abide is what God wills, which is, in turn, the fruit of more disciples being made. Jesus seems to indicate that the central disciplines to abiding are linked to the word of God ("my words") and prayer ("ask"). When Jesus' words abide (dwell extravagantly) in disciples as a complement to their abiding in him, the result is answered prayer.

GLORY OF THE HARVEST

This section of the exegesis reveals the means by which the Father receives glory. God is honored when his disciples make disciples. Disciples are veri-fied when they produce other disciples.

God Honored by Bearing Fruit

8a ἐν τούτῳ ἐδοξάσθη ὁ πατήρ μου, ἵωα καρπὸν πολὺν φέρητε . . .

8a By this my Father is glorified, in order that you bear much fruit . . .

The preposition and dative, singular, neuter pronoun ἐν τούτῳ (by this) looks back to a thought already indicated and forward to the clause it pre-cedes.[145] The phrase, ἐν τούτῳ, refers to the "perfect unity between the Son and the disciple, which results in the disciple's obtaining whatever he asks."[146] God is ἐδοξάσθη (glorified) when one abides in Jesus; his word abides in that one, and that one asks him for what is on his heart. All three actions align (abiding in Jesus, extravagant abiding of Jesus' word in his disciples,

---

143. Lenski, *The Interpretation of John's Gospel*, 1040.

144. Lenski, *The Interpretation of St. John's Revelation*, 1041.

145. Rogers and Rogers, *The New Linguistic and Exegetical Key*, 218.

146. Vincent, *Word Studies in the New Testament*, 250.

and prayer) in order that they bear much fruit. God's preparative methodology for disciple making is revealed: Abide in Jesus, allow Jesus' word to lavishly abide in his disciples, and pray—and his disciples will bear many disciples. In this process and result, God is greatly glorified.

Disciples Verified by Bearing Much Fruit

8b καὶ γένησθε ἐμοὶ μαθηταί.

8b and in order that you become my disciples.

It is in glorifying God (by abiding in Jesus, having his word abide in his disciples—which means disciples surrender to and obey his word—asking him for the things on his heart, and bearing many disciples) that believers in Christ become disciples. According to Marvin Vincent, καὶ γένησεσθε literally means "and ye shall become,"[147] which indicates that Christian discipleship implies progress and growth. It is also translated "you will be"—that is "prove to be"—as "the consequence has a kind of independence (in a final purpose clause) when the future is connected by a subjunctive."[148] Zerwick, however, disagrees: "[There] is no need to interpret [καὶ γένησεσθε] in this manner [that you may bear fruit and (so) you will be my disciples] as the future may be parallel to the subjunctive."[149] Rogers and Rogers state, "If the future is adopted it has a kind of independence: 'and then you will become.'"[150] These comments, taken together with the preferred text (i.e., choosing the option of the subjunctive, "in order that you might be my disciples," as opposed to the future, "you will be/become" or "you will [prove to] be my disciples"), support a meaning that refers to process. Discipleship is an ongoing formation, and as disciples glorify the Father (by abiding in Jesus, allowing his word extravagant dwelling or abiding in them, praying for the things on his heart, and bearing many disciples), they both are and increasingly becoming his disciples.

---

147. Ibid.

148. Blass and Debrunner, *A Greek Grammar*, 187.

149. Zerwick, *Biblical Greek*, 117.

150. Rogers and Rogers, *The New Linguistic and Exegetical Key*, 218.

SPIRIT OF HARVEST

This section of the exegesis describes the attitudes and spirit that harvest both requires and produces. Harvest workers are to minister in a spirit of love, joy, sacrifice, obedience, and friendship.

Love

> 9 καθὼς ἠγάπησέν με ὁ πατήρ, κἀγὼ ὑμᾶς ἠγάπησα μείνατε ἐν τῇ ἀγάπῃ τῇ ἐμῇ. 10 ἐὰν τὰς ἐντολάς μου τηρήσητε, υενεῖτε ἐν τῇ ἀγάπῃ μου, καθὼς ἐγὼ τὰς ἐντολὰς τοῦ πατρός μου τετήρηκα καὶ μένω αὐτοῦ ἐν τῇ ἀγάπῃ.
>
> 9 As the Father loves me, I also love you; abide in my love. 10 If you keep my commandments, you will abide in my love, just as I have kept my Father's commandments and abide in his love.

The verb ἠγάπησέν is the aorist, active, indicative, third person singular ("he loves or [has] loved"). Disciples are exhorted to abide in the love of Jesus (μείνατε ἐν τῇ ἀγάπῃ τῇ ἐμῇ), and they do so by τηρήσητε (you actively keep) continuing to obey[151] or guarding [his commands].[152] Ongoing obedience (i.e., discipline over time) guarantees abiding in the love of Jesus. Obedience is not the end; it is the means. Disciples cannot abide in Jesus and disobey his instructions. Abiding is not spiritual greed or a gluttony of spirituality removed from interaction with lost and suffering people. Abiding in Jesus gives disciples the divine life and power needed for obedience. Disciples stay in the love of Jesus by actively loving other people. Abiding is not an effortless, borderless individuality. "As always, this love is not personal affection, but the being of the disciple for his neighbor that completely determines his own existence. To abide in love . . . means continuing in the love that he has received, in the state of being love."[153] Rudolf Bultmann goes on to say, "To continue in love . . . is not to enjoy the peace of mind that comes from a self-sufficient assurance of salvation, nor is it indulgence in devotions or ecstasy. It is only real in that movement that consists in bearing fruit; it takes place in keeping the commandments."[154] He advocates a robust, active, fruit-bearing response to the love of God that is expressed in obedience to what God commanded. Foremost among those commands

---

151. Louw and Nida, "τηρέω," in *Greek-English Lexicon*, 468.

152. Rogers and Rogers, *The New Linguistic and Exegetical Key*, 218.

153. Bultmann, *The Gospel of John*, 540.

154. Ibid., 541.

is the command to love one another practically and make disciples globally. When disciples abide in Jesus, they receive his love, and his love empowers them to obey his command to sacrificially love others.

Joy

> 11 ταῦτα λελάληκα ὑμῖν ἵνα ἡ χαρὰ ἡ ἐμὴ ἐν ὑμῖν ᾖ καὶ ἡ χαρὰ ὑμῶν πληρωθῇ.
>
> 11 These things I have spoken to you, that my joy may abide in you, and that your joy may be full.

The noun χαρά indicates a state of joy and gladness. "To forestall the notion that obedience is all gloom and doom . . . , Jesus avers, to the contrary, that the goal of his instruction . . . is all about joy."[155] Whitacre writes, "We are in intimate union with him and swept up into his dance for which we were created and which brings the deepest fulfillment and deepest joy to our lives."[156]

Jesus has such joy in the harvest and such joy in obeying the Father who is Lord of the harvest that he guarantees his joy will abide (endure) in his disciples as they abide in him. Joy is the sign and the reward of those who lavish extravagant daily time on Jesus. This joy is not necessarily emotion, but the deep-rooted and sustained exuberance of being swept up into the dance of the God of mission. Jesus spoke these collective truths to his disciples because he knows that in his truths they will find great joy. Abiding in Christ leads to making disciples. Making disciples completes the disciples' joy. The verb πληρωθῇ is a third person passive—literally "he or she is made total or complete."[157] How great is the Father's love for Jesus' disciples! For the assignment he gives them (making disciples) not only glorifies him, but it also brings them the highest level of joy—it completes them.

Sacrifice

> 12 αὕτη ἐστὶν ἡ ἐντολὴ ἡ ἐμή, ἵνα ἀγαπᾶτε ἀλλήλους καθὼς ἠγάπησα ὑμᾶς. 13 μείζονα ταύτης ἀγάπην οὐδεὶς ἔχει, ἵνα τις τὴν ψυχὴν αὐτοῦ θῇ ὑπὲρ τῶν φίλων αὐτοῦ.

---

155. Köstenberger, *John*, 456.
156. Whitacre, *John*, 378.
157. See Louw and Nida, "πληρόω," in *Greek-English Lexicon*, 598.

12 This is My commandment, that you love one another as I have loved you. 13 Greater love has no one than this, than to lay down one's life for his friends.

The verb ἀγαπᾶτε is a present, active, subjunctive. It indicates an ongoing action—"you keep on loving." "It is only when disciples abide in Christ—in his words, in his love—that we shall be able to keep on loving one another"![158] When verses 12 and 13 are considered together, "keeping on loving each other" logically concludes in laying down one's life (dying willingly) for one's friends. "Oddly, Jesus does not spell out what this means in practice. He does not, for example, repeat the command to 'wash each other's feet' ([John] 13:14) nor does he provide any concrete illustration of love for one another."[159] This love for one another must, therefore, encompass everything from the menial to the ultimate—dying for one's friends. The word φίλων is a genitive plural adjective and refers to associates for whom there is affection and personal regard.[160] "The word for friends, [φίλων], is related to a verb meaning 'love' . . . and conveys a greater sense of intimacy than does our modern use of friend."[161] Jesus tells his disciples to love one another as he has loved them. Christ's love would take him to the cross, a literal dying for his current disciples and the disciples yet to be harvested. The implications of this verse for missionary teams are staggering. Jesus expects his disciples to keep on loving one another and the pre-disciples (converts-to-be) through trial and disappointment even to the point of substitutionary death. This love is to be joyfully demonstrated (verse 11). It is the disciple's great joy to lay down his or her life (and will) for his or her friends, team members, and brothers and sisters in Christ.

Obedience

14 ὑμεῖς φίλοι μού ἐστε ἐὰν ποιῆτε ἃ ἐγὼ ἐντέλλομαι ὑμῖν.

14 You are my friends if you do whatever I command you.

"Jesus chose us to be ambassadors . . . first to come to Him, and then to go out to the world and that must be the daily pattern and rhythm of our lives . . . Jesus sends us out . . . to attract men into Christianity."[162] Disciples do this as his friends, "[but] the idea of being the friend of God has also

158. Hendricksen, *The Gospel of John*, 305.

159. Michaels, *The Gospel of John*, 811.

160. Louw and Nida, "φίλων," in *Greek-English Lexicon*, 447–48.

161. Whitacre, *John*, 379.

162. Barclay, *The Gospel of John*, 209.

a background. Abraham was the friend of God (Isa 41:8)."[163] Abraham's friendship with God intertwined with God's missionary purposes. God blessed Abraham to be a blessing to all nations. Friendship with God is inseparably linked with passion for God's glory among all peoples. What endeared Abraham to God was, in part, his refusal to withhold what was most precious to him when God asked for it. Jesus asks his disciples to keep loving one another even to the point of physically and joyfully dying for one another.

The word ἐὰν is a conditional adverb translated "if." If Christians keep loving each other, even to death, they so emulate Jesus in his act of glorious condescension that he calls them friends.[164] Friendship with God must be understood in the Abrahamic context of utter sacrifice (Isaac) and blessing to the nations (Genesis 12). Adoption of God's missionary heart elevates disciples from being his servants to becoming his friends—if disciples do whatever God tells them to do. In the context of the passage, what disciples are to do first is quite clear—abide. From abiding in Jesus comes the wisdom to depend, the will to obey, and the power to bear more disciples.

Friendship

> 15 οὐκέτι λέγω ὑμᾶς δούλους, ὅτι ὁ δοῦλος οὐκ οἶδεν τί ποιεῖ αὐτοῦ ὁ κύριος ὑμᾶς δὲ εἴρηκα φίλους, ὅτι πάντα ἃ ἤκουσα παρὰ τοῦ πατρός μου ἐγνώρισα ὑμῖν.

> 15 No longer do I call you servants, for a servant does not know what his master is doing; but I have called you friends, for all things that I heard from my Father I have made known to you.

The transfer from δούλους to φίλους happens after Jesus reveals all things he heard from the Father. Days away from his crucifixion, Jesus summarized his mission and the missionary heart of his Father by giving his disciples the basic blueprint. The disciples are given the plan and the means. God's plan is for them to make disciples of all nations (the wider context of John's gospel). God's primary means for disciple bearing is abiding. Continuance in (i.e., obedience to) the word and prayer maintains this abiding, which glorifies the Father for the relational union and the disciples that result. Continuance in the word reveals the content of what disciples must obey, and obedience keeps disciples in God's love with the surprising benefit of complete joy. This love (of Jesus for us) and joy (of engaging in what disciples were created

---

163. Ibid., 208.

164. Hendricksen, *The Gospel of John*, 306.

for) gives disciples the power to love one another at great cost. When disciples love one another at great cost, they so endear themselves to the Father that he promotes them from servants to friends because they understand his character, his means, and his ends. No longer unthinking, unknowing instruments, disciples now share a sympathetic union with the Father and ascend the heights of partnership in mission with the Lord of the harvest.[165]

Disciples are true friends of Jesus because they obey what he tells them to do and they understand and participate in his plan to make disciples of every nation. Disciples are true friends of Jesus because they pursue his plan in the very same way he did. Disciples abide in Jesus (as he abided in his Father); disciples abide in his word (as he on his Father's word); disciples ask for the things on his heart (as he asked for the things on his Father's heart); disciples obey him (as he obeyed the Father); disciples receive and pass on his love (as he received and passed on the love of his Father); disciples are joyfully completed in service (as he was joyfully completed); and disciples are empowered to lay down their lives for others (as he laid down his life for us). Union of spirit, heart, method, and experience elevates disciples from servants of God to friends of God.

PARTICIPATION OF HARVEST

In this section, the exegesis reveals how harvest workers are selected.

Jesus Chooses the Workers

16a οὐχ ὑμεῖς με ἐξελέξασθε, ἀλλ ἐγὼ ἐξελεξάμην ὑμᾶς . . .

16a You did not choose me, but I chose you . . .

According to Louw and Nida, ἐγὼ ἐξελεξάμην (I chose) refers to the making of "a special choice based upon significant preference, often implying a favorable attitude toward what is chosen."[166] Jesus did not randomly select his disciples but chose them lovingly and for special purpose. The same words are used by Jesus in Acts 9:15, when he says of Paul, "I have chosen him to serve me, to make my name known to Gentiles." The selection of the disciples was not based on merit. "The ground of God's love for us never lies in us, always in himself, for even apart from his love for us God is love."[167]

---

165. Westcott, *The Gospel According to St. John*, 206.

166. Louw and Nida, "ἐκλέγομαι," in *Greek-English Lexicon*, 361–63.

167. Hendricksen, *The Gospel of John*, 307.

God is love, God loves us, and God loves those beyond us, and the "disciples' status as Jesus' 'friends' is not an idle privilege; it carries with it a solemn responsibility and is granted in the context of being sent on a mission."[168] Disciples are chosen, in love, for mission. Of all the people Jesus could select, he intentionally sets apart disciples in order to lavish upon them love—love for himself and love for the other (the other disciple and other lost sheep). In that lavishing is the opportunity to abide with him, to make disciples, to have extravagant daily abiding in (and forming from) the word, to have prayers answered, to love colleagues, to be completed by joy, to lay down one's life, to understand Jesus' heart, and to share in accomplishing his purpose. Disciples do not select these great opportunities themselves, but Jesus handpicks them himself for these exceedingly great rewards.

Jesus Appoints Workers to Raise New Workers

16b καὶ ἔθηκα ὑμᾶς ἵνα ὑμεῖς ὑπάγητε καὶ καρπὸν φέρητε . . .

16b and appointed you that you should go and bear fruit . . .

The disciples were chosen for a specific mission task. The verb ἔθηκα is an aorist verb in the active tense in the indicative first person singular and refers to assigning a particular task. In this case, the disciples were appointed to bear disciples (ὑμεῖς ὑπάγητε καὶ καρπὸν φέρητε, or "you should go and bear fruit"). "The term 'appoint' . . . probably reflects Semitic usage . . . The same or a similar expression is used in the OT for God's appointment of Abraham as father of many nations."[169] Kostenberger quotes D. A. Carson as proposing this "most naturally refers to the making of new converts."[170] The verb πάγητε ("go") should not be overlooked in importance. Jesus is sending them and exhorting them to make disciples as they move along. "'Go and bear fruit' are closely linked, almost to the point that 'go' functions as a helping verb . . . [The] accent is on . . . 'bearing fruit' in the sense of making new disciples or winning new converts."[171] J. Ramsey Michaels also cites Chrysostom as drawing the imagery of the metaphor of the grapevine extending its branches throughout the world.[172] The sending motif of John's gospel emerges in this injunction. Disciples are sent into all the world to make disciples. This rendering of the text is consistent with the Great Com-

168. Köstenberger, *John*, 459.
169. Ibid.
170. Ibid., 460.
171. Michaels, *The Gospel of John*, 815–16.
172. Ibid., 816.

mission of Matthew 28:19, which also links *going* with disciple making. The linking of *going* and *disciple bearing* emphasizes Jesus' missional intent in this passage.

Jesus Desires New Workers to Abide

> 16c καὶ ὁ καρπὸς ὑμῶν μένη, ἵνα ὅ τι ἄν αἰτήσητε τὸν πατέρα ἐν τῷ ὀνόματί νου δῷ ὑμῖν.
>
> 16c and that your fruit should abide, that whatever you ask the Father in my name he may give you.

The new converts that are made should in turn μένη (present active verb in third person singular). The cycle of harvest comes full circle. Disciples have made disciples as a result of abiding in Jesus. These new disciples in turn abide in Jesus and the harvest cycle begins all over again. "A true disciple prays for fruits, for these fruits are pleasing to God."[173] The answered prayer is again in the context of disciples being made and learning to reproduce. The disciples "have the assurance that Jesus has chosen and appointed them for this activity [to bear disciples] and that the Father will answer their prayers."[174]

Abiding prayer "that whatever you ask the Father in my name, he may give you" (John 15:16) is inescapably linked to mission. About this passage, Piper says, "Notice the amazing logic of this verse. He gave them a mission 'in order that' the Father would have prayers to answer. This means that prayer is for mission. It is designed to advance the kingdom."[175]

Jesus appointed disciples to abide in him. When disciples abide, they produce new disciples. Jesus' intention for these new disciples is that they, in turn, will abide in him and, thus, bear their own disciples. In this ongoing abiding, the harvest is guaranteed and the Father glorified.

Jesus Commands Workers to Love One Another

> 17 ταῦτα ἐντέλλομαι ὑμῖν, ἵνα ἀγαπᾶτε ἀλλήλους.
>
> 17 These things I command you, that you love one another.

---

173. Hendricksen, *The Gospel of John*, 308.
174. Whitacre, *John*, 381.
175. Piper, *A Holy Ambition*, 155.

The word ταῦτα is a demonstrative pronoun that is plural. It "indicates all that Jesus has commanded them is designed to teach them the lesson of mutual love."[176] Westcott, however, disagrees: "This verse must be taken as the introduction of a new line of thought, and not, according to the modern texts, as the summing up in conclusion of what has gone before. On this point the usage in St. John is conclusive against the received arrangement."[177] Textual evidence supports the view of Westcott. Most likely, Jesus sets up his discourse on persecution by underscoring that only mutual love will help the community through the trials ahead.

EXEGETICAL SUMMARY

The premise of this exegesis of John 15:1–17 contends that John's writings are missiological in intent. Jesus is the source of life as the true grapevine (v. 1a). The grapevine is not the nation, religion, or any other entity—only Jesus gives divine life. In Trinitarian unity, the Father plays the role of gardener-nurturer in mission (v. 1b). The branches are disciples, followers of Jesus (v. 2a), who are flexible, pliable, and designed for organic, connected growth—even when transplanted disciples remain constantly connected to Jesus as they spread his gospel to all the world. Disciples in Christ who do not bear fruit are not abiding, because Jesus promised that those who abide bear fruit. Jesus will lift up these non-abiding disciples (i.e., nurtured in one form or another) for a season so they may learn to abide and then bear fruit. Disciples that bear fruit (v. 2b) are cleansed—led through affliction by God—so they may learn to better abide and, thus, bear more fruit. Jesus' word (v. 3) is the primary means of leading disciples to cleansing. To abide means to linger with a person, to dwell with them, to endure. Abiding (v. 4a) is not a place, but a duration of time— a refusal to give way. Abiding is reciprocal constant contact with Jesus. Abiding is both constant communion and concentrated blocks of time with him. Divine life does not come from the branch (v. 4b); the life that bears fruit can only come from vital relationship with Jesus.[178] Fruit is disciples (v. 5a). Just as Jesus was sent to make disciples, so disciples are sent to make disciples. Jesus is divine life, and as

---

176. Rogers and Rogers, *The New Linguistic and Exegetical Key*, 218–19.

177. Westcott, *The Gospel According to St. John*, 208.

178. This text does not imply that abiding bears fruit contrary to (or outside of) other contributing factors. Language learning, relational skills, longevity, opportunity, favor, sovereignty, and a host of other issues contribute to fruitfulness. Some of the complexities of this challenge are detailed in the concluding section under "Operationalizing of Abiding Mission Theory."

his disciples abide on, in, and with him, they will have the life and power to make disciples in turn. Without abiding in Jesus, disciples cannot make true disciples—and to not make disciples is to accomplish nothing.

Disciples who do not abide in Jesus (v. 6) become dry and rigid. If nurtured or restored, disciples learn to abide in Jesus and begin to produce disciples. If they do not learn to abide in him, they become stiff and rigid. If disciples are rigid, inflexible, and unresponsive to his overtures, Jesus does not force them to abide but will let them fall. In that fallen state, they wither until they separate themselves from the grapevine with no ability to draw divine life. There is nothing left for such disciples but to be released from service (or marginalized). Abiding in Jesus (v. 7) is anchored by attentiveness (obedience) to God's word and sharing in God's heart and will through prayer. The disciple's mandate to bear disciples is given so the Father has prayers to answer. When disciples pray for disciples, God answers and produces many disciples through them, and this glorifies himself (v. 8a). When disciples abide in Jesus, allow his word to shape them, and pray for the things on his heart (and receive them), they further glorify God (v. 8b). Followers of Jesus are both disciples already and increasingly becoming his disciples, proving and developing their discipleship. Disciples continue in the love of Jesus (vv. 9–10) by discipline over time in obedience to his words and commands and by loving one another locally as they make disciples globally.

All of the above leads to joy (v. 11). From the well of joy comes sacrificial giving (vv. 12–13). Disciples give their lives for their colleagues and for their disciples, even as Jesus did. Disciples rejoice to die for both their colleagues and pre-converts. It is the missionary call—dying in an effort to save others. Love for Jesus leads disciples to share in his willingness to die for the lost. There is no greater love than this God-sourced missionary love. Those who share God's missionary ambition and participate in the cost are, like Abraham, friends of God (v. 14). When disciples understand God's passion (to abide, to share in his sufferings, to make disciples, to obey his word, to pray his heart, to give him glory, to experience his joy, and to die as Christ did), he is so pleased with them that he elevates them to friends (v. 15). God has chosen specific disciples for this full experience (v. 16a). God's chosen disciples are to go and make disciples (v. 16b). God intends his disciples' disciples to, in turn, abide (v. 16c), which will result in further disciples and an ongoing harvest. God is the guarantor of this renewable effort. God knows this will be a difficult process going forward and so exhorts disciples to continue loving one another (v. 17).

The above exegesis of John 15:1–17 reveals fourteen critical aspects of abiding further detailed in Appendix J.

Section 2

Historical Perspective

THE EXEGESIS IN THE previous section established that abiding leads to disciples. This section examines the historical context of mission agencies during the years 1880 to 1920 and the abiding praxis of exemplar fruitful missionaries in that period. This specific period was chosen as it begins with the end of the "great century" of Christian mission (late 1800s) and ends with the beginning of the "Pentecostal century" of Christian mission (early 1900s). Many missiological issues wrestled with today are but repetition of what greater souls and minds resolved in that day.

Missionary giants Daniel Comboni (Catholic), Samuel Zwemer (Presbyterian), Oswald Chambers (Pentecostal Prayer League/YMCA), Temple Gairdner and Douglas Thornton (Anglican), Lillian Trasher (Assemblies of God), and Lilias Trotter (Independent) all lived in, worked from, or passed through Cairo between 1880 and 1920. With the possible exception of Daniel Comboni (who died in 1881), all of them knew each other and influenced one another. These missionaries were chosen based on their fruitfulness according to the John 15 understanding of making disciples.[1] Disciples are not necessarily converts. Zwemer did not lead Muslims to the Lord according to the historical record, but he discipled a whole generation of missionaries who lived in the Islamic world. Disciples are not necessarily made while the disciple-maker is living. Chambers made more disciples posthumously

---

1. These women and men were faithful to the call of God—and not all saw disciples in their lifetime. Paul points out that some plant, others water, but the Lord brings the increase (1 Cor 3:5–9). Sometimes the example of faithful apostles does not result in converts/disciples immediately but down the road through the ministry of others. At other times, fruitful disciples inspire others to make converts.

through his writings than he did while living. All of the missionaries researched in this study discipled extraordinary numbers of people (whether new converts or those converted long ago) both in their life and after their death.

The next two chapters will answer the following research question: How did fruitful missionaries to Muslim peoples in Egypt and Northern Sudan during the years 1880–1920 abide in Jesus? To establish a foundation for the answer, the research will first investigate the political and ecclesiastical climate of Egypt and Sudan from 1880 to 1920, followed by an overview of biographical information of the selected missionaries. After establishing the historical review, the abiding praxis of the missionaries will be examined to see if their living out of abiding confirms the definition of abiding that emerged from our exegesis.

3

Mission Context of Egypt and Sudan (1880–1920)

THIS PORTION OF THE book examines the historical context of Egypt and Sudan and sets the stage for the exemplary missionary figures that lived in these countries during the period 1880–1920.

MISSIONS CONTEXT OF EGYPT

Missionary activity in the nineteenth century is directly connected to the evangelical awakenings in Europe (particularly Britain) and America in the eighteenth century. In 1763, Henry Venn wrote *The Complete Duty of Man* in which, Paul Sedra notes, Venn argues that "Christ had suffered upon the cross for all and, thus, that salvation was within reach of all."[1] Sedra also mentions William Carey and his work *An Enquiry Into the Obligations of Christians to Use Means for the Conversion of the Heathens* where Carey argues that Christ "has a kingdom that is to be proclaimed in its power to the ends of the earth and that all Christians [have] a duty to engage in the proclamation of the kingdom, whether the time allotted by God for the fulfillment of this purpose be long or short."[2] Carey founded "The Particular Baptist Society for the Propagation of the Gospel Among the Heathen" in the same year, and in 1793 he sailed for India as the first member of the Baptist Missionary Society. In 1795, the London Missionary Society was established, followed by the Church Missionary Society (CMS) in 1799:

1. Sedra, *From Mission to Modernity*, 38.
2. Ibid.

In June 1811, Dr. Cleardo Naudi, a Maltese Catholic, addressed a letter to the headquarters of the CMS in London. He lamented the state of "degradation" into which Eastern Christendom had fallen, and called upon the Anglican church to enlighten the Christian Churches, given the failure of Rome to effect change . . . The Mediterranean Mission then inaugurated would . . . aim at the spiritual revival of the fallen Eastern Churches. Nevertheless, there was, throughout, a broader aim in mind—the conversion of the "heathen" of Asia and Africa. Given limited resources, the CMS was incapable of converting all the Muslims and pagans who rimmed the Mediterranean—but if the existing Churches in such areas were infused with the evangelical ethos, with an uncorrupted Christian spirit, then perhaps, both by example and through missionary zeal, they could contribute to the conversion of the "heathen" themselves.[3]

In 1801, the British defeated the French in Egypt (the 1802 Treaty of Amiens nominally returned Egypt to Ottoman control). Wellington defeated Napoleon at Waterloo in 1815, breaking the power of the French in the Mediterranean forever. This opened the door, with respect to safety and communication, for greater British missionary presence on the Mediterranean rim. William Jowett was made the CMS Literary Representative for the Mediterranean and visited Egypt in 1819, 1820, and 1823, and proposed that both Alexandria and Cairo were crucial beachheads for the gospel.[4] In 1824, the Ottoman Sultan forbid the importation of Scripture into his empire, but Muhammad Ali (wanting the favor of the European powers) was more tolerant to religious activity and the *firman* (imperial decree) of the Sultan was not honored in Egypt.[5] Egypt offered security and freedom of movement; this was irresistibly attractive to European and American mission boards.

The earliest record of missionary endeavor in Egypt is by the Moravian Church, "which had its beginning in 1752 and lasted for thirty years."[6] Several early Moravian missionaries died. "The results of their devoted labors are found in the individual lives they touched and quickened," since they "undertook to establish no ecclesiastical organization."[7] In 1825, CMS sent five German missionaries from Basle seminary to Egypt—including Samuel

---

3. Ibid., 39.
4. Ibid., 39–40.
5. Ibid., 40.
6. Watson, *The American Mission in Egypt*, 130.
7. Ibid.

Gobat who afterwards became bishop of Jerusalem—but discontinued the mission in 1826, discouraged at the lack of results.

The United Presbyterian Mission began in 1854 as a result of a resolution at First Presbyterian Church of Allegheny on May 21, 1853.[8] Thomas McCague and his wife arrived in Cairo on November 15, 1854, and James Barnett (from Syria) joined them nine days later.

Much of the focus of evangelism in the early years of the Presbyterian mission was on the Coptic population. In 1867, the British protectorate allowed the Coptic Church to tour the country and forcibly recruit any children of Copts who converted to Christianity for the army.[9] The young church survived the hostility, and between 1870 and 1880 the Presbyterian Church in Egypt grew in members (from 180 to 985), in attendees (from 438 to 2,083), and in schools (from 12 to 44). During the rebellion of 1882, "although the Moslems around them threatened to murder all the Christian men and appropriate their wives and daughters and property; yet during all these troublous times, not one of these Protestant Christians was harmed, nor were their services interfered with."[10]

By 1895, the mission oversaw 33 churches and 119 schools, and had more than 8,886 persons in Sunday worship. In 1903, the Presbyterian missionaries heard of their colleagues in India who resolved to reach India by appealing for 180 new missionaries. This startling strategic hope encouraged the United Presbyterian Mission to believe for the "actual evangelization of Egypt . . . After long, careful and prayerful consideration . . . an appeal was issued . . . to the church in America for 280 new missionaries."[11]

The CMS left Egypt in 1862, but reopened its work there twenty years later (1882) when F. A. Klein, an Arabic scholar and literary man, transferred from Palestine; and then, in 1888, F. J. Harpur, a doctor, transferred from Arabia to Cairo. They initiated the two main means of reaching out to Muslims for both CMS[12] and other agencies that would follow their lead:

---

8. The reason for the resolution was fourfold: three of the reasons were linked to finding refuge (health reasons) and rest (political strife) for Presbyterian missionaries in Syria; only the fourth reason was stated "to meet the spiritual needs of Egypt." Watson, *Egypt and the Christian Crusade*, 153. See also Watson, *The American Mission in Egypt*, 152.

9. Ibid., 167–68.

10. Ibid., 198.

11. Ibid.

12. Early CMS policy was to confine itself to work among Muslims, but this was not to the exclusion of partnering with Copts who converted and joined the effort.

medicine and literature. The CMS mission in Cairo was seen as a base for advance up the Nile into Sudan.[13]

The North Africa Mission[14] (a non-denominational mission of British origin) worked in Morocco, Algeria, Tunis, Libya, and Egypt, entering Egypt in 1892.[15] On December 6, 1892, the mission agencies in Cairo agreed to form the Egyptian YMCA. Four nationalities (English, Egyptian, Syrian, and Greek) were involved, and on January 9, 1893 the YMCA in Alexandria opened its doors. The English, Germans, and Egyptians joined the association and focused on soldiers from the start.[16] The Egypt General Mission (Independent) began work among Muslims in 1898. A German mission, called Sudan Pioneer Mission, intended to work into Sudan among Bisharin Arabs and Nubians from the Egyptian city of Aswan. The Canadian Holiness Movement and the Pentecostal Bands of the World missions began work in Egypt in 1899.[17]

Most missionary methods in Egypt during the period 1880–1920 involved general service (medical, professorial, educational), itinerant bookselling, evangelism in reading rooms, the visitation and education of secluded women, and literature distribution. Challenges during this period arose from the formalism of the Protestant church (especially among second-generation believers), animosity between Copts and Muslims (and its prejudice that began creeping into the church), and the resistance of both the British government and the Islamic community to evangelism. Heather Sharkey says:

13. Watson, *The American Mission in Egypt*, 200.

14. In 1905, Annie Van Sommer and Arthur T. Upson, two British missionaries connected to the North Africa Mission, founded the Nile Mission Press (NMP) in Egypt to produce evangelistic literature in Arabic for Muslims. The press was based in Cairo but coordinated from Tunbridge Wells, England. See Sharkey, *American Evangelicals in Egypt*, 90.

15. The North Africa Mission was founded in November 1881, when their first mission station was established in Morocco by George Pearse, H. Grattan Guiness, and Edward H. Glenny. See Steele, *Not In Vain*, 15.

16. *Fifty Years*, 306.

17. Lewis Glenn notes that other missions to Egypt included the Holland Mission (1868), the Peniel American Mission (1897), Bethel Orphanage (1898), and Church of Scotland Mission to Jews (1858). Smaller independent missions also began working in Egypt at that time—some of them precursors to the Assemblies of God. "On January 21, 1905, L. E. Glenn and company of workers started for Egypt to open a missionary work" (*Missionary Travels in Bible Lands*, 35). Glenn and friends were a part of the Nile Valley Mission out of Bedford, Indiana. The Missionary Holiness Herald and The Vanguard publication helped solicit prayers and finances for this independent holiness endeavor.

The euphoria, confidence, and bravado that had distinguished missionaries after 1882 was subsiding by the time World War I ended. After 1918, American Presbyterians in Egypt showed persistence but greater caution as Muslim nationalists stood up to challenge the aspects of Christian missionary work—notably, evangelization among Muslims—they regarded as not only inappropriate and repugnant but subversive.[18]

Historians have long contended that World War I negatively affected European missions as the "Christian" sending nations mercilessly killed each other. "But while the war weakened the mainline Protestant missions, it strengthened the evangelical vision of American independent 'faith missions', sponsored by conservative, fundamentalist Protestant church groups, who saw in its apocalyptic destruction a sign of the millennium to come."[19] An outstanding feature of the time was the willingness of the mission agencies to work together. This was evidenced by the Cairo conference of 1906, the Edinburgh conference of 1910 (with a focus on Islam), and the Lucknow, India conference of 1911.[20] All three of these conferences celebrated an ecumenical approach to mission among Muslims. External pressure often forges unity. For the missionaries in Egypt and Sudan from 1880 to 1920 this was certainly the case.[21] Ironically, much of the pressure came from the Imperial British regime.

Many British missionaries and Coptic Christians were perturbed by the policies of British rulers. It appeared to them that British "neutrality" was in actuality a catering to a Muslim majority. Their charges were not groundless. Copts were kept from high offices they once held, not allowed representation on provincial councils; and were taxed to support schools in which Islam was taught. As Friday was made the legal holiday, they

18. Sharkey, *American Evangelicals in Egypt*, 95.

19. Ibid.

20. Lucknow 1911 refined plans for pooling resources to train missionaries, share advice on methods, and produce a Christian literature for Muslims not only in Arabic but also in languages such as Persian and Urdu that were widely used by Muslims. Conference leaders also resolved to establish a joint international and interdenominational study center in Cairo (The Cairo Study Center) to train Protestant missionaries in Arabic and Islamic studies for work throughout the Islamic world. See Sharkey, *American Evangelicals in Egypt*, 92.

21. Though Andrew Watson of the American Mission (Presbyterian) wrote in 1897, "The entrance of the C.M.S. and the N.A.M. into a field so long occupied by us, has been regarded as a breach of mission comity, and some correspondence has taken place on the subject between them and our Board, the result of which has not yet transpired." Watson, *The American Mission in Egypt*, 407.

were obliged to work on Sunday. Missionaries found themselves restricted from the Sudan and the Memorial fund for Gordon College, given by many who expected the Christian ideals of Gordon to be observed, was used for a college in which the Bible was excluded and the Quran included. Many British administrators had little sympathy for either missions or the Christians of the land.[22]

This context in Egypt influenced the mission context of Sudan. In the period from 1880 to 1920, Sudan was not much more than an extension of British rule in Egypt.

MISSIONS CONTEXT OF SUDAN

The first to enter Sudan with missiological intent were the Catholics. "After the battle of Omdurman (1898), Bishop A. M. Roveggio, the vicar apostolic since 1895, began pressing for permission to re-establish the Catholic presence in Sudan."[23] Life in Sudan was harsh and missionary longevity was rare.

Interest in the Sudan after its conquest by Egypt was also shown by the church, but just like the European traders, missionaries fell victim to the harsh conditions of the White Nile region. In 1846, after the White Nile had been opened up to navigation, Pope Gregory XVI created the Vicariate Apostolic of Central Africa, and by 1848 a mission had been established at Khartoum. A year later it received permission to penetrate into the White Nile region as far as the Equator. In 1853, a mission was established near Godokoro among the Bari tribe. However, the harsh climate, hostility of the natives, and lack of financial support forced the missionaries to give up in 1860.[24]

After the Catholic mission's failure in 1860, "an attempt by the Franciscans to revive the vicariate failed at an enormous cost of missionary lives lost through disease. One of the survivors, Daniel Comboni was made vicar apostolic of Central Africa in 1872."[25] He had immense influence on Catholic mission to the Sudan.

The evangelicals entered Sudan next. "In 1885, the CMS had established Gordon Memorial Mission, dedicated to evangelizing the Sudanese,

22. Vander Werff, *Christian Mission to Muslims*, 168.
23. Daly, *Empire on the Nile*, 250.
24. Moore-Harell, *Egypt's African Empire*, 11.
25. Daly, *Empire on the Nile*, 250.

which functioned for a season at Suakin in 1890. In 1898, even before the fall of Omdurman, the CMS approached the Residency for permission to enter the Sudan."[26] Permission given, Lord Cromer granted a large tract of land to the CMS mission, but finding missionaries to enter Sudan proved difficult. L. H. Gwynne was eventually appointed army chaplain to Church of England (which removed him from direct missionary activity but kept him in Khartoum). CMS missionaries turned their attention to the south.[27]

Shortly after CMS expressed interest in Sudan, the American Mission (also called United Presbyterian Mission) began to investigate work in Egypt's southern neighbor:[28]

> In 1899, the United Presbyterian Mission sent two if its missionaries (Andrew Watson and J. K. Giffen) to Sudan to report on the possibility and propriety of opening up work in that country. Later J. K. Giffen, H. T. McLaughlin, Ralph E. Carson, and G. A. Sowash (all missionaries serving in Egypt) were transferred. The Sudan mission is the child of the Egyptian Mission.[29]

The Presbyterians joined the Anglicans and the Catholics in Khartoum as entities permitted but not welcomed by the British authorities. "Catholics [were] mostly Italians and Austrians of a peasant background, while the Protestants were mainly lower middle class Britons and Americans of a fundamentalist outlook, single minded and earnest. British officials, from Cromer down, were almost to a man Anglicans."[30] Kitchener treated Catholics and Protestants in Northern (Muslim) Sudan poorly:

> On October 11, 1898, Cromer and Kitchener met a representative of CMS in Cairo, who requested permission to send a medical mission to Khartoum. "There could be no objection to establishment of missions at Fashoda and southward," he was told, but "among the Mahomedan population" this would be "very undesirable." [The CMS were uninterested in Fashoda but saw it as a possible indirect way to Khartoum]. It was not until December 1899 that an advance party, Dr. F. J. Harpur

26. Ibid.

27. Ibid., 252.

28. Back in 1883, a book-selling expedition had ventured into Sudan and sold 462 copies of the Scriptures. The rise of the Mahdi shortly thereafter made access into Sudan difficult, if not impossible. In 1896, the Egypt mission, aware of England's desire to reconquer Sudan raised the question of mission response. See Elder, *Vindicating a Vision*, 100–1.

29. Watson, *The American Mission in Egypt*, 197.

30. Daly, *Empire on the Nile*, 250.

and the Rev. L. H. Gwynne, arrived in Khartoum. At about the same time Cromer set down the principle that was to govern missionary activity during the Condominium: that it would be allowed only in the non-Muslim South . . . for fear of the popular reaction in Egypt and the Sudan. He cautioned Bishop Blyth [Anglican Bishop of Jerusalem whose diocese included Egypt and Sudan] that "to encourage missionary enterprise" in the Northern Sudan would, "incur a very grave responsibility" . . . Blyth claimed to share Cromer's objection to immediate missionary activity but argued that to control such activity in the future an administrative structure was needed.[31]

Like their CMS colleagues, the American Presbyterian Mission, refused permission to work in the North, began work in south Sudan in 1901. Generally under mission policy (caused by duress from the British rulers), missionaries were sent to the south, not primarily to convert or even educate, but simply to kept out of the north.[32] In 1905, the "Holiness Movement" of Canadian Methodists approached the Sudan agent in Cairo but was discouraged as were the Pentecost Bands of the World Mission in 1913.[33] In 1914, the beginnings of WWI negatively affected Catholic presence in Sudan (more than it did Protestant presence) as several Catholic missionaries were Austrian. The Governor General of Sudan restricted their access, and as a result stations shut down and recruitment ceased.[34]

As in politics, so in mission, Sudan is the little brother to Egypt. Mission work in Sudan between 1880 and 1920 was an overflow of the established missions in Egypt. The British policy of segregation and spheres of influence made mission to Muslims in Sudan more challenging than in Egypt (Christian mission was not allowed in the north, and Islamic mission was restricted in the south).

NOTABLE MISSIONARIES TO MUSLIMS IN EGYPT AND SUDAN (1880–1920)

Seven notable and exemplary (for the disciples they made) missionaries who lived in or worked out of Sudan and Egypt are introduced in this section.

31. Ibid., 251.
32. Ibid., 259.
33. Ibid., 253.
34. Ibid., 259.

Daniel Comboni

Daniel Comboni was born March 15, 1831 at Limone near Lake Garda in Brescia, Italy and baptized the next day. At age 12 he began training for the priesthood and missionary service under the tutelage of Father Nicholas Mazza in Verona, and at age 18 he dedicated himself to missions in Central Africa. Ordained to the priesthood on December 31, 1854, Comboni was commissioned with the Mazza Institute expedition to Africa in 1857. He and five priests sailed from Trieste, Italy to Alexandria, Egypt. There they boarded a steamer christened *The Morning Star* and headed up the Nile River to the Sudan.[35] The mission failed due to sickness, and, broken in health, he returned to Italy in 1859.

In 1860, Comboni traveled to Aden, Yemen, to rescue young African slaves who were accepted into the African college of the Mazza Institute. Returning via Cairo (after spending 1861 in Sudan), he was given charge of the former African slaves for three years. In 1863, he went to Germany where he made "contact for the first time with the 'Cologne Society,' which had been formed for the ransom and care of African slave children."[36] In 1864, while in prayer, he was inspired with a "Plan for the Regeneration of Africa"[37] and promoted the plan across Europe. He traveled to Egypt in 1865 and 1866 to begin a partnership with the Franciscans. The collaboration failed, and the Mazza Institute rejected Comboni and abandoned its mission ambition. In 1867 he founded his own mission called the Missionary Institute for Africa, arriving in Cairo in 1868 to set up base. His intention was to educate Africans to return as indigenous workers to their Central African homelands. By 1871, dedicated to missions in Africa, he launched his motto "Africa or Death" at the Congress of German Catholics in Mainz.[38] On May 21, 1871, "Rome raised the whole vast expanse of Central Africa to the rank of prefecture, entrusting its evangelization to the Verona Fathers."[39] The next year he was named Pro-Vicar Apostolic of Central Africa.

Comboni set up two colleges in Cairo in 1873 and took control of the mission in Khartoum. Expansion of the mission (known as the Missionary Societies of the Verona Fathers and the Verona Sisters) was rapid and included stations at Berber (1874), El Obeid, and Dilling (1875). "On July 2, 1877, Pius IX raised the prefecture of Central Africa to vicariate status and

35. Russell, *Africa's Twelve Apostles*, 219.

36. Lozano, *The Spirituality of Daniel Comboni*, xix.

37. Referred to as the "Piano" (The Plan).

38. Lozano, *The Spirituality of Daniel Comboni*, xxi.

39. Russell, *Africa's Twelve Apostles*, 232.

nominated Comboni as first Bishop."[40] In 1879, he commissioned a multinational missionary team from Verona to Africa and in 1880, expanded the two college facilities in Cairo. In 1881, he made a final tour of Sudan and explored the Nuba Mountains in the hope of opening a new frontier of mission. On October 4, Comboni, weakened by travel and saddened at the death of many young missionaries,[41] fell deathly ill with fever and died on October 10, 1881 in Khartoum.

Samuel Zwemer

Samuel Marinus Zwemer was born in Vriesland, Michigan, on April 12, 1867. His father and mother were Dutch immigrants and pastors of a small church among the Reformed congregations in West Michigan.[42] In 1870, the family moved to Milwaukee. Zwemer was one of eleven children: six girls (one, Nellie, spent forty years as a missionary in China) and five boys (four entered Christian ministry). In 1873, the family moved to Albany, New York before returning to Michigan. During these years, he attended "the preparatory department of Hope College and continued until he received from the college the A.B. degree."[43] As a boy, he loved to read and read so much that his peers called him, "Lazy Sam."[44]

In 1886, Zwemer heard Robert Wilder of the Student Volunteer Movement speak. He became one of the first to enter the movement and later became one of its leaders. In summer 1886, he worked as a colporteur for the American Bible Society. On June 22, 1887 he graduated from Hope College, and after graduation he returned to traveling and selling Bibles, hoping to place a copy of Scripture in every Michigan home. Later that year, he entered New Brunswick Seminary (later Rutgers University in New Jersey) and studied medicine in preparation for missions work. In 1888, Samuel preached his first sermon to a congregation of ethnic people in a small church. During this time, he also gave many talks on missions in various seminaries and first began to think of forming a non-denominational mission to Arabia. James Cantine, a friend and fellow visionary, "graduated a

40. Ibid., 237.

41. From 1860 to 1864 alone, forty-four Catholic Missionaries would die in the Sudan. See Russell, *Africa's Twelve Apostles*, 222.

42. "[In Zwemer's childhood] the major decisions of the home were all made after seasons of prayer . . . Three times a day, at each meal, there was Bible reading and prayer." Wilson, *Apostle to Islam*, 21.

43. Ibid.

44. Ibid., 22.

year before him and was to precede him to the Near East to begin the study of Arabic."[45] The Classis of Iowa ordained Zwemer as a missionary after his graduation from seminary in 1890. Dr. John Lansing, Cantine, and Zwemer presented their plan for an Arabian mission to the Board of Foreign Missions and the General Synod of the Reformed Church but were told funds were inadequate to support the current missionaries.[46] Undeterred, Zwemer sailed for Beirut where he joined Cantine in Arabic study with the encouragement of the venerable Dr. Cornelius Van Dyke, Dr. H. H. Jessup, and others from the Syria Mission of the Presbyterian Church, USA. From there, he and Cantine traveled to Cairo to meet with Dr. Lansing, planning and praying over where in Arabia to establish their mission.[47] They settled on Basrah, Iraq (1891), before opening stations in Bahrain (1892), Muscat (1893), Amara on the Tigris, north of Basrah (1895), and Nasariyeh (1898).[48]

In 1895, the CMS mission in Baghdad received two young missionary ladies from Sydney, Australia. Disembarking at Basrah, Zwemer escorted the ladies to Baghdad. A short time later, on May 18, 1896, Amy Elizabeth Wilkes married Zwemer in the British consulate in Baghdad.[49] The Zwemers served in Basrah until their furlough in 1897, when their daughter Katherine was born in Spring Lake, Michigan. A second daughter, Ruth, was born three years later. Both girls died within one week of each other of dysentery in Bahrain in 1904.[50] Five other Arabian Mission colleagues of Zwemer died in the field between 1898 and 1906.

In 1905, Zwemer entered a new phase of mission—raising funds for the Arabian Mission and the Student Volunteer movement. He did so until the Cairo 1906 conference (an ecumenical investigation into the work of reaching Muslims) led to Edinburgh 1910 and Lucknow 1911. Then came the request for him to head to Cairo in 1912 to oversee a training school for

45. Wilson, *Apostle to Islam*, 32.

46. The Arabian Mission was organized in 1889 but adopted later (1894) by the Reformed Church, "although retaining its separate financial status." Jessup, *Kamil Abdul Messiah*, 85.

47. Paul Harrison's reply when asked why missionary societies were not at work in Arabia: "I don't believe God has given enough divine stubbornness to anyone except Dutchmen to stay on and work in Arabia." Quoted in Wilson, *Apostle to Islam*, 49. "It is quite true," Harrison added, "that one who combines the stubbornness of the Dutch and the inquisitive American spirit and the zeal of a pioneer for Christ is not easy to stop." Quoted in ibid., 63.

48. Jessup, *Kamil Abdul Messiah*, 85.

49. Wilson, *Apostle to Islam*, 47.

50. The Zwemers had four other children: Nellie, Raymond Lull, Amy Ruth, and Mary Moffat.

missionaries to the Muslim world.[51] The Reformed Mission Board agreed to this strategic redeployment as long as he spent some time traveling in the United States on their behalf for the solicitation of funds and personnel. In Cairo, he edited the periodical *The Muslim World*,[52] worked with the Nile Mission Press, wrote many of his books, and served the various missions in training, teaching, speaking,[53] and vision casting. "He taught in the Theological Seminary, preached frequently in Arabic and English, and was intensely zealous and active in various forms of work for the Muslims."[54] From Cairo,[55] he ventured across the Muslim world to teach, encourage, and exhort the Christian community towards the task of reaching Muslims with the gospel.[56]

In 1918, J. Ross Stevenson, then president of Princeton Theological Seminary, invited Zwemer to become a member. He eventually accepted the call to chair the History of Religion and Christian Mission department in 1928.[57] He taught there for eleven years before moving to New York City in 1939. In 1937, his wife Amy died suddenly, and he was remarried to Mar-

---

51. Zwemer wrote an article "The Tale of Three Cities" in *The Missionary Review of the World*: "Mecca represents the unoccupied fields of Islam, and challenges faith and heroism. Constantinople, with its mosque of St. Sophia, appeals to our loyalty. We must win back what is lost of the Church of Christ. And Cairo is the city of opportunity, of the open door and the beckoning hand. Mecca represents Islam as the excluder, behind closed doors, defying the entrance of the Christ; Constantinople, Islam as the intruder into the domains of the King; Cairo reminds us that in Africa Islam is the great rival faith, and that here must be fought to the finish the struggle for a continent. The three cities voice the appeal of three continents, Asia, Europe, and Africa, to be freed from the thralldom of Mohammed and welcomed into the glorious liberty of the children of God." Quoted in Wilson, *Apostle to Islam*, 84.

52. "No agency can penetrate Islam so deeply, abide so persistently, witness so daringly and influence so irresistibly as the printed page." Charles R. Watson of the American University in Cairo, quoted in Wilson, *Apostle to Islam*, 53.

53. "A great part of Zwemer's time was spent speaking in conferences. He had been largely responsible for the first general conference of missionaries to the world of Islam held in Cairo in April 2006." Wilson, *Apostle to Islam*, 49.

54. Ibid., 84.

55. After three months in Cairo, Zwemer wrote on December 26, 1912: "My three months' residence here in this great metropolis has already confirmed my judgment that it is the one strategic place in the Moslem world from which we can influence every Moslem land, persistently and irresistibly, through the printed page." Quoted in Wilson, *Apostle to Islam*, 80.

56. For example, a visit to the various mission stations of North Africa was planned with Dr. John R. Mott in 1922.

57. Wilson, *Apostle to Islam*, 209. "The students gave Zwemer the nickname of 'Uncle Sam' . . . evidence that the students had taken him into their hearts and considered him a professor who understood their point of view" (ibid., 86).

garet Clarke in 1940. In 1949, the mission he helped found at 23 celebrated its sixtieth anniversary in Kuwait. On April 2, 1952, ten days before turning 85, he passed away.[58]

Zwemer was an engaging man.[59] "His face caught attention, and his eyes seemed always sparkling with fun. The prominent Dutch features would break into a friendly smile at the slightest provocation."[60] "His over-flowing sense of humor would bubble up at almost any time . . . [He] loves any sort of jokes, and he does his share of laughing and laugh making. [After a long day of ministry] Zwemer, out of his experiences from Michigan to Arabia, is setting the table agog and the fun becomes hilarious."[61] He was blessed with an inquisitive mind, an extraordinary capacity for work,[62] a controlled temper, and a twinkle in his eyes, which marked the abundant good humor of his nature.[63] He had "indomitable perseverance, especially in the things where he was certain that Christ would be served. Outstanding traits were determination, courage, and faith."[64] Most impressively, he lived his theology; he did not just hold it in theory. Although Zwemer favored a direct approach with Muslims,

> he did not offend Moslem hearers or readers in most cases, for they found he had a very deep and sincere respect for all Moslems and their beliefs and a broad love for them and all men. This love was his fundamental motive and guiding star, even in times of controversy . . . with all his zeal and straightforward

58. Ibid., 245.

59. Once in Cairo, Zwemer was asked to preach to the British soldiers. When he arrived at the camp he found a tent that could hold 300 only accommodating eight. "Zwemer went outside the tent and in a loud falsetto voice, heard throughout the camp, he gave the Muslim call to prayer. The men came running from all over the camp to see what was happening. Zwemer ushered them into the service and held them spellbound throughout." Wilson, *Apostle to Islam*, 61.

60. Wilson, *Prophet*, 19.

61. Ibid., 58–59.

62. "[Zwemer] had the most acquisitive mind that I ever met . . . He had an abundance of fresh illustrations for any theme on which he was speaking. This made him a fascinating teacher. He also had an inventive mind, fertile with fresh plans for the work. Almost too much so, in fact for practical work. In a committee meeting, his mind would scintillate with new ideas that would commend themselves to the rest of us. But perhaps after we had decided on a plan that we would follow, we would meet again a little later, and he would seem to have quite forgotten the plan he had suggested and on which we had agreed, and would have a whole batch of new plans." Wilson, Apostle to Islam, 84–85.

63. Ibid., 242.

64. Ibid., 243.

advance he seldom had trouble, but on any number of occasions was received by Muslim leaders with honor and respect.[65]

His indomitable spirit, constant joy, eternal vision, tireless pen, faithfulness in trail, and love for Master, missionary, and Muslim rightly earned him the title "Apostle to Islam."[66]

Oswald Chambers

Oswald Chambers was the fourth son of Clarence and Hannah Chambers.[67] One of nine children, he was born on July 24, 1874 in Aberdeen, Scotland where his father was pastor of Crown Terrace Baptist Church. When he was 5, the family moved to Stoke-on-Trent, later to Perth, and ultimately to Southgate, London. At 10, he was "merry and irresponsible, [and] showed little trace of the intense mental concentration that distinguished his character later in life."[68] A gifted artist, he attended the Art School in Kensington where he obtained the Art Master's certificate. In 1895, he returned to Scotland for the Arts Course at Edinburgh University and became a prizeman in fine art and archaeology.[69]

Chambers found it hard to make a living through his art and harder still to be satisfied by anything save intimacy with God himself. On February 16, 1897 he left Edinburgh to begin ministerial training in Dunoon. He studied under Duncan McGregor who had started his own Bible school, the Gospel Training Center, in 1893.[70] From 1897 to 1906 he was based there, alternatively teaching and preaching, undergoing a crisis of faith that was

65. Ibid., 242.

66. Though Zwemer is not known to have led many Muslims to the Lord, he profoundly impacted several through discipleship and teaching. One example is Kamil, a Syrian convert who traveled in Arabia with Zwemer. He was martyred only two years after his conversion. H. H. Jessup says of Kamil, "Prayer seemed his special delight. I have never met a person, who from the outset, seemed so peculiarly taught of the Spirit of God." Jessup, *Kamil Abdul Messiah*, 16. Traveling through a storm with Zwemer, Kamil testified: "We were in a sad state and protected ourselves with prayer and singing praises, and in supplication to God that he would look upon us in compassion" (quoted in ibid., 31). Kamil prayed regularly and loudly so Muslims could hear. Kamil prayed with and for Muslims. Telling of an encounter with a Muslim man who had a tumor in his abdomen, Kamil recounts: "I then kneeled with Mr. Zwemer at the sick man's feet and prayed to God, asking that he would answer us in honor of the Son of his love, the Lord Jesus Christ" (quoted in ibid., 37). Zwemer's influence on Kamil was profound.

67. Young, foreword to *Oswald Chambers*, by Bertha Chambers, 13.

68. McCasland, *Oswald Chambers*, 27.

69. Young, foreword to *Oswald Chambers*, by Bertha Chambers, 15.

70. McCasland, *Oswald Chambers*, 66.

unresolved until he fully surrendered to God in 1901—an experience he linked to the baptism of the Holy Ghost.[71]

From 1906 to 1907 Chambers traveled to America and Japan, captivating congregations with his teaching and preaching. In 1907 the Pentecostal League of Prayer asked him to provide leadership, which he did until 1911.[72] On May 25, 1910 he married Gertrude "Biddy" Hobbs. He first met her in his brother's church in Eltham and fell in love with her on the SS Baltic from Liverpool to New York. Biddy was "a devoted woman who was also an expert stenographer, a fact which would mean much in the years to come."[73]

On June 13, 1907, "Chambers' article titled 'Missionary Ignorance' appeared in God's Revivalist. In it, he spoke his mind on the tragedy of sending young missionaries into difficult foreign assignments without adequate preparation."[74] Four years later he addressed that tragedy by opening the Bible Training College in Clapham Common, London on January 12, 1911. The College was a residential one where students and staff lived, studied, and ministered communally. The focus of the college was mission and ministry preparation with C. T. Studd as a guest lecturer. Indefatigable, Chambers taught the courses, ran a correspondence Bible Training Course, published articles for American revivalist magazines, and continued preaching around the country. When World War I erupted in 1914, he was sobered by the hour and by the implications of a fallen world. "Oswald's own intercession led him to a momentous choice. 'Lord, I have decided before thee to offer work with the forces; undertake and guide me in each particular.'"[75] Thus resolved, Chambers applied to work for YMCA in Zeitoun, Egypt, as a chaplain to British soldiers stationed in Egypt.

Oswald and Biddy became parents of Kathleen Chambers on May 24, 1913. Oswald went ahead of his wife and daughter to Egypt, as war conditions did not permit them to accompany him immediately. Travel permission granted, his family joined him, and he spent the last two years of his life ministering to British and foreign troops in Egypt. When he died in 1917, a

---

71. Chambers struggled to come to a personal intimacy with the one about whom he so eloquently shared. His struggle was not so much for intellectual understanding of the truths he proclaimed as much as it was a longing for assured communion with the object of his postulation. See McCasland, Oswald Chambers, 89.

72. The Pentacostal League of Prayer was a religious organization founded by Richard Reader Harris devoted to spiritual holiness and spiritual revival. The League organized prayer and revival meetings around the United Kingdom. See ibid., 92.

73. Wiersbe, 50 People Every Christian Should Know, 321.

74. McCasland, Oswald Chambers, 123.

75. Ibid., 198.

simple telegram was sent to England: "Oswald in His presence."[76] Chambers is buried in Cairo. Biddy began taking copious notes of his teachings, talks, and lectures back in 1911 and continued the practice until his passing.[77] Her faithfulness and persistence after his death produced twenty-eight books.

Temple Gairdner

William Henry Temple Gairdner was born in Ayrshire, Scotland, in 1873 to a Scottish father and English mother. His father—a physician and president of the Royal College of Physicians—was disciplined, focused, and honorable, with a formidable intellect.[78] His mother was elegant, witty, dramatic, and passionate. Gairdner was equal parts of both. He went to St. Ninian preparatory school at Moffat in 1882 and to Oxford for university (Trinity College in 1892). He had a passionate love for Scotland and England.

Gairdner's years in Oxford coincided with the end of the Oxford movement, "the dangerous point in its story when men spoke well of it."[79] Though the Oxford movement (an inheritance of the late eighteenth/early nineteenth century awakenings) was in decline, the Student Volunteer Movement had just started.

At this juncture in his life, tragedy struck. Gairdner's brother Hugh fell ill, and for two weeks he watched him slowly die. He returned to Oxford and sought out men who "made no secret of their love and faith."[80] He talked with them and watched them. Seeing eternity firsthand, he decided the only life worth living was radical.[81] He was converted and deeply in love with

---

76. Ibid., 15.

77. Chambers had a keen appreciation for truth well expressed in print and was fond of saying, "Probably the most lasting of all preaching is with the pen" (quoted in ibid., 255).

78. As a result, Gairdner welcomed ideas, longed for truth, and loved a good argument. See Padwick *Temple Gairdner of Cairo*, 35.

79. Ibid., 17.

80. Ibid., 23.

81. In a letter to his son (concerned about radical Christians in his day), Gairdner said of his Christian university friends: "Their shibboleths were terrifying, their narrowness a byword, but upon them something of divine fire had descended, and they stuck at nothing that they could see to be the will of Christ." He said: "They see a few things clearly, and other things not at all; those things they will insist on with an insistence which blinds them to other aspects. Everything will be black or white with them; no shading of any sort. And their vocabulary will be to match. BUT, I say again, these people have to be reckoned with. Was I not in the midst of them, and one of them at Oxford? And as I look round the world I see everywhere that it is these men (perhaps mellowed and developed now) who are doing the big things in the world—the

Jesus: "I stayed up a day or two just to enjoy solitude with the unseen Lover. And when I went down to Glasgow, I did not go alone."[82] This passionate intimacy marked him his whole life:[83]

> Probably no friend of his who ever heard Temple Gairdner say the Name "Jesus" in ordinary talk can forget it. He used the Name very little: it was too sacred to him . . . Yet now and again something in a conversation would induce its use, and always it came out with the shy yet unconcealable note of a lover."[84]

He was so in love with Jesus, his natural reserve could not contain his exuberance and the "impossible was happening to him [street witnessing in Oxford] because he was a man in love."[85] In 1893 he attended a meeting of the Keswick convention and was called to missionary service.[86] He signed the declaration of the Student Volunteer Missionary Union: "It is my purpose, if God permit, to become a foreign missionary."[87] After completing his studies in 1896, he agreed to another year of lay work at Oxford and from 1897 to 1899 traveled for the Student Volunteer Movement (organizing and speaking).[88]

---

big things for mankind, and God, and the Kingdom of Christ." Quoted in Padwick, *Temple Gairdner of Cairo*, 20–21.

82. Padwick, *Temple Gairdner of Cairo*, 26.

83. "Men often asked to be introduced to him," says T. E. Alvarez, "because of the brightness which was an atmosphere about him wherever he went." This quite unconscious shining out of an inner illumination was one of his marks through life. Padwick, *Temple Gairdner of Cairo*, 29.

84. Ibid., 26.

85. Ibid., 29.

86. Gairdner returned to Keswick in 1896, the year he was disappointed to not get a first in his exams. There God confirmed his missionary call. "There, on his first morning he retired alone for a 'long time in church.' The transaction that took place in the silence of the empty church by the lake was momentous. As he meditated he heard some words of the Gospel addressed to himself with utterly personal force. 'Canst thou drink of the cup that I drink of and be baptized with the baptism wherewith I was baptized?' Gairdner knew that he must answer. He said unto Him, 'I can.' Jesus said unto him, 'Thou shalt.'" Ibid., 45.

87. Ibid., 29.

88. He was not impressed with the flabbiness of lifeless organizing committees. He commented there was only one way to keep life in an organization: "There is only one thing—fire the centre. The core, the five or six men in dead earnest, must become in more earnest and draw in the next circle, and then the next, and so on, into the life of seeking after God." Quoted in ibid., 55–56.

On his public speaking, an observer commented: "He would begin in a very and commonplace way, so that the censorious would say 'There is nothing here'; when suddenly in a flash there would come an utterance, so it seemed, from the Throne of

R. E. Speer and John R. Mott impacted him deeply. His 1894 diary comment on Mott's sermon "The Man Christ Jesus" says, "The Personality which, when we were shown it, burned our hearts is alive, the same, present, our Friend and Lover. I was constrained to nestle into Jesus as never before."[89] The respect was mutual. Speer and Mott were both impressed with him.

> He impressed me with his natural enthusiasm, his responsiveness to exacting demands in the realm of spiritual discipline, and to the stern challenges sounded out in regard to the extension of the reign of Christ. It is given to but a few men to share in laying the foundations of a movement, which within their own lifetime profoundly and extensively influences for good the life of their own nation and the welfare of mankind. Gairdner was one of a small group to whom was given this distinction.[90]

During these years of travel, Gairdner met Douglas Thornton. Thornton became a lifelong friend and co-worker, a man he loved as his own soul, a man whose untimely death proved one of the largest losses of Gairdner's life. The two were soul mates.

> Their close working friendship recalls historic combinations of men whose twin genius united extensive and intensive, prophecy and scholarship, the world of action and the world of ideas . . . Thornton the prophet reached his ideas by great intuitions, knew they were right, and was not over-careful in the logical support he gave to them. It was Gairdner's task to fill in the logic and show the sweet reasonableness of what looked like some wild leap.[91]

Thornton was commissioned as a CMS missionary to Cairo in 1898. Gairdner wrote him: "I shall help in separating you for your life mission to Islam . . . May you be glorified with the glory of Jesus—that is the glory of self-loss, of the cross. May you spend and be spent. May God honor you by giving you to drink of Christ's Cup baptizing you with Christ's baptism."[92] Gairdner joined Thornton in Cairo in 1899 and spent two years studying

---

God itself, the inspired word of the authentic man of God, lightning in a dark world." Quoted in ibid., 53.

89. Ibid., 48.
90. Ibid., 49.
91. Ibid., 128–29.
92. Ibid., 61–62.

Arabic.[93] On February 16, 1901 he was ordained a CMS minister at St. Mark's in Alexandria by Bishop Blythe and was ready to begin ministry to Muslims in earnest. Two challenges slowed his vision: (1) he lacked a marriage partner, and (2) he "suddenly . . . found himself in a mission with a secretary (leader) who was a saintly invalid, obliged to live outside the city, and haunted whenever new proposals were made, by the invalid's instinctive dread of seeing work grow beyond his strength to handle."[94]

He overcame the first challenge through prayer and a letter to childhood friend Miss Margaret Mitchell, a CMS missionary assigned to India. Her assignment was graciously changed to Palestine so she could study Arabic. They married in Nazareth on October 16, 1902. Gairdner wrote of the marriage, "Please God these things will make something heavenly, something spiritual and ethereal in our relations one to another. Something that God may have pleasure in and use to His own glory."[95]

The second challenge was overcome in time. Bishop Gwynne ultimately testified, "[Gairdner] was cleverer, abler, knew more than I, yet he served me; and his tenderness, patience, and absolute loyalty caused deep affection and emotion. Though he was never seen in the gatherings of the mighty, he was one of the biggest men in the Church of England."[96]

From 1902 to 1907, Gairdner and Thornton worked in close concert in the work of evangelism, teaching, apologetics, and ministry in the established church. Gairdner's love for Muslims, Arabic, and the Lord was evident.[97] He used music and drama to communicate the gospel,[98] and used

93. After Gairdner was assigned to Cairo, "he began to see before him the stupendous system of Islam, a system of devotion, of thought, of social life, of law, entrenched, impressive, and deliberately defiant of the Spirit of Jesus. Cairo he saw now as the very heart of that Islamic life." He wrote to his father "Cairo is my destination for the present and perhaps for good. Though I am ready to go further, I have an idea that I shall not go. I believe that Cairo is the important centre: good work done there would certainly be felt in the Sudan. Cairo is the centre of Islam, par excellence. It is to Islam that I go—not to any particular phase of it . . . To Cairo, then he went, and Cairo became his city, half loved, half hated, but his own. The love came first . . . And with all the outward ordinariness of life in a city full of telephones and electric trams, committees and tourists, he was yet aware of a sweet, sickening poison in the air, a spiritual atmosphere tainted by a hidden foulness—the palpable influence of thousands of lives enslaved in the sensual. 'Cairo is a subtly deadening place,' he said." Ibid., 73.

94. Ibid., 75.

95. Padwick, *Temple Gairdner of Cairo*, 89.

96. Ibid., 286.

97. "We need the song note in our message to the Moslems . . . not the dry cracked note of disputation, but the song note of joyous witness, tender invitation." Gairdner, quoted in Padwick, *Temple Gairdner of Cairo*, 158.

98. "He loved to sing hymns. A favorite was 'And I love my Lord Jesus Above

his mind and pen to declare the unsearchable riches of Christ. His ability in Arabic was legendary. On one occasion, "for an hour without a note he had addressed a critical crowd [in Arabic] of a thousand men, giving them Christ in such a manner as to make every man solemn and no one angry."[99] He balanced a love for Muslims with a hatred of Islam. On the treachery of Islam, its betrayal and coercion, he said, "It is Satanic. I never felt as I have this week the fact of the hideous existence of a kingdom of darkness and of evil. It has come down on us like the night."[100] He felt those who follow Jesus should do so unashamedly. When a Muslim seeker asked why he could not follow Christ secretly and outwardly comply with Islam, he and Thornton said that was only laughing at Christ.[101]

After Thornton's death in 1907, Gairdner's administrative duties in the mission increased. He produced and edited evangelistic works, hymnals, and other literature. He provided leadership and pastoral care to the wider missionary community and consulting expertise to translation efforts. He lectured at the Cairo Training School along with Zwemer. He traveled and taught and prayed and preached at a seemingly inhuman pace. He did it with great joy and strength derived from a happy heart in Jesus and a loving environment in his home. "[His] humour was an affectionate humour. His laugh had more love in it than that of any man . . . if you could make him laugh you were embraced by it."[102]

In 1910, his mission recognized his mind and creative genius. He was granted a year of study leave to consolidate his learning and help speak for and shape the mission. He embarked on his studies by first learning German so he could study German theologians on their own terms. He flung himself into the study of Islam and Arabic literature. From 1911 to 1914, he continued to lead and mold the mission community in Cairo through both his character and his teaching, revolutionizing the way Arabic was taught in Egypt and initiating what would become the language department of the American University in Cairo. From 1914 to 1918, he served as the secretary of the CMS in Cairo, and his days were filled with administrative decisions. Despite the weight of the role, he was still young at heart as seen

---

Everything.' The lover glowed and shone from his whole aspect." Ibid., 26.

99. Padwick, *Temple Gairdner of Cairo*, 190.

100. Padwick, *Temple Gairdner of Cairo*, 95.

101. In one particular case where a seeker was agonizing over the cost of public confession, the seeker had a vision where he was encouraged to stand for Christ. Later he found that very night Thornton and Gairdner were up all night—until 3 a.m.—praying for him; they were praying at the exact time he had the vision. See ibid., 141.

102. Ibid., 41.

through his love for children, the piano, and imaginative stories and songs.[103] "His masters were partly mystified and partly delighted at his unpredict-able way of doing things, with a little flicker of humour playing over all his work."[104] Constance Padwick noted this commentary from one of Gaird-ner's contemporaries:

> I think some of us just missed his friendship, because we were paralysed by his unusualness. You never knew what he would think or do. Certainly no one in our circle can ever have pro-voked more thought or cut adrift more self-complacency. "Probably he was a little too big for the missionary world to take in," says an observer from another mission.[105]

In his administrative duties, he understood the privilege of being un-der authority. In her work on Gairdner, Padwick included these words from Bishop MacInnes:

> And the marvel is not only that Temple Gairdner could not ever say a word that was disloyal to his Master, but that the other man who was with him could not either. That was Gairdner's strength, the practice of the presence of Christ, and from there it flowed, as a full and even tide, his unconscious, unceasing, yet wholly compelling influence.[106]

From 1918 to 1924 Gairdner assumed a missionary statesman role in Cairo. He was instrumental in building unity, discipling young missionaries, mentoring Egyptian leaders, developing missiology, speaking truth in love through his seminars, teaching, or leading prayer meetings. He exhibited a love for life, music, activity, sport, learning, culture, language, and people, and he was madly and consistently in love with Jesus.

Temple Gairdner died on Ascension Day, May 22, 1928. He had learned a lesson about death when his best friend, Thornton, died. At that time he wrote, "The opposite of joy is not sorrow, but sin. Pure joy and pure sorrow can live together."[107] As Gairdner lay dying, a visitor said, "I found myself coming out of his room filled with a spontaneous and an unusual joy . . . Time and again one left that room with an impelling sense of joy."[108] He was so aware of the presence of Christ as he lay dying, he said, "Everything

103. Ibid., 57.
104. Ibid., 81.
105. Ibid., 76.
106. Ibid., 187.
107. Ibid., 325.
108. Ibid.

in the room says Glory."[109] When asked about an epitaph for his grave, Lady Gairdner chose one word: "Satisfied."

Douglas Thornton

Douglas Montagu Thornton was born in 1873. His mother died when he was five, which led him to be shy and socially awkward. Recognizing intellectual promise in his son, Thornton's father provided the best education possible; at age seven he went to preparatory school at Rottingdean and at fourteen to Eton in Marlborough. When Thornton was thirteen, his elder brother Cecil became gravely ill and died. His passing profoundly marked Thornton. It underlined his salvation and clarified his call to ministry.[110] Gairdner writes, "At Cecil's funeral, as they were returning from the grave, Douglas's godmother said to him, 'Now Douglas, you carry on the work that Cecil[111] had in his heart to do for God.' And he did."[112]

From Eton, Thornton went to Trinity College at Cambridge. He joined the Student Volunteer Movement, regularly attending the "weekly missionary meeting of the Cambridge Missionary Union."[113] He defied the status quo and evangelically pursued immigrant Indian students in ways seen as less than decorous by the prim standards of upperclassmen. He was stubborn and fixed, "a man of one idea and one aim; but as that aim was all inclusive, it can hardly be called narrow."[114] His one aim was that all people should be saved and every nation evangelized, and he doggedly pursued that aim no matter what anyone thought of him. In 1896 he joined the staff of the Student Christian Movement and applied his energy to serving that organization and inspiring students in secular and religious colleges to respond to the call for workers among unreached peoples. Upon his being commissioned to Egypt, the General Secretary of the Student Christian Movement said, "There is hardly a department of the Movement's work which does not show traces of his influence."[115]

---

109. Ibid.

110. Reflecting on his brother's death (by thanking God for his own health), Thornton realized he never really thanked God for sending Jesus to die for his sins. "So there and then I did so," he wrote in later years, "and then and there I gained assurance of forgiveness, which I have never lost." Quoted in Gairdner, *D. M. Thornton*, 9.

111. Thornton had one child, a son named Cecil—named for his deceased brother.

112. Gairdner, *D. M. Thornton*, 10.

113. Ibid., 20.

114. Ibid., 2.

115. Ibid., 37.

In Cairo in 1898, Thornton began his Arabic study with characteristic singleness of purpose. A visionary, he kept the end in view. The end of language study for him was the evangelization of the world, which "would, beyond question, have been . . . 'planets,' had the revelation of the Kingdom of Heaven reached beyond our little earth."[116] In Cairo for only six months, he sent strategic plans to the home office, advocating a focus on the revitalization of the Coptic Church and its invaluable partnership in reaching Muslims. In 1899, he married Elaine Anderson in Cairo.

The visions that Thornton saw for missions work in the first six months proved to be uncannily prescient. He spent the rest of his life initiating or attempting to initiate them.[117] Gairdner lists those ministry goals as Sudan evangelization (using Egypt as a base), Coptic ministry (missionary training), evangelization of Cairo's educated elite, literature evangelization, education, and missionary training (in Cairo to reach other fields).[118] Thornton spent the next nine years in pursuit of these objectives. "If he sometimes went too fast and was blind to the limitations imposed by his means and materials, that was probably inevitable in the nature of things. After all, it is the function of the driving wheel to drive."[119]

Thornton could see over the horizon. Most Middle East missionary efforts focused on revitalizing decaying ancient churches that could in turn evangelize Muslims. While not forsaking this vision, he saw greater potential in the reverse: "Give us a living church of Moslem converts here, and they will, I believe, lead the way to the Easterns[120] to greater activity for Christ."[121] Thornton had the same far-reaching vision for Cairo—as a means not an end. Gairdner shares this quote: "Our work, however, is not by any means confined to Cairo, or to Egypt. It has always been my hope and prayer that we might reach Al Azhar [University] students from far and wide, and this is being realized."[122] He understood that to reach elite students who studied at the premier educational institution in the Muslim world was also to reach their families in their sending countries. He recognized the uniting power of Arabic and dreamed of ways that Arabic literature could penetrate where no expatriate missionary could go.

116. Ibid., 76.

117. Ibid., 124.

118. Ibid., 125.

119. Ibid., 126.

120. I.e., the Orthodox Church.

121. Gairdner, D. M. Thornton, 151.

122. Ibid., 153.

In 1906, Thornton and Gairdner secured the old dwelling of Arabi Pasha, the revolutionary Egyptian Nationalist General of the 1880 uprisings. Spacious "Bait Arabi Pasha" (House of Arabi Pasha) became a residence for both families and a center for teaching, dialogue, evangelism, Bible study, and literature distribution. In 1904, Thornton conceived the idea of a published periodical, "Orient and Occident," intended to "reach more than the student class only, with articles for young and old, Sheikh and Effendi, on religious and on general subjects, in two languages, and illustrated."[123] He worked tirelessly through 1905 to see the magazine from development to printing to distribution to writing. He collapsed into a well-earned furlough in 1906.

Thornton had difficulty resting, and his 1906 furlough became a marathon of meetings and mobilization, planning and strategic thinking. The last of which was a paper presented to the senior members of the university of Oxford on "Cairo as a Key to the Muslim World." In it he elucidated all the challenges of Cairo and gave a warning of the emergence of a fanatic Pan-Islamism, "dominating the land, sooner or later to produce another revolution, and possibly a world-movement under the banner of Islam, which will push back the cause of evangelism of Moslem lands for centuries."[124] His remarks ended with—

> But there is a brighter and perfectly possible picture—with Cairo as a centre of Christian light and learning, a metropolis to which all Oriental Christians and many Mohammedans will strive to send their sons for their highest education, a workshop whence divinely hewn tools can be sent as instruments of blessing throughout the Orient, a press which turns out Christian literature in many a Mohammedan language, and not least, a home where Christ is known and loved, and followed and adored.[125]

Thornton returned to Egypt full of plans for the wide dissemination of "Orient and Occident" and with vision for an exploratory trip to the Sudan. His health allowed two tours of Upper Egypt but not a visit to Sudan. His journey to Upper Egypt convinced him that it was both possible to work with the established churches indirectly (to help them reach Muslims) and to work directly with Muslims themselves.

---

123. Ibid., 206.
124. Ibid., 244.
125. Ibid.

And his final objective was, as the final objective of his Society was and is, the evangelization of Moslems. This direct aim has never lost sight of or relaxed for a moment. The indirect methods were only made possible through and by keeping on working at the direct object. Thornton knew that the whole of the unique influence of the Church Missionary Society upon the other Christian bodies in Egypt was entirely due to their knowledge that the direct aim was its only aim. No prejudice therefore existed against its combining indirect with direct methods—influencing Christians as well as influencing Moslems. Thornton kept his eye steadily fixed upon both aspects of the question.[126]

When Thornton and his wife became engaged, he told her of his passion to be a "preacher-prophet" all the time. Weakened from the pace of a demanding life and his peripatetic tour of southern Egypt, Thornton succumbed to pneumonia. Descending into delirium, alternately prophesying and preaching, his last discernible words were, "I must have Friday for the Moslem meeting," and then, "The work." He became unintelligible, but his spirit remained fiery. He preached himself hoarse in a language only angels could understand—a preacher-prophet to the end. He died on September 7, 1907 at age thirty-four.

Lillian Trasher

Lillian Hunt Trasher was born in 1886 in Jacksonville, Florida. She moved to Boston as a young girl and again to Brunswick, Georgia. When she was ten, she heard the salvation testimony of neighbor Ed Mason; it stirred her spiritual curiosity. In February 1887, on the way home from school, she paused in the woods and cried, "Lord, I want to be your little girl." She was quiet a while and then blurted, "Lord, if ever I can do anything for You, just let me know and I'll do it!"[127]

Trasher studied one year at God's Bible School in Cincinnati and served as a pastor for a short time in the college town of Dahlonega, Georgia, where she testifies, "God blessed my efforts there very much indeed."[128] In 1909 she went to work at the Faith Orphanage and Bible School near Asheville, North Carolina under Mattie Perry, and in May 1910 she and Tom Jordan were engaged. Ten days before the wedding, she and a friend went to hear a missionary from India, and God called her to be a mission-

126. Ibid., 253.

127. Howell, *Lady on a Donkey*, 22.

128. Assemblies of God World Missions, *Letters From Lillian*, 98.

ary. Trasher told Jordan immediately; he replied that he would wait for her. She gently insisted that he could not, for what she was called to do would take decades; they must separate. "[God] let me have the privilege of giving up all for Him," she said.[129] God miraculously provided the finances and on October 8, 1910, she and her sister Jennie set sail for Egypt.

Trasher arrived in Egypt on October 26, 1910 and she made her way to Asyut where she was to assist Reverend Dunning in his work.[130] In 1911, she agreed to look after an unfortunate baby whose mother died and whose father planned to throw it into the Nile. Trasher took the baby and cared for it that night in the home where she lived with an Egyptian host family. The malnourished infant cried most of the night, and the host family protested that the baby was too noisy and must leave.[131] She replied, "If the child must go, then I will go, too."[132]

With only three months experience in Egypt, Trasher rented her own room and kept the baby—an orphanage was born. In 1915 she secured a modest property, and by 1916 the orphanage family included fifty boys and girls. By 1941, 2,700 meals per day were served, and in the 1960s the orphanage housed 1,500 orphans and served 4,500 meals per day on a campus of more than eleven buildings.[133] In 1981, George Assad wrote that the orphanage sat on twelve acres of land, consisted of "13 buildings, which include dormitories, a beautiful church, the primary school building, dining room, bakery, storerooms, clinic, offices, water tower, and an electric engine. We have workshops for carpentry, sewing, and knitting, and swimming pools and playgrounds for recreation."[134]

As the orphanage grew, so did the needs. As a matter of principle, Trasher never turned anyone away. She solicited funds from local believers and merchants, she prayed for miraculous provision, she corresponded with supporters in America, and she worked very hard with her own hands. The orphanage went through trials of finances, disease (1947 cholera epidemic), and government intrusion, but always emerged victorious, largely due to Trasher's faith and courage. Trasher was often in "danger of being attacked

---

129. Ibid., 99.

130. Ibid., 32.

131. In defense of the Egyptians, it should be noted that in the early years, the majority of all funds for the orphanage came from Egyptian contributions, as it has done as of 2012.

132. Christie, *Called to Egypt*, 43.

133. Ibid., 44.

134. AGWM, *Letters From Lillian*, 122.

by Arabs, who often spit at her and yelled obscenities in the streets."[135] But her indomitable spirit frequently carried her through times of risk.

> One night, there was a terrific fight as four hijackers attacked a hashish smuggler who, with his wife and baby, was going by donkey into the interior to peddle the dope. Miss Lillian leaped into the battle, scorning the flashing knives, kicking, whacking, yelling in Arabic. She chased the hijackers away, got the woman and her baby into the orphanage, called the police, who carted off the body of the smuggler, who had been slashed to death in the fray. The woman and her child are still in the orphanage.[136]

She had many names coined for her. President Nasser called her "Nile Mother," and others referred to her as "lady on a donkey," a reference to her circuit-riding fundraising in the early years. Her most beloved name was "Mama Lillian." Many current pastors of the Assemblies of God Church in Egypt are the fruit of her vision and legacy. After fifty years of faithful service, she died in Egypt on December 17, 1961. She once said, "I feel sure that the next generation will be very different because all of those who have passed through our doors will know how to train and educate their children in the ways of the Lord."[137] Her favorite fable summarized her life:

> My work reminds me of a fable of a little boy who was crossing the desert alone. He became very thirsty so he was obliged to dig in the ground with bleeding fingers until he came to water. He drank and went on his weary way.

Each time he became thirsty he dug holes and his hands became more torn and bleeding. At last he reached the other side, exhausted and fainting, his clothes hanging in dusty rags.

Some months later he looked across the desert and saw a happy little boy coming with his hands full of fresh flowers. The child was coming the very same way which he had traveled. He looked at the strange sight in perfect amazement. When the little boy arrived, he asked him how it could be that he had crossed the awful desert and looked so fresh and cool. The child answered, saying, "Oh, the way is beautiful. There are many small wells out of which spring lovely, cool water, and around each of these wells there are flowers and shady bushes and soft green grass. I had no trouble at all in crossing!"

---

135. Beatty, *Nile Mother*, 11.
136. Ibid.
137. AGWM, *Letters From Lillian*, 39.

The first boy looked down at his own scarred fingers and knew that it was his suffering which had made the desert bloom and had made the way easy for other little boys to cross. But no one would ever know to thank him or to ask who had dug the wells, but he knew and was satisfied.[138]

Lilias Trotter

Lilias Trotter was born in London in 1853 to Alexander and Isabella Trotter. Lilias was devoted to her father who encouraged his children from an early age in both scientific and artistic pursuits.[139] She had a gift for art, and in 1876 in Venice, she received the attention of famed art critic John Ruskin. She was thirteen, and Ruskin fifty-five. He agreed to tutor her, and a pure, unusual friendship began. In 1874, The Broadlands, one of England's stately homes, hosted one of the first conventions for "the deepening of spiritual life, the forerunner of the Brighton and Keswick Conventions."[140] She attended this meeting as she did the Moody meetings of 1875. Both meetings profoundly marked her. She no longer felt she could pursue an art career and began to volunteer with the Young Women's Christian Association.

In 1876, Trotter went to Switzerland with her mother and sister, attended a convention (where she preached her first sermon in German), and toured Venice with Mr. Ruskin.[141] In 1879, Ruskin again volunteered to personally train her and open the world of art for her—a promise he was positioned in society to fulfill. Art thrilled her soul. It was agonizing to lay down her unique talent and love for God's call. A voyage to Norway in 1880, an operation in 1884, and another visit by Ruskin in 1885 highlighted her ten-year service with the YMCA on Welbeck Street. Near the end of this period, two members of the YMCA expressed a desire to serve in foreign missions (one in India, another in China), but when she prayed, "the words 'North Africa' sounded in her soul as though a voice were calling her."[142] She attended a meeting about another mission opportunity when "at the close someone stood up and asked, 'Is there anyone in this room whom God is calling for North Africa?' She rose quietly and said, 'He is calling me.'"[143]

138. Ibid.

139. Stewart, *The Love That Was Stronger*, 13.

140. Ibid., 17.

141. Pigott, *I. Lilias Trotter*, 9.

142. Ibid., 15

143. Ibid.

On March 15, 1888, Trotter left for Algiers with three friends. They spent their days studying Arabic, praying, reading, meeting with expatriates, and making friends in the Arab quarter. On May 15, she received the news of her sister's sudden death. Days included walks around town with Arabic and French evangelistic literature, ministry visits to the ships in harbor, meetings for expatriates, and more Arabic study. Trotter returned to England in 1890 for a four-month rest, and when she arrived back in Algiers she found a residence on Rue Du Croissant that became the base for her peripatetic mission activity for the next thirty-two years. With a ministry base established in Algiers (with five women total), she dreamed of expanding the work south into the desert. In March 1894, together with Helen Freeman, she traveled over land to Biskra, Touggourt, and ultimately to Oued Souf, a small oasis town west of the Tunisian border.[144] Another five-month journey to the Southlands was undertaken in 1895; it both invigorated and depleted Trotter, resulting in a well-deserved furlough in 1896.

When she returned to Algiers in 1896, she entered one of the most discouraging phases of her ministry. The French government restricted missionary activity, and local sorcerers attacked new converts through curses and black magic.[145] Trotter organized outreach for young boys who ran the streets and alleys and for Muslim ladies who visited relatives' tombs on weekends. In June 1897, Kate Smith (missionary with North Africa Mission among the Kabyle in Djemaa Sahridj) experienced a filling of God's Spirit on the return from a conference in Switzerland. She returned

> ... with an overwhelming sense of power and joy. Upon arrival in Djemaa, she shared her joy with her fellow workers who likewise experience the same Spirit touch, praying and praising together until their hearts melted into one. Lilias later wrote that one after the other, mission workers, French helpers, and the four Kabyle lads living at the mission station "broke down, in confession and surrender, as the sweet breath of God's Spirit swept over them."[146]

This filling of the Spirit allowed the missionaries to press through the tough times to the victory ahead.

Itinerant ministry to emerging stations filled much of 1900 to 1902. In 1903, setbacks nearly brought the work to a halt; these setbacks were not overturned until March 1906, when an additional home was acquired in El Biar. A new mission station opened in 1909 in the western province of

---

144. Rockness, *A Passion for the Impossible*, 134–35.

145. Ibid., 160.

146. Ibid., 162.

Oran, and ten new members joined the Algerian Mission Band (the name given to the collection of workers under Trotter's leadership) during 1911 and 1912. By Trotter's twenty-five-year mark in Algeria, the Algerian Mission Band was quarterly conducting 1,422 meetings and 2,409 industrial trainings, offered 614 medical services, had 1,486 hospitable hostings and 54 resident guests, had made 818 visits to station villages, and distributed 78 Scriptures and 381 tracts.[147]

World War I (1914–1918) hampered ministry to outlaying stations in the south. In those years Trotter turned her attention to literature and translation. By 1913, she realized that the Nile Mission Press in Cairo was strategic for Arabic and French literature across North Africa. Traveling to Cairo in November,[148] Trotter and her companions joined a course taught by Zwemer, Gairdner, and George Swan. Zwemer taught apologetics, Gairdner taught phonetics, and Swan taught Arab mysticism. Swan's teaching opened Trotter's eyes to the possibility of reaching Sufis and influenced her interactions with them.[149]

The years 1920 to 1922 ushered in a period of freedom unrealized to this point and coincided with the growth of the mission band and an increase in local converts. 1923 marked thirty-five years of Trotter's ministry in Algeria, and she concentrated the next years on administering her mission and personally reaching out to Sufi mystics. This was an unusual thing for a woman, but possible due to her advanced age and sterling reputation among Arabs. On August 27, 1928, Lilias Trotter passed away. Members of the mission band had gathered around her sickbed singing "Jesus Lover of My Soul" when Trotter

> looked out the window and said, "A chariot and six horses!" "You are seeing beautiful things?" asked Helen Freeman. Lilias looked up and spoke her last words: "Yes, many, many, beautiful things." She stretched out her arms as though she would hold them all in her embrace, then slowly lifted her hands in prayer. Almost immediately she became unconscious, and in perfect calm she drew her last breath and went Home.[150]

When Trotter died, the Algerian Mission Band consisted of thirty missionaries in fifteen mission stations or outposts. Trotter was, according to

---

147. Ibid., 249.

148. Trotter said of Cairo, "One feels Cairo is the powerhouse of forward movements." Quoted in Pigott, *I. Lilias Trotter*, 150.

149. Pigott, *I. Lilias Trotter*, 150.

150. Rockness, *A Passion for the Impossible*, 324.

Dr. Christy Wilson, "one hundred years ahead of her time."[151] In 1964, the Algerian Missions Band merged with North African Ministries. North African Ministries in turn became Arab World Ministries, which merged with Pioneers in 2011. Lilias Trotter was one of the greatest pioneers of mission to the Muslim world.

151. Ibid., 327.

4

Abiding and Mission Effort to Muslims in Egypt and Sudan (1881–1920)

ACCORDING TO THE EXEGESIS of John 15:1–17 (see section 2), abiding in Jesus leads to making disciples. The contention of this dissertation is that missionaries who abide in Jesus will make disciples. This chapter synthesizes the personal and corporate abiding praxis of disciple-making missionaries Daniel Comboni, Samuel Zwemer, Oswald Chambers, Temple Gairdner, Douglas Thornton, Lillian Trasher, and Lilias Trotter to see how they abided in Christ. The biographical record of these missionaries shows that they all made disciples—some disciples were from Muslim backgrounds, some were young missionaries, and some were Christians impacted by their lives and writings after they passed.

This chapter assumes there is mystery in the process. Rather than working to define the mystery, this discussion probes how these missionaries practiced abiding, not how they made disciples. Following the logic of the dissertation, the critical point to learn is how to abide. If missionaries learn to abide, Jesus promises they will bear disciples.

PERSONAL ABIDING

The personal abiding of these missionaries can be organized into six general categories that emerged from a synthesis of the exegetical findings. Those categories are: (1) continuance in the presence of Jesus; (2) intentional blocks of extravagant daily time with Jesus; (3) priority on the word and prayer; (4) disciplined approach; (5) corporate praxis; and (6) strategic inspiration.

Always in the Presence of Jesus

The lives of Comboni, Zwemer, Chambers, Gairdner, Thornton, Trasher, and Trotter all share ongoing communion with Jesus. None regulated his or her walk with Christ to fixed times. All experienced intimacy in ongoing communion—striving to ever be in the presence of God. This experience had implications on their mission praxis. "The missionary vocation, as Daniel Comboni lived and understood it, entails an essential relationship with Christ Jesus."[1] David McCasland noted that Chambers agreed, saying, "Unless the life of a missionary is hid with Christ in God before he begins his work, that life will become exclusive and narrow. It will never become the servant of all men, it will never wash the feet of others."[2]

Potentially, Zwemer directly or indirectly influenced the Church's response to Islam more than any other man or woman. "Wherein lay the dynamic of so powerful a life? It was a life in God. The motive force came from constant communion with the Creator through His Son Jesus Christ."[3] Though less well known than Zwemer today, Gairdner was a contemporary and friend of his. Padwick shares the result of Gairdner's unceasing fellowship with Jesus:

> And the marvel is not only that Temple Gairdner could not ever say a word that was disloyal to his Master, but that the other man who was with him could not either. That was Gairdner's strength, the practice of the presence of Christ, and from there it flowed, as a full and even tide, his unconscious, unceasing, yet wholly compelling influence.[4]

Gairdner said of Douglas Thornton, "But into that secret place where the soul meets with its Lord, who shall intrude? The direct and conscious communion between the Spirit of Douglas Thornton and Christ's Spirit, *this*, and only this, can account for the strange intensity with which he sought first the Kingdom of God."[5]

---

1. Lozano, *The Spirituality of Daniel Comboni*, 30.
2. McCasland, *Oswald Chambers*, 101.
3. Wilson, *Apostle to Islam*, 239.
4. Padwick, *Temple Gairdner of Cairo*, 187.
5. Gairdner, *D. M. Thornton*, 90.

Whether in the intensity of focus in service or breadth of influence in mission, the source of the power was the constant communion these men and women had with Jesus; they were always with him. One day after watching her children respond to a crisis, Trasher had a revelation: "With great depth it came to Mama that her hundreds of children were doing only what they had seen her do, both in times of plenty and in times of stress. They knew she prayed without ceasing."[6] Trasher's individual habit of always being in the presence of Jesus directly impacted her mission and her disciples. Miriam Huffman Rockness notes that Trotter had the same realization:

> It has come these days with a new light and power, that the first thing we have to see to, as we draw near to God day by day, is that "our fellowship is with the Father and with His Son Jesus Christ." If we can listen in stillness, till our souls begin to vibrate to the thing He is thinking and feeling about the matter in question, whether it concerns ourselves or others, we can from that moment begin praying downwards from His throne, instead of praying upwards toward Him.[7]

For these men and women of mission, the starting point of their abiding was unbroken communion with Jesus. They loved to be with him. Jesus was their best friend and their constant companion, and they strove to never leave his presence. Intimacy with Jesus helped them frame decisions and responses; intimacy with Jesus helped them sense what to do and how to speak. These missionaries spoke from the place that they aimed never to abandon—the simple and glorious presence of Jesus.

Intentional Blocks of Extravagant Daily Time with Jesus

These seven missionaries could be considered mystics, but it is also true that they scheduled daily time with God. For Comboni and his missionaries, this regimen included daily spiritual exercises including "a one-hour meditation in the morning, Holy Mass, a fifteen-minute examination of conscience before lunch and before rest in the evening; holy Rosary, visit to the Blessed Sacrament and spiritual reading."[8] Zwemer insisted on daily blocks of time set aside for God and brushed aside alarmist worries about legalism. "Those who are staggered and offended when they are told by the saints of the ages

---

6. Howell, *Lady on a Donkey*, 175.

7. Rockness, *A Passion for the Impossible*, 305–6.

8. Mondini, *Africa or Death*, 122.

that man should spend hours upon hours alone with himself and God, need only to recall the prayer life of our Lord."[9]

Zwemer and colleagues lived out this principle. "We find that he continued the hour of prayer and Bible reading from noon to one o'clock, which had been established the first year in Seminary. Before a major address for the Student Volunteer Movement he records, 'Felt very weak spiritually, but prayer was strengthening.'"[10] Chambers agreed with Zwemer and remarked, "There are certain times of the day when it not only seems easier, but it is easier to meet God. If you have ever prayed in the dawn you will ask yourself why you were so foolish as not to do it always; it is difficult to get into communion with God in the midst of the hurly-burly of the day."[11]

Each of these missionary leaders modeled an abiding praxis that started with "always communion" with Jesus that was fortified by daily blocks of concentrated time with him. Padwick shares the story of an Egyptian friend of Gairdner: "I was very much struck by the simplicity of his personal life . . . I often used to go to his room and find him kneeling on the bare stones. One day I thought I would go to see him, and I found him kneeling there on the stones, so I came away without his hearing me. Two hours later I went back . . . he was still kneeling there."[12]

While Gairdner was a kneeler, Thornton was a pacer. "His house lay on the northern edge of the city and it was his delight to go up to the roof and pace up and down, and meditate, and pray."[13] The example of both men was profound on their Egyptian disciples. Similarly, Lillian Trasher imparted to her young disciples a love for extended, extravagant time in the presence of Jesus. She said of her orphanage wards:

> The most wonderful sight I ever saw in my life was when I followed the noise up to the housetop. There were dozens and dozens of little girls shouting, crying, talking in tongues, rejoicing, preaching, singing—well, just everything you can think of—praising God! Several of the children saw visions . . . It is as if a mighty fire has struck us. Nothing can stop it . . . The children pray in the fields, on the canal banks, and in all the rooms. The house and grounds have become "a house of God."[14]

9. Zwemer, *Taking Hold of God*, 53.

10. Wilson, *Apostle to Islam*, 32.

11. Chambers, *Prayer*, 42.

12. Padwick, *Temple Gairdner of Cairo*, 82.

13. Gairdner, *D. M. Thornton*, 117.

14. AGWM, *Letters From Lillian*, 17–18.

Trotter was intentional about her daily lavishing of extravagant time on Jesus.

> Lilias was a "Mary" more than a "Martha," in spite of the demands of her work. How inspiring to note that this pioneer's lifestyle carved out "a quiet place near to the heart of God." Whether retreating to Fortification Woods in Algiers [with her Bible] every morning from 7:15–8:30, drawing strength from hearing God speak in the solitude of the Sahara Desert, retiring to a rooftop room or *melja*, or on her intentionalized "two weeks alone with God" every summer in England or Switzerland, Lilias knew what the one thing needful was.[15]

The daily devotion of these men and women had a profound impact on mission. First, as influential leaders, they modeled what was most important to their followers. Comboni taught his missionary trainees to daily linger with Jesus. Zwemer exhorted missionaries serving across the Muslim world to prioritize Christ in their daily schedules. Gairdner and Thornton impressed upon a generation of Egyptian believers (both from Christian and Muslim backgrounds) that the most important hours of the day were the ones spent with the Bible and in prayer. Trasher raised an army of intercessors who were grounded in the Scripture and dedicated large portions of their day to God. Trotter led an entire mission into the life-giving rhythm of daily and seasonal resting in Christ. The praxis of these missionaries was observed and emulated by those they influenced. The ripple effect on mission underlined the most important activity a missionary could take up—to lay down his or her schedule and revel in the presence of Jesus.

A Priority on the Word and Prayer

Examining how these daily blocks of time with Jesus were spent reveals that the two most common elements were the word of God and prayer. Some of the seven missionaries wrote in a journal, some painted, some sang, and some read devotional literature. But without fail, all spent the majority of their daily extravagant time with Jesus in the Scripture and in prayer. This focus on Scripture and prayer impacted their mission in important ways.

This focus for Comboni led directly to a Pentecostal experience of empowerment. Prayer and Bible study revealed his limitations and fostered an urgency to be empowered by God's love through God's Spirit. John Lozano notes that his superiors said:

15. Rockness, *A Passion for the Impossible*, 15.

We believe that there was more to our missionary's zeal than the simple effect of a meditation on the universality of redemption and on the love of Christ for sinful humanity. It came rather, from a charismatic experience, an essential part of the life experiences which awakened his vocation. The love of Christ for souls forcefully took possession of him. It was a Pentecostal experience.[16]

For Zwemer, the impact of abiding through Bible study and prayer manifested itself in his public ministry. "He believed with all his heart in the whole of the Bible as the word of God . . . The Bible was so much a part of his life that thought and word seemed naturally to take the form of Biblical phrase."[17] In his speaking, witnessing, and teaching, Scripture flowed from him effortlessly, as he expended great effort to take in Scripture on a daily basis. Daily focused time in prayer also had a mission effect. "Back of all this intense activity was his own quiet walk with God. He was a man of much prayer. That was the secret of his buoyancy of spirit, infectious laughter, fund of good stories, clasp of hand and sparkling eyes; all were eloquent of his love for men, born of his love for his Savior."[18]

Standing against common thinking and trends, Chambers referred to the Bible constantly in his public teaching and preaching. He also insisted that ideologies and experiences—no matter how appealing—had to conform to the Bible. The Bible was central to him. McCasland notes that Chambers taught:

The end and aim and meaning of all sanctification is personal, passionate devotion to Jesus Christ. Keep bold and clear and out in the bracing facts of His revelation world, the Bible. Never compromise with those who water down the word of God to human experience, instead of allowing God to lift up our experience to His word.[19]

Gairdner emphasized the day-to-day role of the Spirit empowering the service and mission tasks that believers would not ordinarily choose for themselves. He wrote that the Holy Spirit was given

to give us the wonderful (but unseen and unrecognized and uncounted and un-praised) power in prayer (for the mouth of the Spirit-filled man is the mouth of Christ in prayer), to enable

16. Lozano, *The Spirituality of Daniel Comboni*, 35.

17. Wilson, *Apostle to Islam*, 241.

18. Wilson, *Prophet*, 239.

19. McCasland, *Oswald Chambers*, 109.

us to do His will perfectly from day to day, even if that will is unseen and unnoticed suffering, loneliness, loss of fame and ambition, failure if you like.[20]

Daily prayer, according to Gairdner, led to daily direction and daily empowerment—an empowerment that was not only for the grand and miraculous, but also for the mundane and difficult. It was daily time in prayer and the Bible that empowered both the sublime and the suffering. For Thornton, moral conviction and guiding values were forged in the furnace of daily prayer and Bible study. He wrote to his fiancée, "Help me to be true to my past convictions, wrought out on my knees, and in the presence of the life and Book of Christ."[21]

Trasher's methodology centered on a dissemination of the word from which she daily fed. She wrote in her letters, "[The children] are getting the Word of God, and sometime, somewhere it will spring up and bear fruit, if not in them, then in their children. The Word of God is alive and will not die. We were not asked to give the results; that is for God to do."[22] Trasher felt the Bible was the power, and her mission aim was to get the Bible into the hearts of her children. Trotter's personal prioritization of daily time in the word and prayer informed all her decision making. "Lilias [Trotter] put the highest priority on spending time completely alone with God, studying his word with a heart open and receptive to His voice—an activity requiring utmost commitment from her, given the many demands on her time."[23]

The devotion of these seven missionaries to daily times in the word of God and prayer impacted mission in three ways: First, it provided them the ongoing content of their prayers, preaching, teaching, and writing. Second, it provided the sensitivity and discernment for the numerous small decisions that they were required to make on a daily basis and the occasional momentous one. Third, faithful daily time with the word and in prayer renewed them in the Holy Spirit and gave them repeated power, passion, and energy for the task at hand.

A Disciplined Approach

Conjoined to the daily practice of Bible reading and prayer is the discipline and organization needed to maintain such ambition. "The missionaries

20. Padwick, *Temple Gairdner of Cairo*, 105.

21. Gairdner, *D. M. Thornton*, 66.

22. Assemblies of God World Missions, *Letters From Lillian*, 88.

23. Rockness, *A Passion for the Impossible*, 187.

[Comboni and his team] and religious of the time understood community as a disciplinary reality. Living in community meant being subject to the same discipline and creating a detailed timetable in which acts of piety were included."[24] Comboni and his missionary team realized that abiding in Jesus was not all ecstasy. Abiding in Jesus includes times and seasons that are dry and unexciting. The brief mountaintop experiences are made possible by disciplined and difficult ascent. Wilson shares a portion from Mrs. Zwemer's diary:

> It was in Persia that we learned a new version of an old proverb: "Late to bed and early to rise makes a missionary healthy, and wealthy, and wise." One medical missionary in charge of a large hospital spends two and a half hours daily in prayer and Bible study—no wonder that his paper on "Spiritual Cooperation" read at the Tehran Conference deeply moved us all.[25]

These missionaries understood that intimacy with Jesus included faithful waiting on him, enduring times of silence, and maintaining a schedule and a regime even in the absence of emotion and feeling. The busier these mission leaders became, the more responsibility given them, the more demanding and pressing the need, the more careful they were to discipline themselves to daily rendezvous with Jesus. This was true of Chambers.

> In the face of increasing demands on his time and energy, Chambers stringently maintained his early mornings alone with God . . . Oswald's morning hour with God was the only undisturbed portion of his day . . . In summer Chambers usually rose by 5:30 a.m. to have his time alone until everyone met for prayers at 7:15.[26]

The result of these missionaries' determined discipline were a profound influence on their organizations and a broader mission philosophy. Padwick notes that Dr. Mott, cofounder of the Student Volunteer Movement, says of Gairdner,

> He impressed me with his natural enthusiasm, his responsiveness to exacting demands in the realm of spiritual discipline, and to the stern challenges sounded out in regard to the extension of the reign of Christ. It is given to but a few men to share in laying the foundations of a movement which within their own

24. Lozano, *The Spirituality of Daniel Comboni*, 108.

25. Wilson, *Apostle to Islam*, 131.

26. McCasland, *Oswald Chambers*, 244–45, 257.

lifetime profoundly and extensively influences for good the life of their own nation and the welfare of mankind.[27]

Thornton disciplined himself with one central idea in view—the work of the glorification of Jesus among the peoples who did not know him. All other pleasures (pure as they may be) were subservient to this aim. "[Thornton] sought first the Kingdom of God and his righteousness . . . every hour, every waking thought, every journey, every holiday, every letter, every talent, every interest, was dedicated to the one cause."[28] In Trasher's ministry, a time arose when she became very concerned for the spiritual life of the girls in her orphanage. She rebuked their lack of discipline and devotion; they repented and cried. One of the more difficult girls approached Trasher and said, "Mama, I am going to start a Prayer Army among the girls and I shall put my name the very first on the list."[29] The girls responded to her rebuke and example, and dedicated themselves to the discipline of prayer focused on reaching the lost. Trotter agreed with her contemporaries on the centrality of disciplined prayer.

> Prayer had always been an essential spiritual discipline for Lilias. She was convinced the band could not survive the hostile spiritual atmosphere, much less succeed in their mission, without the divine guiding and empowering that comes from intimate fellowship with God.[30]

Another aspect of discipline common to these pioneer missionaries was the experience of personal suffering. In suffering they realized a sweet and sustaining intimacy with Jesus. For Comboni,

> The sense of being misunderstood and lonely arose in his last years . . . [He] felt he had somehow been abandoned by the very people in charge of the works he had founded . . . It is interesting to note that it is during these last years that his theology on the relationship between the cross and the works of God becomes most explicit and insistent. At the same time, his letters during these last months speak of identification with Christ and reflect a lively and tender love for the Lord.[31]

---

27. Gairdner, *D. M. Thornton*, 49.

28. Ibid., 87.

29. AGWM, *Letters From Lillian*, 37.

30. Rockness, *A Passion for the Impossible*, 15.

31. Lozano, *The Spirituality of Daniel Comboni*, 19.

Zwemer experienced the tenderness of Jesus after his two daughters died in Bahrain. Chambers, surrounded by soldiers in the midst of war, constantly encountered loss. From that context he wrote:

> Remember, what makes prayer easy is not our wits or our understanding, but the tremendous agony of God in redemption. A thing is worth just what it costs. Prayer is not what it costs us, but what it cost God to enable us to pray. It cost God so much that a little child can pray. It cost God almighty so much that anyone can pray. But it is time those of us who name His name knew the secret of the cost.[32]

Temporal suffering helped Gairdner understand God's suffering and the cost paid to secure freedom, even freedom in prayer. The death of his brother and his best friend, along with the tragic passing of others, affected him. "The mission did attain in these years the spirit of a family in which love and freedom of speech were both conserved. And one of the welding forces was the shock of repeated sorrow, for in Gairdner's first years of married life there were several tragic deaths in the little group."[33] Thornton's disappointment stemmed from the brutal realities of mission labor.

> There is something very deadening about the first stages of a missionary life ... the contrast between aspiration and reality ... in the hard glare of the Orient, romance may quite easily wither away. Only the spirituality, the roots of which are far beneath the surface, stretching deep down to a spring of the Living Waters, has a chance of maintaining its freshness and strength.[34]

Trasher was no stranger to pain. She was forced to call off her wedding ten days before the wedding day, seventy of her children were forcibly taken from her and returned to Muslim homes, and she occasionally became deathly sick. Her telling response to a grave sickness was, "This illness was the best lesson I have ever had in my life."[35] Trotter's father died when she was twelve. During that period of grief, her sister wrote about her, "She simply shed a constant light over her home" through the "very hardest thing in her life," and God brought her "soul into blossom."[36]

These missionaries faced tragic loss, and all emerged from tragedy sweeter. This sweetness—wrung from the bitterness of suffering—was

32. Chambers, *Prayer*, 21.

33. Padwick, *Temple Gairdner of Cairo*, 127.

34. Gairdner, *D. M. Thornton*, 127.

35. AGWM, *Letters From Lillian*, 23.

36. Rockness, *A Passion for the Impossible*, 50.

possible because all disciplined themselves to communion with Jesus daily. Fixed times of meeting with Jesus prepared them for times of darkness and seasons of silence. The end result of their discipline was sweetness of soul and the capacity to minister to others.

Corporate Praxis

Missionaries differ in personality, capacity, and spirituality. To affirm that everyone abides is to acknowledge that, while corporate abiding must have conformity to have purpose, individual abiding must be idiosyncratic to be nutritional. Lozano notes that Comboni affirmed the harmony of the communal and individual approach:

> Prayer . . . must be adapted to the conditions of the individual. It is only natural, then, that each person should make it in the place, time, and form that is most profitable . . . Prayer is not [only] a private matter . . . When we enter and form part of a community of faith, and hence of prayer, the whole group becomes co-responsible for the prayer life of each of its members, and when this life seems to be weakening in a member, it is a legitimate cause of concern of the community and its leaders.[37]

Corporate abiding is richest when individuals (in his or her own fashion) approach corporate time prepared by his or her own devotional experience. In the context of missionary teams, "everyone" indicates that everyone gives Jesus extravagant personal attention, everyone (from his or her context and culture) personalizes how he or she interacts with Jesus, and everyone comes together for corporate abiding times as well. Zwemer pointed to the preciousness of these corporate times of prayer.

> One of the most vivid recollections of the early years of our mission is of the hours we spent in prayer together, first in the Seminary dormitory, then on the slopes of the Lebanons . . . and afterwards in Aden and Basrah and Bahrein . . . We always coveted the whole of the promised land and our eyes were beyond its coasts.[38]

One missional advantage of corporate abiding is that disciples learn from each other how better to pray. McCasland shares a story that Chambers wrote about his old friend John Cameron:

37. Lozano, *The Spirituality of Daniel Comboni*, 108.
38. Wilson, *Apostle to Islam*, 239.

How he knew God! How he talked with God! And how he
taught me out on those hills—at midnight, at dawn light, and
at noonday have I knelt before that old veteran in prayer. Truly
it was a great goodness of God to allow me to know such men.
I learnt a bigger stride, the stride of the mountains of God, with
these royal, elemental souls.[39]

Gairdner is noted for teaching others to pray. A visiting Bishop at
Gairdner's church sensed the presence of Christ when the body went to
prayer, "which means, I suppose, that those who worship there had learnt
to pray. Possibly the training of that congregation was the Canon's greatest
work."[40]

Mission contexts, especially severe ones like the Islamic world, demand a corporate multi-lateral approach to prayer and service. Thornton affirms that he "had the privilege of learning how to think and read and work
with as much accuracy as possible by contact with many various minds,
whose habit it was never to do things by halves, but to take every step after
thorough deliberation and constant prayer."[41] Thornton was a better missionary on account of collaborating in prayer with others.

Trasher discovered that teaching others to communally abide in Christ
was one of her greatest works:

Last Sunday afternoon there was a great outpouring of the Spirit
of God at our church and the children prayed for nearly three
hours. Dark came but the lights were not turned on at once. I
was kneeling on the platform wan when I looked up I could
see hundreds of little forms with raised hands, calling out to
God in one volume of prayer . . . I don't think I ever had seen
before what my call really meant. All the wonder of it was shown
to me in a new way; all of the sacrifices of the past years and
the hardship seemed to melt into nothing as the glory of the
call of God was shown me. He has allowed me to be the one to
open this home of light and comfort for such a great mass of
praying children. Nothing life could have given me could have
compared to this![42]

Trasher's young praying community was her legacy and her reward. A
highlight for Trotter was the breakthrough of the Holy Spirit in a meeting
attended by all the mission agencies in Algeria:

39. McCasland, *Oswald Chambers*, 115.

40. Padwick, *Temple Gairdner of Cairo*, 284.

41. Gairdner, *D. M. Thornton*, 167.

42. AGWM, *Letters From Lillian*, 48.

> One after another nearly all of those gathered put away all hindrance and unbelief, often with broken-down confession before God and man and, through the grave and gate of death, went out into a new world of deliverance and downright sanctification. On the last day there was a sweep of the Spirit through the room . . . and, one after another the last strands of unbelief gave way in soul after soul. We could only wonder and praise. It was the Lord's doing.[43]

These missionaries personally learned to abide in Jesus. They also led their communities into the presence of Jesus. As these missional communities spent time in the presence of Jesus together, they deepened precious unity, found new strength, and received fresh vision. These missionaries sharpened one another by seeking Jesus together, and the sum effect on mission efforts is immeasurably positive.

Strategic Inspiration

A striking finding in a review of these missionaries' abiding distinctive is their conception of the nature of prayer. They did not consider prayer as preparation or empowerment for missions; they considered prayer the primary work of mission. Comboni endeavored to pass this on to his missionary trainees:

> "They must pray and have faith, and pray not just with words but with the fire of faith and charity. This is how the undertaking in Africa was planted. This is how our Religion and all the missions in the world were planted." Comboni distinguishes prayer, as he understands it, from simply recited prayers.[44]

His point was that all missions in the world were planted not as a result of prayers of faith and love, but by prayers of faith and love. Wilson writes about the primary role prayer played in the influence attained by Zwemer:

> [He] had attained for himself a strength of faith that could move mountains. Never did his faith stumble at the power of God to do the impossible . . . Through prayer and service he was used to call out and equip bands of men and women for the most difficult mission fields of the world. Such a faith was not gained or maintained without a struggle.[45]

43. St. John, *Until the Day Breaks*, 79.
44. Lozano, *The Spirituality of Daniel Comboni*, 101.
45. Wilson, *Apostle to Islam*, 241.

Zwemer's prayer and service were indistinguishable. He did not see prayer as cursory or as a precursor to the task. He viewed prayer as the main task and all other efforts supplemental. Wilson relates the story of a missionary to Muslims in China who shared an exhortation given by Zwemer to a group of workers.

> [Zwemer] would again refer to the all-important ministry of prayer and urge upon us all that we take the needs of the Chinese Moslems, as well as Moslems all over the world, upon our hearts more than ever in the past . . . We dare not be careless in the matter of intercession. All the plans and organizations suggested will be of no avail and will not result in the conversion of one soul to Christ unless it be accompanied by our prayers in the all-prevailing Name of Jesus Christ our Lord.[46]

Chambers expressed the same sentiment in his characteristic style. "We are all Pharisees until we are willing to learn to intercede. We must go into heaven backwards; that phrase means we must grow into doing some definite things by praying, not seeing."[47] He believed that prayer was the definite work—primary kingdom achievements were initiated and completed through intercession. Similarly, Gairdner believed prayer not only illuminated (making understanding possible), but it also instructed (prayer actually explained). Padwick shares an anecdote from an Egyptian believer from Muslim background that Gairdner discipled:

> He would come on his bicycle every day for a fortnight, and stay two hours to teach me. When we came to the chief points of dispute between the two religions, he would not teach me till we had prayed together. "In prayer, all things are explained," he told me. And he taught me to keep silence awhile before entering into prayer. I felt he loved me for myself, not because I might become a Christian only, and in this I found he was like Christ. And he loved our children and always played with them.[48]

Early in ministry, Gairdner came to an understanding of the simple secret of prayer's primal functionality. Returning to England for a short furlough, weary and spent from missionary labor, he walked to sea coast and communed with God.

> [He] shouted in prayer to the God of that wind to blow with the rushing west wind of His Spirit into [his] and make it as

46. Ibid., 156.
47. Chambers, *Prayer*, 59.
48. Padwick, *Temple Gairdner of Cairo*, 142.

healthful and free and blowy as that gale from the sea. No one
was there to hear and [he] shouted praise in a sort of madness. It
was splendid. Ten years fell off [him] on that sea wall. There is a
secret for eternal youth—the eternal renewing of the regenerate
heart—the daily becoming "as a little child"; that is the secret.[49]

His discovery was that prayer prepared the way for strategic thinking, prayer prepared the messenger for strategic action, and prayer was the
primary strategy. He also discovered that daily abiding with Jesus, in all of
its passion and reality, was the way to stay fresh and supple in the rigors of
life and ministry. Gairdner tells of Thornton's similar conclusion: "I became
conscious I could lead other men, but had no power to do it. Never shall I
cease to be thankful that I got to Keswick that summer. For God showed me
that the power of the Holy Ghost was needed in my life."[50] Through prayer
times at Keswick, Thornton realized that he was absolutely dependent on
the Holy Spirit. Seeking after the Spirit became the experience of strength
itself, not merely its genesis.

It took these seven missionaries time to realize that prayer did not only
reveal and empower the strategy—it was the strategy. Trasher admitted the
following in her letters:

After 48 years in Egypt, I have found the hardest days were the
first days ... young, untried, full of zeal and energy, but I had
not been tested. I first had to learn how to trust God for a stamp,
a railway ticket, a suitcase, all such small things.[51]

Only after she realized that the primary work was done in prayer
through trust was she able to sustain the pace and load of her responsibilities. She learned how to do more by doing less. As she focused primary
energy on prayer, God took care of numerous issues and she was able to
achieve what he left for her to do. Prayer not only reveals and empowers
strategy, but prayer is the primary strategy and activity of mission.

The abiding praxis of the seven missionaries researched (Daniel
Comboni, Samuel Zwemer, Oswald Chambers, Temple Gairdner, Douglas
Thornton, Lillian Trasher, and Lilias Trotter) evidence all aspects of the
definition of abiding resulting from our exegesis in the first section of this
book. All communed with Jesus all the time. All dedicated blocks of time
to lavish extravagant attention on Jesus. All spent the majority of those
blocks of time in the word and prayer. All disciplined themselves and their

---

49. Ibid., 152.
50. Gairdner, *D. M. Thornton*, 26.
51. AGWM, *Letters From Lillian*, 109.

followers to spend time with Jesus (and experienced suffering in the process). All engaged others in a communal celebration and interaction with Jesus. All found time with Jesus to be the strategy, not just empowerment for the strategy. As a result, all seven missionaries produced disciples, and their disciples in turn produced disciples. History attests to these men and women's lasting impact on missions.

Section 3

Field Research

THIS SECTION BUILDS ON the biblical exegesis of John 15:1–6 and the historical examination of the abiding praxis of seven missionaries in Egypt from 1880 to 1920.

Three social science methods were utilized to probe into the personal abiding practices of team leaders of church planting teams in Muslim North East Africa and into how they led their teams in corporate abiding. A semi-structured interview process asked questions concerning personal abiding to a sample set of multinational team leaders who worked in various countries under various mission agencies. Second, Q methodology was used to ask two questions (each via its own Q-sort) to those team leaders concerning their teams' corporate abiding; Q-sort 1 queried what the teams actually do and Q-sort 2 queried what was valued. The third research tool was a self-administered electronic survey sent to team members of the interviewed team leaders that probed into the impact the abiding of team leaders has had on team members.

Field Research

5

Methodology

THIS CHAPTER CONTAINS AN overview of the different research methods and details how these methods are used in the research process.

OVERVIEW OF RESEARCH METHODOLOGY

The research methodology used in this section includes both qualitative and quantitative methods. The primary social science methods used were semi-structured interviews, Q-sort surveys, and a self-administered electronic survey. This integrated approach empowers the methods to complement and verify one another. The objective of this research was to understand the abiding praxis of team leaders and the influence that their abiding has both on teams and on missions.

Semi-structured Interviews

Twenty-three team leaders[1] (both male and female) from North East Africa (Sudan, Kenya, Somalia, Djibouti, Comoros, Zanzibar, and Egypt) were selected for interviews. A written list of questions was compiled and field-tested on men and women with leadership experience before being revised.[2]

---

1. Originally there were twenty-four interviewees selected, but was unable to make the interview appointment. Therefore, the resulting total of twenty-three semi-structured interview transcriptions are numbered 1–5 and 7–24.

2. "In situations where you won't get more than one chance to interview someone, semi-structured interviewing is best . . . Semi-structured interviewing is based on the

The interviews were held progressively in three different countries—Kenya (July 2012), Egypt (September 2012), and Sudan (August 2013). In each location interviewees were asked the same questions with the interview tool being slightly adjusted to reflect arising data before usage in the next location.[3] Those interviewed represented the following mission agencies: Frontiers, Global Missions Service (GMS), Assemblies of God World Missions (AGWM), Youth With A Mission (YWAM), Antioch Ministries International (AMI), the International Mission Board (IMB), African Inland Mission (AIM), Inter-serve, Pioneers, Operation Mobilization (OM), and Staying on the Spot Ministries.

According to Patton, "the fundamental principle of qualitative interviewing is to provide a framework within which respondents can express their own understandings in their own terms."[4] Respondents came from nine different countries (United States, Canada, Sweden, Finland, Sudan, Brazil, Lebanon, Egypt, and England) and included fourteen females (of twenty-four total),[5] of which only one was single. These semi-structured interviews accommodated the different communication styles of the respondents, allowing for more accurate findings. Each interview lasted between forty-five and seventy-five minutes, which is well within the norm for semi-structured studies.[6]

---

use of an interview guide. This is a written list of questions and topics that need to be covered in a particular order." Bernard, *Research Methods in Anthropology*, 205.

3. "The interview questions are written out in advance exactly the way they are to be asked during the interview . . . Any clarifications or elaborations that are to be used are written into the interview itself. Probing questions are placed in the interview at appropriate places. The basic purpose of the standardized open-ended interview is to minimize interviewer effects by asking the same question of each respondent. Moreover, the interview is systematic and the necessity for interviewer judgment during the interview is reduced. The standardized open-ended interview also makes data analysis easier because it is possible to locate each respondent's answer to the same question rather quickly and to organize questions and answers that are similar." Patton, *Qualitative Evaluation Methods*, 202.

4. Ibid., 205.

5. "The interview questions are written out in advance exactly the way they are to be asked during the interview . . . Any clarifications or elaborations that are to be used are written into the interview itself. Probing questions are placed in the interview at appropriate places. The basic purpose of the standardized open-ended interview is to minimize interviewer effects by asking the same question of each respondent. Moreover, the interview is systematic and the necessity for interviewer judgment during the interview is reduced. The standardized open-ended interview also makes data analysis easier because it is possible to locate each respondent's answer to the same question rather quickly and to organize questions and answers that are similar." Patton, *Qualitative Evaluation Methods*, 202.

6. "The individual or depth interview is a conversation lasting normally for one to

Other Qualitative Research

Semi-structured interviews are a form of qualitative research. Qualitative research is "any kind of research that produces findings not arrived at by means of statistical procedures or other means of quantification."[7] Even though statistics and math are not obviously used, qualitative research is still analytical. Juliet Corbin and Anselm Strauss point out, "Major components of qualitative research are data, analytic or interpretive procedures, and written/verbal reports."[8] All semi-structured interviews were recorded with the interviewees' explicit permission and then transcribed. The interview transcriptions were literal, but excluded pregnant pauses, audible, but nonverbal stutters and hesitations, laughter, and inaudible expressions. Themes[9] were identified through a memoing process,[10] and findings were derived from the analyzed themes. Bernard affirms, "there is no single method for [analyzing texts]. Some of the major traditions of text analysis include hermeneutics (interpretive analysis), narrative and performance analysis, schema analysis, discourse analysis, grounded theory, and content analysis."[11] This research employed grounded theory method in deriving findings from the semi-structured interviews.

Grounded Theory Methodology

Corbin and Strauss define grounded theory as:

> [O]ne that is inductively derived from the study of the phenomenon it represents. That is, it is discovered, developed, and

---

one and a half hours." Ibid., 51.

7. Corbin and Strauss, *Basics of Qualitative Research*, 17–18.

8. Ibid., 20.

9. "Qualitative analysis of qualitative data. Interpretive studies of texts, like transcriptions of interviews . . . You focus on and name themes in texts. You tell the story, as you see it, of how the themes are related to one another and how characteristics of the speaker or speakers account for the existence of certain themes and the absence of others. You may deconstruct the text, look for hidden subtexts, and, in general, try to let your audience know—using the power of good rhetoric—the deeper meaning or the multiple meaning of the text." Bernard, *Research Methods in Anthropology*, 428.

10. "The key to making all this work is called memoing. Throughout the grounded-theory process, you keep running notes about the coding and about potential hypothesis and new directions for the research. Grounded theory is an iterative process by which you, the analyst, become more and more grounded in the data. During the process, you come to understand more and more deeply how whatever you're studying really works." Ibid., 463.

11. Ibid., 449.

provisionally verified through systematic data collection and analysis of data pertaining to that phenomenon. Therefore data collection, analysis, and theory stand in reciprocal relationship with each other. One does not begin with a theory, then prove it. Rather, one begins with an area of study and what is relevant to that area is allowed to emerge.[12]

As the transcribed interviews were studied, memoing was used to identify key themes and concepts. These themes were collated together and cross-referenced against one another in order to determine where broad consensus could be formed. Where there were multiple repeated thematic assertions a finding would emerge and was recorded.[13] Bernard lays out the mechanics of grounded theory. They appear deceptively simple: (1) Produce transcripts of interviews and read through a small sample of text; (2) identify potential analytic categories—that is potential themes—that arise; (3) as the categories emerge, pull all the data from those categories together and compare them; (4) think about how the categories are linked together; (5) use the relations among the categories to build theoretical models, constantly checking the models against the data—particularly against negative cases; and (6) present the results of the analysis using exemplars, that is, quotes from interviews that illuminate the theory.[14] Bernard simplifies the theory down to the identification of themes in the text and the "coding [of] the texts for the presence or absence of those themes. Coding turns free-flowing texts into a set of nominal variables."[15] These nominal variables derived from the interview texts become the major findings of the research.[16] Corbin and Strauss refer to this same process as open coding, which they define as "the process of breaking down, examining, comparing, conceptualizing, and categorizing data."[17] Kathy Charmaz explains, "Coding starts the chain of theory development. Codes that account for our data take form together as nascent theory that, in turn, explains these data and directs further data

---

12. Corbin and Strauss, *Basics of Qualitative Research*, 23.

13. "The grounded theory approach is a set of techniques for (1) identifying categories and concepts that emerge from text, and (2) linking the concepts into substantive and formal theories. The approach was developed by sociologists (Glaser and Strauss 1967; Strauss and Corbin 1990) and is widely used to analyze ethnographic interview data." Bernard, *Research Methods in Anthropology*, 463.

14. Ibid.

15. Bernard, *Research Methods in Anthropology*, 463.

16. "Grounded-theory research is mostly based on inductive or 'open' coding. The idea is to become grounded in the data and allow understanding to emerge from close study of the texts." Ibid., 464.

17. Corbin and Strauss, *Basics of Qualitative Research*, 61.

gathering."[18] "In vivo coding" then is the reading of the text and underlining or highlighting things as it is being read, using phrases to name themes. (Numbers or mnemonics can also be used.) Corbin and Strauss describe in vivo coding as "the words/phrases used by the informants themselves, catchy ones that draw your attention."[19] Michael Agar points out that "the trick is to try and develop categories from the way the informants talked, rather than imposing a set from outside."[20] He goes on to affirm "there's nothing necessarily wrong with imposing categories—you may do that later. But that's not what the early phase of ethnography is all about."[21]

Themes can have sub themes, and tables can be created that include interviewee data (age, sex, occupation, length on field). This data can then be examined by age/category/gender/experience to see frequency of thematic repetition. At some stage in the process, one arrives at theoretical saturation, and no new themes emerge.

Q Methodology

This portion of the chapter on Methodology presents further details on Q methodology.

General Principles

Q methodology is an advanced form of pile-sort survey and "can be understood, in its most basic form, as a simple derivation or inversion of the statistical technique known as factor analysis."[22] Watts and Stenner explain that in Q methodology there "is ordinarily no definitive hypothesis or theory being tested and hence there are no definitive expectations about the study findings."[23] Job Van Exel and Gjalt de Graaf quote Stephen R. Brown, stating, "Q methodology provides a foundation for the systematic study of subjectivity, a person's viewpoint, opinion, beliefs, attitude, and the like."[24]

Paul Stenner, Deborah Cooper, and Suzanne Skevington reveal, "Q methodology was developed by William Stephenson . . . as a means of

---

18. Kathy Charmaz, *Handbook of Qualitative Research*, 515.

19. Corbin and Strauss, *Basics of Qualitative Research*, 20.

20. Michael Agar, *The Professional Stranger*, 104.

21. Ibid.

22. Watts and Stenner, *Doing Q Methodological Research*, 5.

23. Ibid., 174.

24. Van Exel and de Graaf, "Q Methodology: A Sneak Preview," 1.

gaining access to subjective viewpoints."[25] William Stephenson developed Q methodology to improve research into the science of behavior. It has grown into a tool that can quantitatively measure and analyze qualitative data. Stephenson described Q methodology as "a set of statistical, philosophy of science, and psychological principles"[26] that would lead to the reformulation of factor analysis while avoiding the excesses of reductionism. What makes Q methodology unique is that it combines quantitative and qualitative methods. It uses a quantitative method to study qualitative data. R. M. Baker makes a case that Q methodology can accurately evaluate subjective material and is "appropriate to questions about personal experience . . . and matters of taste, values, and beliefs."[27]

Watts and Stenner point out that "all Q methodological studies are characterized by two main features: (1) the collection of data in the form of Q-sorts, and (2) the subsequent intercorrelation and by-person factor analysis of those Q-sorts."[28] Q-sorts are a collection of items provided by the researcher that the interviewee subjectively arranges along a continuum. Stenner, Cooper, and Skevington point out that the methodology provides "a model of [the interviewee's] viewpoint on the issue under study."[29]

Q methodology is distinguished by factor analysis. Factor analysis allows "any shared modes of engagement, orientations, or forms of understanding to be detected."[30] Stephenson brought "the methods of correlation and factor analysis into the laboratory and clinic,"[31] thus making it possible for qualitative data to be researched objectively. Essentially, Q methodology uses a quantitative method to examine subjective and qualitative data, probing for currents and trends (factors) that are commonly held, though unseen, throughout a study group.

Specific Application

Twenty-seven team leaders were chosen to participate by Q-sort from nine different nationalities (American, Swiss, Sudanese, Canadian, German, Brazilian, Egyptian, Korean, and Dutch). Seventeen respondents were male and ten female. Ten different mission organizations were represented including

25. Stenner, Cooper, and Skevington, "Putting the Q into Quality of Life," 2162.
26. Stephenson, *The Study of Behavior*, 1.
27. Baker, "Economic Rationality," 2343.
28. Watts and Stenner, *Doing Q Methodological Research*, 178.
29. Stenner, Cooper, and Skevington, "Putting the Q into Quality of Life," 2162.
30. Stenner, Dancey, and Watts, "Understanding of Their Illness," 442.
31. Stephenson, *The Study of Behavior*, 9.

Frontiers, GMS, AGWM, YWAM, Antioch, IMB, AIM, Inter-serve, Pioneers, OM, and Staying on the Spot Ministries. Those interviewed worked in Sudan, Zanzibar, Somaliland, Djibouti, Kenya, Egypt, Comoros, Morocco, India, and Jordan. Each participant was asked to sort forty-eight statements about corporate abiding within his/her team from the practices the team did least often to those done most often. They were then asked to sort the same statements again along a different dimension—from those they value least to those they value most. The first question involved the abiding praxis of their teams: How did they lead their team in abiding in Jesus? The second question probed into what they valued in corporate abiding (whether or not it was practiced). To reduce the possibility of fatigue among team leader couples who participated in semi-structured interviews and two Q-sorts, spouses alternated between the semi-structured interview and the Q-sort survey. Whichever spouse completed the Q-sort survey was the opposite spouse who sat for the semi-structured interview.

The rationale for researching the abiding praxis of church planting teams is twofold: (1) to cross reference abiding practices with fruitfulness (disciple making) of said teams; and (2) to use fruitful teams abiding praxis as a baseline for coaching and assisting other less fruitful teams.

Practically, a Q-sort is very simple. In this research forty-eight statements about corporate abiding were written on forty-eight individual cards. In this particular research there were two continuums. The first was "do this often / hardly ever do this," which provided the range for the current corporate praxis of team abiding. The second was "very important / not important," which provided the range for what the team leader thought was most valuable in corporate abiding settings. The Q-sort was done twice: the first time to research what the team leaders actually did (Q-sort 1), and the second time to research what the team leaders valued (Q-sort 2). For Q-sort 1, a grid with forty-eight large squares was placed on a table. The first step for the sorter was to go through the stack of forty-eight statements (one statement per card) and place those cards in one of three piles: (1) If the card mentioned something the team leader did often in the team setting, he or she placed it to the right; (2) if the card mentioned something the team leader rarely did, he or she placed the card to the left; and (3) items periodically done were placed in the middle. Starting with the pile on the right (practices done often), the team leader placed the cards on the right-hand side of the grid, arranging them by frequency, starting with the top farthest right column, and working vertically downward to the end of that column before beginning the next vertical column. As the team leader placed the cards, he or she was allowed to shift the cards as he or she felt appropriate. There were less opportunities (two) to the extremes of the scale to place cards than at the middle (nine), thus leading the responder to identify what was practiced most often and vice versa. Each card had a number that was recorded according to its place on the grid. When this process was completed for Q-sort 1 (frequency of practice), the cards were cleared off the grid and shuffled.

The process was repeated for Q-sort 2, which asked the question of value. Rather than arranging the statements by frequency, the team leader arranged them by value. The practices he or she most valued were placed in a pile on the right, least valued on the left, and neutral value in the middle. A similar process to Q-sort 1 was followed. There were less opportunities (two) to the extremes of the grid to place cards than at the middle (nine), thus leading the responder to identify what was most valuable and vice versa. Each card had a number that was recorded according to its place on the grid.

Remote Surveys

The self-administered remote surveys were distributed through the internet to the team members of team leaders who were interviewed by either semi-structured questions or Q-sort surveys.[32] The survey consisted of three essential forms of questions: short answer, multiple choice,[33] and close-ended.[34] These surveys were electronically returned to the researcher where they were analyzed and compared for thematic similarity. Two forms of analysis were used: grounded theory and memoing for the short-answer questions and statistical averaging for the close-ended and multiple-choice questions. The essential question addressed by the remote survey was the effect of the team leader's abiding on team members. A qualitative approach

32. "The questionnaire is a self-administered interview. Questionnaires can be distributed in person to individuals or groups, or can be mailed to selected potential subjects . . . Closed or fixed-choice questions are relatively easy to code but can be restrictive . . . The greatest advantage of questionnaires is that they are the cheapest form of interview and the most likely to preserve subject anonymity. Their greatest disadvantage is that they require literacy in the respondent and demand exquisite clarity in the instructions and questions." Grosof and Sardy, *A Research Primer*, 145.

33. Multiple Choice Response Item: "A question or statement comprised of: (1) a stem, which is the question or statement itself and (2) the possible responses, sometimes called foils. The responses may form a scale or be categories only. Usually the respondent is instructed to select one response only, but in some situations, is allowed to choose more than one." Sproull, *Handbook of Research Methods*, 198.

34. Closed-Ended Question: "In a closed-ended question, respondents are offered a set of answers and asked to choose the one that most closely represents their views." Frankfort-Nachmias and Nachmias, *Research Methods in the Social Sciences*, 233.

(grounded theory) was used to identify themes, which were then coordinated into concrete findings.

A sampling of twenty team members (nine men and eleven women) from the team leaders who were interviewed completed the self-administered electronic surveys. Eighteen of the responders were American, one was Swiss, and one described herself as "bi-cultural." All twenty responders were either with Frontiers or AGWM. Seventeen had a bachelor's degree, one a masters, one an associates, and one a high school diploma. Team members had served in Tanzania, Sudan, Comoros, Egypt, and Djibouti. Length of service ranged from several months to several years. More than 75 percent of the survey responders were in their twenties. The rest were in their thirties.

Concerning respondents' views of the baptism in the Holy Spirit, three believed it happens at salvation and is repeated, one believed it happens at salvation and is not repeated, one believed it happens after salvation and is not repeated, fourteen believed it happens after salvation and is repeated, and one was unsure but determined to keep asking for ongoing fillings.

Ethics

Each interview included an explanation of interviewee rights. All who were interviewed signed a consent form for both their and the interviewer's protection. Booth explains the necessity of these precautions, "When researchers study people, they may inadvertently harm them—not just physically but emotionally, by embarrassing them or violating their privacy."[35] The interview consent forms for the semi-structured and Q-sort interviews are included in Appendices E and F.

SUMMARY OF RESEARCH METHOD

Three primary social science methods were used in this research: semi-structured interviews to research how team leaders personally abide, Q-sort surveys (a double application to research both how teams corporately abide and what team leaders value in corporate abiding), and a self-administered electronic survey to research how the personal abiding of team members has been affected by the abiding of team leaders. This integrated approach, utilizing both qualitative and quantitative methods, assists the investigation of the impact of abiding praxis, both personal and corporate, on church planting missionaries (particularly team leaders) in Egypt and Northern Sudan.

35. Booth, *The Craft of Research*, 87.

6

Findings From Abiding Praxis of Team Leaders

THE INTERVIEWS WERE TRANSCRIBED and then memoing was used to identify themes. These themes were collated using grounded theory method to discover the findings below.

FINDINGS

In this section, twenty-nine findings will be presented. These findings are not arranged in order of importance, but according to the sequence of questions in the semi-structured interview. Two findings (17 and 23) address a corporate function of abiding. They are included here, as they emerged from an interview about personal abiding.

Table 7.1: Summary of Findings from Abiding Praxis of Team Leaders

1	During the daily rhythm of spending time with Jesus, Bible reading and prayer were the most common elements of abiding and were mentioned by every respondent.
2	The Bible is the cornerstone of abiding.
3	The most common framework for lingering with Jesus is an extended block of time in the morning.
4	Active listening is an integral part of abiding.

5	Worship (listening to music, playing guitar, singing in the local language, praise) is a strong common denominator for those who daily abide in Jesus.
6	The average block of time spent abiding in Jesus exceeds one hour per day.
7	Music plays a vital part in ongoing abiding (all-day communion).
8	Contexts of pressure and overwhelming lostness help focus continual attention on Jesus.
9	Outside activity (exercise and nature) helps keep lines of communication with Jesus open.
10	Those who abide in Jesus experience a steady growth in depth and length of their abiding time.
11	Those who spend extravagant time with Jesus on a daily basis are not satisfied or complacent; they want more of Jesus, specifically to hear his voice and to be intimate with him.
12	Abiding is sweetest when life is hardest or about to become harder.
13	Jesus takes the initiative in abiding. He invites, befriends, guides, and becomes the source of mission.
14	Abiding in Jesus increases the sense of missionary effectiveness.
15	When missionaries stop abiding, even for short periods, their attitude and tolerance for difficulty diminish.
16	Abiding gives missionaries content, energy, creativity, and longevity.
17	The most common corporate practice of abiding is prayer.
18	Solitude does not play a prominent role for most leaders of church planting teams (to their regret).
19	Legalism is not common to those who are intentional about prolonged abiding times.
20	The structure of abiding time and place (whether it is rigid or flexible) depends on the personality of the abider.
21	Suffering improves the quality and quantity of abiding.
22	Abiding strengths of other cultures provoke a Godly jealousy.
23	Corporate abiding is a living demonstration that missionaries not only need Jesus, they also need each other. There are several key things that happen in corporate abiding that do not normally happen in individual abiding, namely laughter, gifts of the Spirit, loud worship, and perspective.

24	Abiding gives humbled and dependent leaders the content of what they share with others and leads to a prominent role for the word doing the work of mission.
25	Abiding gives overwhelmed leaders what they do not naturally have.
26	The most common fruit of the Spirit experienced by the respondents as a result of abiding were peace, joy, and patience.
27	For Western missionaries, there is no significant connection between dreams and intimacy with Jesus. It is more common for non-Western missionaries to experience intimacy with Jesus through dreams. Most of the missionaries who experienced intimacy with Jesus in dreams are female.
28	Abiding's primary effect on church planting strategy is guidance (peace and direction) on what to do and what not to do, who to be and who not to be.
29	Abiding is taught by mentors and by Jesus.

Finding 1

During the daily rhythm of spending time with Jesus, Bible reading and prayer were the most common elements of abiding and were mentioned by every respondent. Some respondents did more of one or the other (Bible reading and prayer), but all did both. Journaling, devotional reading, listening/meditating, and singing were all mentioned frequently. Memorizing Scripture and praying in the Spirit were mentioned infrequently. There was always variety according to personality and season of life. One free-spirited woman working in Somaliland commented, "I do spend the majority of my time praying and being quiet or singing. I'm not the heaviest studier of a bunch of Bible." Bible and prayer, however, were not male-dominated phenomena. A woman who works in Sudan revealed how she spends her abiding time: "Praise, probably twenty minutes, and then probably an hour of Scripture reading and meditation. Then usually about 20–30 minutes of prayer time." Representative of the whole was a forty-one-year-old American who said that of his two-hour abiding time, he spends at least an hour of it reading the Bible. While there was a wide variance of other disciplines in the daily rhythm of spending time with Jesus, the overwhelming commonality was Bible reading and prayer. Bible reading and prayer make up the base set for all abiding.

Finding 2

The Bible is the cornerstone of abiding. The Bible as the source for prayer emerged from the research as an indisputable finding. Responders did not tend to pray in what is normally called intercession (praying through a list), but instead spent most of their time in prayer praying the Scripture back to God. A Dutch woman working in Cairo said, "Because I could spend hours and hours in traffic, I really pray often. But I feel I don't feed myself enough with the Bible to fuel [my] prayers again." A Lebanese woman working in Sudan asserted, "I think that you cannot abide in God without reading the Bible." An American with Frontiers who works in Sudan revealed, "I always start reading Scripture then do some time listening and praying specific things that I feel God puts in my heart." An American male with YWAM affirmed, "The study of Scripture would be, I mean, it is kind of the core. I start by reading Scripture. The Lord speaks to me through Scripture. God guides me through Scripture. I reflect on Scripture, and I pray the Scriptures. So central." While both Bible reading and prayer are common, what is unique is the centrality of the Bible as the content of missionary prayers. A single American woman called to work among Arabs declared, "Well, I guess [the word] directs my prayers a lot of the time. It reminds me of people to pray for or things in my own life I need to pray for . . . The word is my main time, my main thing." A male with eighteen years of ministry experience shared, "My prayer life seems to be responsive to what I am dealing with personally or what I have just read." A team leader agreed, "Sometimes my prayer time is stimulated by going through my memory verses. And then sometimes [those] structure my prayer time."

A team leader in Somalia commented on *Lectio Divina*.[1] "You read a small portion over, and over, and over, and over. And you look for anything that stands out to you, like a Scripture or words, and then you focus on that. And you try and meditate on that and just walk away with it. You know, pray over that part that stands out to you." The word and prayer were invariably mentioned together, but the word much more often than prayer. The essential finding is that the word is the core of the discipline of abiding. Abiding is the word plus worship, the word plus silence/listening, the word plus journaling, the word plus fasting, and, most commonly, the word plus prayer. The word is the one constant in the abiding of missionaries in Islamic Northeast Africa.

---

1. Traditional Benedictine practice of scriptural reading, meditation, and prayer. There are four movements: read, meditate, pray, and contemplate.

Table 7.2: References to the Disciplines

Spiritual Discipline	References in 23 Semi-structured Interviews
Reading the Bible	45
Praying	39
Meditation/Contemplation	10
Worship/Singing	10
Listening/Silence	7
Reading Devotionals	7
Writing in Journals	7
Memorizing Scripture	6
Listening to Music	6
Fasting	3
Praying in the Spirit	2

While variety was expressed in the personal application of abiding, it became thematically apparent that the Bible played the unifying and central role. An American in Sudan said, "[The word and prayer] are the two main things . . . but I also do reading of books." A fifty-five-year-old administrator of a Sudanese school confessed, "The heart of abiding for me is reading the word, and then listening." A Brazilian with AIM affirmed, "Reading Scripture is number one. Prayer as well." A team leader in the Comoros agreed, "[The word of God] would be the dominant [role]. Like it would be where I spend the most time." A woman with twenty-four years of ministry experience asserted, "[The word of God] is very critical. I feel like I need a word for the day to speak to me, and I feel like it's very important that I keep reading until I find something that speaks to me for that day." A wife with two children working in Zanzibar clarified, "I think the word of God and prayer are most important . . . But lately, at least, the word of God has become more important because I am standing on it more."

Finding 3

The most common framework for lingering with Jesus is an extended block of time in the morning. The majority of those interviewed favored one extended block of time in the mornings. Mothers of small children formed an exception to this theme; they tended to spend time with Jesus as the rhythm of their lives allowed. A few responders divided their abiding time into morning and evening blocks. One Finnish mother put it this way, "The most effective time for me is during the morning hours. Not very early, but when everybody leaves the house and I need to do something in order to get that house in a little bit of order. At least where I am going to spend my time, otherwise I can't concentrate. But it should be during the morning hours." A Brazilian father commented, "I usually wake up early before there are things to do and usually have half an hour. And then I try to have my devotion in the evening, before going to bed . . . about twenty minutes to a half an hour as well."

Finding 4

Active listening is an integral part of abiding. Research revealed that abiding in Jesus critically involves times of quiet listening to what Jesus wants to say. Abiding time does not need to be filled with the active reading or praying of the abider. One woman with twenty-eight years of experience working with Somalis said, "I get up in the morning and I stare, and sometimes God talks to me [laughs], and sometimes I just stare." An American working in Sudan who holds a PhD in engineering affirmed, "I probably read for half an hour to forty-five minutes. I probably pray for the remainder of it (total of two hour block). Maybe some singing in there. Maybe some contemplating in there or just listening." Abiding requires time for the seeker to be at rest, waiting for the initiation of God. A common mistake is to not allow God time to speak.

Finding 5

Worship (listening to music, playing guitar, singing in the local language, praise) is a strong common denominator for those who daily abide in Jesus. Those who linger with Jesus do so in an interactive manner, with verbal adoration and singing playing key parts. Research revealed a worship theme common to most responders. Some sang their own songs; some listened to music; some made their own music; and some lifted their voices in audible praise. A forty-four-year-old Lebanese mother related, "I just meditate on one thing. I love to tell the Lord how much I love him. I love to tell him I'm so thankful for the blood of Jesus." A Sudanese man testified, "I have long periods of praise. In the car I play a lot of worship music. I work with a lot of projects in the house, but all the time praise and worship. This gives me power that is not normal. Sorry, even in the bathroom I sing, and God gives me new thoughts." Worship is a normal, necessary response of those who live in difficult contexts. It forms an essential part of the respondents' everyday abiding.

Finding 6

The average block of time spent abiding in Jesus is over one hour per day. Abiding time varied from twenty minutes to two hours per day, with an average time of sixty-four minutes per day (from a sample set of twenty-three missionaries). Of the twenty-one respondents who were comfortable giving an average time, two spent twenty to thirty minutes per day abiding, eight spent thirty to sixty minutes per day abiding, eleven spent sixty to a hundred and twenty minutes per day abiding. The majority of responders spent more than an hour every day abiding.

Table 7.3: Time Spent Abiding Per Day

Number of Respondents	Average Time Abiding Per Day
2	20–30 minutes
8	30–60 minutes
11	60–120 minutes
	64 minutes/day (average)

Finding 7

Music plays a vital part in ongoing abiding (all-day communion). Fourteen of twenty-three respondents (61 percent) directly mentioned the impact of worship or music on their ongoing communion with Jesus. A thirty-nine-year-old male in Sudan said, "I'll be moved by a song, and I will feel God is speaking to me about something." A mother from the Netherlands remarked, "At times there is a certain song, you think, oh, it touches you, so the song stays with you." A male Sudanese Arab explained, "I sing in a very gentle way, and I see the way the Lord loves me. Sometimes I sing many songs and feel a greater blessing. I sing a lot and it leads to strong prayer. And if a person was walking next to me, he would think I was crazy. But it is for the Lord!" Across all nationalities, singing in worship is a primary way team leaders experience the presence and comfort of Jesus all day long.

Finding 8

Contexts of pressure and overwhelming lostness help to focus continual attention on Jesus. When missionaries live in hostile contexts, an unexpected blessing is that oppression aids workers to constantly abide. In these environments, constant, repeated, internal prayers for guidance and help are an essential way that respondents commune with Jesus. Ongoing abiding is usually connected to ongoing need. A male worker in Kenya explains, "It is just continually praying or continual thoughts, asking him for wisdom or asking the Holy Spirit for direction." A team leader in the Comoros adds, "I consistently try to pray as often as I think of it during the day. Either it's just a quick thing of thanksgiving or a prayer for someone or 'I love you Jesus' or things like that." Often these prayers are short little petitions for help, prayers for survival. A sixty-year-old woman who works in the Horn of Africa confesses, "Often it is just calling for help or guidance, protection." Sometimes the initiation of an activity helps spark communion. A Sudanese team leader reveals, "In all the day when I will start anything, I pray that I will do these things right." These "breath" prayers are for the most part quietly, internally prayed.

Those who work in hostile climates do not hide that they commune with Jesus all day long, nor do they wait for private times of prayer. An American engineer in Sudan commented, "During the work day, praying with people who we feel have needs. I've stopped telling people that I'll pray for them later. I want them to hear me pray for them right then. And that gives the Lord an opportunity to perform a miracle. It also shows the Muslim what a conversational prayer is like and personal relationship." An American woman in Sudan relates, "When a thought or person comes into my mind, that I take a moment and pray a prayer for them. 'Jesus help them, speak into their life.' Just being aware." A team leader with the IMB declares, "I like for my daily life to basically be a conversation." This respondent mentioned the joy of being so absorbed with Jesus that he is not even conscious of others around him. Another gentleman with seventeen years of ministry experience phrased it this way:

> I'll bring the Lord into my decisions, when I'm trying to process an email or trying to prepare to meet with somebody to discuss anything, a business issue all the way to a counseling issue. I'll take time and ask the Lord to help me in the decision and open my heart to the Spirit to try to be aware of what he wants me to do in the situations. In addition, when I'm talking to somebody, sharing the gospel, while they speak or even during my time, I'll

ask the Lord to please help me in this process. Where I hope I'm
not relying on my intellect to do it.

An Egyptian who leads one of the Bible Societies in Egypt said, "It
is not separated that I have one hour and then I start life. That is what I
call walking with Jesus . . . One hour, maybe that is, you prepare yourself to
walk with Jesus, but that is not the only time you do it. So eating, drinking,
answering my email. It is the spirit I live. It is what I consider my walk. It's
not a separated piece of my day and the rest of the day is business." When
workers are surrounded—and often overwhelmed—by needs and by lost
men and women, they find it easier to constantly commune with Jesus. A
married American woman in Egypt explained, "I'm much more aware of
lostness around me, so in taxis and as I'm walking by a mosque, as I'm passing people, thinking about relationships, I'll be in prayer for them all day
. . . just the lostness of people." Contexts of pressure, oppression, and overwhelming numbers of lost people aid workers in communing with Jesus all
day long.

Finding 9

Outside activity (exercise and nature) help keep lines of communication
open with Jesus. Repeated breaks for prayer in the course of the day is the
exception. The vast majority of respondents did communion on the move,
while washing dishes, cleaning the house, exercising, walking to work, driving, listening to others, and answering emails. Walking or driving to work
were repeatedly mentioned as times of communion. A Swedish team leader
in Sudan shared, "Nature inspires me, so when I hear the birds singing or
something, that often brings sort of worship for Jesus." A Brazilian leader
commented that "trying to observe and see the beauty of God, even in small
things" helps him continually to commune with Jesus. The implication is
that it is more difficult to commune with Jesus for those who are inside and
do not exercise. Physical activity (outdoors where possible) makes a positive
contribution to an ongoing awareness of the presence of Jesus. In difficult
contexts, the presence of Jesus is not always directly felt; sometimes it is
apprehended by faith. A Dutch mother admits:

> I didn't feel that I was very close to Jesus. I had to always . . . in
> my mind say, "By faith I know he's here with me" . . . and you
> know you hear sermons where God is gonna cut you off. You
> start believing that . . . but the Lord is not harsh. He will lift.
> That . . . makes me love Jesus even more than being afraid of

him, especially when we're on the mission field and people ask you what you do. And sometimes I don't know what I do and I've been trying to survive and take care of my family . . . If I can teach my children to love Jesus, to depend on him, and to love him and walk in his ways, I will be so happy.

This research showed that an ongoing awareness of the presence of Jesus was enabled by an active lifestyle. Ongoing communion sometimes needs to be assumed by faith, and yet as a leader from Finland who has served in Sudan for twelve years said, "Often when you pray about something, you will notice what he says and kind of trust what Jesus says to you. Or often . . . through other people."

Finding 10

Those who abide in Jesus experience a steady growth in depth and length of their abiding of time. Of those interviewed, 83 percent (nineteen out of twenty-three) indicated that their time abiding with Jesus was quantitatively more—much more—than in years past. Among the four whose abiding time did not quantitatively increase were those who had young children. Abiding (especially for mothers) changes after children, being less scheduled when children are young, but longer and more regular when children are grown or in school. An American mother with AGWM in Sudan explains:

When I had children, I had a scheduled time, but it was shorter. But I felt I would take advantage of more menial tasks . . . I felt the Lord was with me driving, in running kids to and from games or whatever. I felt like the Lord was with me just constantly through the day . . . I felt it was more then—a more natural flow when I had kids . . . I did like it when I had kids, but I'm really enjoying it now. Yeah, I just feel like it's deeper now.

A mother in Zanzibar candidly admits that her favorite season of abiding was not when the kids were young "because [she] could never have a schedule." But at the same time, mothers never regretted the child-rearing season. A Lebanese mother in Sudan testified, "But I think now having children—I think my understanding of love and sacrifice and all that has . . . made me, on the inside, understand much more [about the Lord]."

When the interviewees were asked why they spent more time abiding now than before, the answers centered on three main variables: teaching (having been exhorted to abide), pressures of context, and season of life. One mother in Sudan stated she had "more time myself with Jesus [now that the children have moved on]." Another father with YWAM in Sudan who has young children shared that he spends less time abiding now. "I would say typically before marriage and before kids it was an hour to two hours a day. Young kids and marriage, it is a half hour to an hour a day." A recently married Sudanese woman confides:

> I think after I married I have a lot of things I am supposed to do, but I know this is not right, this is wrong; but yes, I am busy—more than before. I'm not happy about that, but I feel that . . . After being married in Sudan, in our culture, it means that most of my time is not for me or for what I would like to do.

Much of the increase in abiding time was connected to a greater sense of need. A woman working with Frontiers in Egypt expressed, "If I am going to [be involved with Muslim background believers], I need to be praying more . . . like the last time since summer there wasn't much demand and then I feel like, oh, I go down in my times with Jesus. There's less need . . . It helps you to be more disciplined because you feel the need." A young mother who had recently arrived in Somaliland shared, "I'm walking with more of a sense that the Lord is with me and everything. And I think I'm carrying bigger things so I'm constantly talking to him about it." This sense of need was a common factor behind increased length of abiding with Jesus. An unmarried team leader with AGWM communicated she spends "much more [time with Jesus now] . . . just because I realize how much more I need the word and I need to meditate on the word."

A married team leader with Frontiers agreed. "I feel like it's different here . . . I have more frequently, longer amounts of time with Jesus . . . Five years ago I wouldn't have ever spent two hours just waiting on the Lord. I feel like especially in my time here, that's something that I've really been stirred to." Seasons of life have a direct impact on length of fixed abiding times. A husband with the IMB in Sudan explained, "Our lives have seasons in them and we've kind of moved into a new season as our kids have gotten a little older and we're able to do a little bit more and we've learned how to cope with all the different things that we have to keep up with." A team leader from Brazil concurred. "There are times when I spend more time fasting than others. There are times when I'm more like reading the Bible than praying. There's others when praying more than reading the Bible. So I see more variation in things I do. I had seasons where I would like—my devotion time would be longer or it would be shorter."

This research showed that while there is allowance for seasons of life (primarily connected to having young children), the vast majority of those living in Muslim North East Africa spend more time with Jesus now than they did a few years ago. The primary reason for the increased time with Jesus was an increased sense of need for help.

Finding 11

Those who spend extravagant time with Jesus on a daily basis are not satisfied or complacent. They want more of Jesus, specifically to hear his voice and to be intimate with him. Seventeen of twenty-three respondents (71 percent) articulated a clear hunger for more time abiding in Jesus. Prominent was a desire for more intimacy with Jesus, more dialogue (hearing his voice), and more quietness of soul (stillness and rest). The essential finding is that none of the respondents were satisfied with their abiding time. All were hungry, longing for something more. Many ongoing desires were mentioned (wisdom, creativity, obedience, children's salvation, desire to be like Jesus, intercession, desire for change, reflection on Jesus, honor for Jesus, more Bible, more Scripture memorization, more supernatural encounters, prayer, meditation, structure, prayer in Spirit, corporate prayer, writing, etc.), but a common hunger was for stillness, quietness, and the capacity to hear better—for more dialogue and closer intimacy with Christ. An American woman in Sudan declared her desire "to be pressed into what He is saying that I can recognize it right away and I obey it just as quickly. I would like [my abiding times] to be more stilled . . . to get myself settled. That is an ongoing struggle of me—to quiet my spirit long enough to be able to do that."

A married woman with experience in both Burundi and Egypt put it this way, "I would like . . . to feel less rushed so I have more time to sit and wait and not to think." A Lebanese wife and mother expressed the longing that "[she] would like to . . . hear him more . . . [to] feel that he's planning my day with me . . . I would like that he would tell me more specific things . . . how to reach out or how to pray for others, even for my family. Rather than me being the clever one . . . thinking of something." A Sudanese woman expressed, "I would like to hear clearly, sometimes I am confusing in the hearing the voice of God . . . I would like to speak with Jesus. I know I speak with him but I would like also to hear from him clearly and rightly." A man working in the Comoros agreed, saying he longed for more intimacy. "I long for—like I really would love to feel like it's just this double, two-way dialogue going back and forth. And just hearing the Holy Spirit as I'm going through my day." Men and women, single and married, experienced and fresh on the field, from Sudan, Somaliland, Zanzibar, and Egypt all expressed a longing to better hear the Lord. This longing to better hear the voice of the Lord is connected to a longing for intimacy with Jesus. A male Sudanese leader said he longed for friendship with God: "That he is my friend. And I am his friend. That is, he is my Father and I am his son, but there is no one that feels like we do between us. That is, I feel an intimate relationship. I feel him very close to me." A male American, "I long for the closeness primarily . . . [for] the fellowship of the Spirit. I desire that more and think about that more than the more ability or power in ministry." A woman in Zanzibar said she longs "for [her abiding] to be a relationship and not just me, one-sided—to hear his voice." A woman in the Horn of Africa said, "[I long for] hearing his voice more in my life rather than me talking to him so much. I would like to hear more what he has to say." The more that missionaries in Islamic Northeast Africa spent time with Jesus, the hungrier they became for more of him, particularly to hear his voice.

Finding 12

Abiding is sweetest when life is hardest or about to become harder. Most respondents' favorite season of abiding was when they were young or un-married or married but without children or when they were going through difficulty. Being young gave them more time for Jesus. Being in hardship made them desperate for him.[2] This research also discovered that a call to mission brought abiding intimacy,[3] and that preparation times were particularly sweet, even if they were stretching. Fourteen respondents directly commented on the difficulty of sustaining a regular and long structured abiding time after marriage and/or when young children were in the home. None of the respondents said that having children in the home lengthened their set abiding times. Many commented on other aspects of God (during the parenting years) that were made real to them through the menial tasks of the day. Having less structured abiding time is normal for parents of small children (especially mothers).

2. As one responder said, "We've been married for eleven years and we have wanted to have children and we haven't. It's just been some difficult times of depending on the Lord. But I feel like through it there have just been aspects of God's character that I've understood that I wouldn't have. It's just desperation in me. It's been beautiful, even though it's horrible."

3. "[I felt closest to Jesus] when the Lord called [my wife] and I to Sudan, and we had talked about it and began to process it . . . that was one of the sweetest times because I needed him. My life was changed and I needed his help to process. The second time is being here in Sudan and feeling the pressure of workload, family life, and Islam. And knowing that Jesus was the only way to combat those things and those would be the two different times."

Hardship often led to missionaries' favorite season of abiding in Jesus. One American wife and mother relayed that her favorite season of abiding "was in Cairo during language study because it was so humbling, so soul crushing. I needed something to build myself up . . . That was sustenance. I remember that; those were good moments with the Lord." An American man in Khartoum stated his favorite abiding time came through the hardship of "knowing how small I was in comparison to the task at hand, knowing I needed the Lord and then knowing I needed to build people to help me." An American working with Somalis in Kenya said his favorite season of abiding was "during the last six months of itineration, when I really had to depend on God . . . It made me just want to get more into him and be more dependent, so it was just a sweeter time for me because it was just coming down to I needed him more. And so it was just that time of dependence that I could really enjoy abiding during that time." A woman working in Somaliland declared her favorite season of abiding to be during "a lot of lonely times, a lot of hard times. A couple close friends passed away." A Finnish leader with Inter-serve mentioned how "the Bible has become really living in the difficult times." Not only do hard times aid in making abiding in Jesus sweeter, the anticipation of change or coming challenges also made walking with Jesus enriched. A leader with the IMB in Khartoum declared: "There have been times in the past where it seemed like there were risks that we were taking or that I wasn't sure of the outcome of something that I was doing. There was like a reward at the end of it in spite of the risk . . . or because of the risk, that really I felt like God was especially close to us at those points."

A Dutch missionary with Frontiers agreed. "[My most intimate times with Jesus] would be in the times of big changes. As we were [discussing] about coming to the field or not, or maybe just before marriage, just before deciding if we have our first child or not, decision times when you long to hear from God before you make your decision. Times of crisis also." Those who experienced trials on the field looked back at them with a certain fondness, since difficulty has the potential to make abiding in Jesus sweeter.

Finding 13

Jesus takes the initiative in abiding. He invites, befriends, guides, and becomes the source of mission. Abiding is commonly thought to be something men and women do in their pursuit of God. This research found that Jesus takes initiative for abiding in his followers. An American with YWAM in Sudan said, "Jesus is more faithful in his abiding in me than I am in my abiding in Jesus . . . I think Jesus has been faithful to be in my life, to be in my heart, to be watching over me, to be walking with me. Oftentimes calling me when I am distracted." A Brazilian in Sudan concurred, "[In] many challenges I have been facing, I see that Jesus is with me, he's abiding in me and he is opening doors." A single American woman in Sudan mentioned, "He abides in me by really speaking to me and drawing me closer to him by improving or working on things in my life." Those interviewed expressed that not only does Jesus take the initiative for the abiding relationship, but he also is more faithful than believers can be. One woman in Sudan puts it this way:

> His faithfulness . . . even when we aren't faithful, that he is . . . even when I think like, "Oh, I want to spend two hours today [with him]" and things get busy and instead he just shows up and speaks to me when I'm washing dishes and I wasn't expecting it. Or just the simple ways that he surprises me with his presence when I wasn't looking for it. I just feel like he's so faithful to make a way, even when I don't give him space to do it.

Abiding becomes a response to the initiative of God, and this removes the pressure and the legalism from the process. An American in Sudan reflected, "His love never fails. The inner witness that I am his child and he still loves me is the most prominent reality. He hasn't left me." This abiding of Jesus in the workers (even as they were intentional about abiding in him) produced fruit and favor in ministry. A woman in Sudan testifies:

> When I spend time with Jesus and then go to the English club that I teach and I am sitting with those Muslim women, and I feel Jesus abiding in me in those moments where they are asking me questions about life and they are asking me what truth is in their marriage, and I sense his presence so thick in that moment, that I know the words I am saying are words of encouragement to them and helping them understand who he is.

Another single woman who is a teacher in a Muslim-dominated elementary school details how abiding led to effective ministry.

> I definitely see the Lord gave me a lot of creative ideas for my classroom that I was able to share the gospel more with the kids . . . The Lord really gave me creativity, and yeah, I really felt like I was really sensitive to the Spirit too. So yeah, during that time [favorite season of abiding] I just remember the Spirit directing me so instantaneously in the classroom, and I think that was a

direct result of just the sweet time with Jesus that I spent in the mornings.

This research showed that multiple missionaries experienced Jesus taking the initiative for their abiding, which resulted in more effective and powerful ministry. Jesus' abiding in missionaries functionally means that he actually sources and accomplishes the work of mission. A Swedish woman in Sudan shares:

> Sometimes in interactions with people and their comments, you realize this wasn't me, it was Jesus, through me. Like one time . . . a [Muslim] teacher came up to me and whispered, "I love your smile. You have Jesus." And I thought, that smile wasn't my smile—because I was very frustrated at the time. But she could still see Jesus in me. And that was Jesus.

An American male expressed Jesus abiding in him as: "When I'll make a mistake and try to do things in the flesh, and realizing how offensive that can be and realizing how sweet Jesus is and how he can change things by me just being a vessel. Allowing him to pour out of me rather than self-accomplishing things is the sweetest thing for me."

This research showed that the results of Jesus' abiding in missionaries are works and words that are directly from him. A leader in the Horn of Africa stated, "I think it is a goodness that doesn't originate with me . . . There are good thoughts that I have that haven't come from me, I'm sure." A missionary in Sudan relates, "[Jesus'] abiding in me [is lived out when] I try to give grace where it is not deserved, to look for non-human ways to give grace. The human reaction would be to react and pounce, but rather to give grace instead is one of the ways [Jesus abides in me]." A team leader in Egypt offers, "[I experience Jesus' abiding in me by] being an extension of him. I know that's a direct correlation to my time with him, my intimacy with the Holy Spirit." A Dutch mother adds:

> When I feel his presence and I'm just a wiser parent. Or I can give counsel to people and I see it's really not me; it's Jesus in me. When you feel just MORE, when you can say the times when you feel out of—you don't know what to do and suddenly you feel, "Oh, Jesus is here, the Spirit is here." And then suddenly things happen and you really realize this is not my own power.

All the initiative for abiding does not rest on the missionary. This research finds that Jesus himself takes the initiative to abide in missionaries and to become the source of their ministry.

Finding 14

Abiding in Jesus increases the sense of missionary effectiveness. This research showes that the more missionary leaders abide in Jesus, the more they sense effectiveness in their outreach and ministry. A Portuguese leader testified to the increase of the Lord in him after abiding. "I felt I was able. Jesus is in me; I have the Holy Spirit now, because I am being able to be free of things that by myself I'd never be able to . . . He was abiding in me. He was helping me." An American male with the IMB confessed, "[If I don't abide], I have less capacity. I function more out of my human nature if I'm not relying on Christ, if I'm not spending time with him. And I tend to function much more out of the relationship with him if I am spending time in him." This same gentleman pointed out, "In the work that we do, relationships are the key to success and I think the relationships are less efficient if I'm not abiding." An American female with AGWM shared, "[In the season when I was closest to the Lord], I felt like I was fruitful, I felt like I was shining for Jesus, and people grew." Numerous respondents testified that abiding in Jesus accounted for a positive difference in ministry—even among resistant peoples. A leader with Frontiers in Sudan stated: "A few years ago, I would have thought that the soil that we're working in is just really hard soil and it just needs tilling. I think that's partially true but I really feel like now is the time for harvest and I do feel that there's definitely a correlation between abiding and being in the presence of Lord and harvest."

A Sudanese woman who helps her husband lead the OM team in Sudan asserts that it was her abiding in Jesus that opened the door for her to have effective Bible studies among Muslim women.

> A lot of [Muslims] here, they heard there is Christianity but they don't know anything about that. And in that time I spent time [abiding in Jesus], because we have a lot of time, I spent time and I read a lot and when I read it, I share it with these ladies and when, we have like a group, I make like a group. I didn't make it, they come to me and they ask me and I say, "Okay, let us sit together and read." I'm reading from the Bible what I can know and after that I share. This is, I have effect in that time.

Abiding in Jesus not only helps with external ministry, it also aids internal stability. A team leader in Sudan noted, "I notice the more consistently I abide, the less the foothold the enemy has in my mind and the less ability he has to distract me from our point, our reason for being. If I abide more, it feels like the focus is sharper. Whereas, if I miss abiding days, things become fuzzy and convoluted."

Capacity for sharing increases when abiding is prioritized. A team leader in Somaliland stated, "Every time I feel a great sense of the Lord really being with me, then I feel there's more to give and share." An American leader reflecting on his ministry to Muslim background believers (MBBs) in Sudan links his fruitfulness to his abiding time. "I attribute the opportunities I had to the abiding time I was doing. I just had more opportunities than I ever had before . . . I felt so good about where I was and what I was doing and just feeling a part of God's work. And I felt I was growing the most, too, during that time." This research finds that abiding in Jesus has a noticeably positive effect on the missionary's subjective sense of the quality and quantity of their mission work.

Finding 15

When missionaries stop abiding, even for short periods, their attitude and tolerance for difficulty diminish.[4] Almost all respondents mentioned the negative effect on their attitude if they did not consistently abide. A woman in Cairo confirmed, "[If I don't abide with Jesus on a daily basis], I get frustrated with myself." A Lebanese team leader revealed that when she does not abide, "I become critical or negative . . . I'm less patient." An American woman concurred, "[If I don't abide], there's definitely a rapid decline in my attitudes and in my emotional energy and just my interactions with other people in general—it snowballs." A different American female related, "[When I don't abide], well, there's just something missing . . . You just don't have peace. You left your shoes in the closet, and you're missing something in your life, and you're just not prepared."

The limitations resulting from a lack of abiding are not restricted to a single gender or culture. An American male said, "I notice a direct correlation with anytime I don't abide in the Lord. I end up feeling like I hurt people or push too hard or try to become too efficient or organized. I miss the human element, the relational element of things if I don't abide with the Lord. He helps me see the people."

An Egyptian leader admitted, "[When I abide in Jesus, it helps me] not to feel irritated because someone else will get the praise." A team leader in Khartoum shares, "You are in a much better frame of mind to address your day when you live in the Muslim world when you have spent time with Jesus. I don't honk as much or shake my fist." A male team leader in

---

4. Abiding should not be confused with relationship with Jesus. According to John 15:6, it is possible to be a branch (a disciple as the exegesis in chapter 3 shows) and not abide. It is possible to be "in Christ" and not abide in him.

the Comoros admits, "[Without abiding,] I'm less patient. My mind is more prone to wander." Research reveals that all people, regardless of culture, age, or gender, evidence a noticeable decline in both effectiveness and morale when they cease to abide in Jesus. One woman in Sudan expresses,

> If I am not abiding in him daily, and specifically for a specific period of time . . . if I don't do that then I just feel so lost during the day. I feel like I'm not focused . . . I can't make decisions nearly as well as I normally can, and I feel like "Wow! What's going on?" until I realize, "Oh! I didn't really spend time with the Lord today." There is definitely a link between spending time with him and making decisions, being aware spiritually of what is around me . . . Definitely abiding in the Lord focuses my mind; [it] starts the day right for me . . . with a good attitude.

Perhaps most succinct was the candid self-evaluation of a team leader in Somaliland: "I'm a horrible person, especially if I don't abide." While there is a demonstrable negative effect on the lives and ministries of those missionaries who stop abiding, there are no considerable negative effects (limitation) from abiding. Four respondents mentioned that the discipline of abiding requires the forfeiture of sleep, while others mentioned other good or neutral things were given up (TV time). Others mentioned that intentional abiding occasionally required the rescheduling of appointments or the deferment of tasks. One American woman expressed a positive restriction resulting from abiding in this manner. "Well surely, hopefully, there are limitations—like the Lord keeping my mouth shut at certain times." An American working with YWAM in Sudan explained, "Sometimes I choose to do more abiding and less work. I would say I never regret when I have longer quiet times. Maybe I get less done in the day, but maybe there is more quality in what I get done that day." A veteran in the Horn of Africa puts it succinctly:

> Oh, I think sometimes I think the fact that we have to spend so much time with devotions on a busy day kind of irks me, you know, but it's not like I missed an appointment with the president because we were doing devotions or anything like that. It is a discipline and that does not come without cost. But it is not a serious cost and I am sure it is well worth it.

This research shows that while a cessation of abiding has immediate and ongoing negative effects, there are no discernible limitations of consequence for those who spend extended daily time abiding in Jesus.[5]

5. An American male who holds a PhD in engineering explains, "[The more I abide,

Finding 16

Abiding gives missionaries content, energy, creativity, and longevity. Abiding is not only a replenishing (restoring what has been drained in the course of life and ministry), abiding in Jesus is the source of missionary life. A mother from the Netherlands explains, "When people are around, I feel like I need to be with Jesus . . . because I [need something] to give." An American team leader, who was a layman before being called to mission, states, "I depend on the Lord completely in my own heart because I feel I don't have specific [theological] training. So I cling to the Lord in that, and I feel like he's the one who has to give me capacity since I haven't had any real training." The contexts of mission—particularly the harsher Islamic contexts—tend to overwhelm the stoutest heart. Even an accomplished woman in ministry humbly submits, "[Abiding] has made me aware of my need for Jesus and my time with Jesus, which shows me how those who don't know Jesus, how desperate they are in their life, how much more they need to experience who he is." A Christian Arab in Cairo put it this way, "[Abiding is connected to quality of mission] because God gives visions, gives ideas, gives creative ways of how to do things. Not only that, but God also gives you people with these creative ideas." A leader of a Frontiers team in Sudan shares:

> Working and living life here [in a Muslim context] takes a lot of energy, and my emotional and spiritual energy [are] hugely related to the time I spend with the Lord. I definitely find that my reserves get depleted quickly, and to be able to get filled with him, I feel like then I have the energy to go out and spend time with people, and if that isn't there, it affects every area.

An AGWM church-planting team leader in Sudan echoed this sentiment—God gives the energy and resources that enable people to serve others. "The more time I spent with Jesus, the more time I felt prepared in some way to do the time to get the close relationship . . . When you're close to the Lord, you have more to give out. I have figured out that when I do give Jesus the time, and settle into it and rest my brain, that he'll bless that."

The divine energy and creativity supplied through abiding is critical, for it contributes to missionary longevity. A Brazilian team leader affirms, "[Abiding helps] even to stay on the field, to persevere . . . I feel that Sudan is a daily challenge. I believe I have been here so far because he's the one keeping us here, providing and working our emotions and challenges that

---

the more I have time for]; in other words, somehow, what I needed to get done that day is never [negatively] impacted [when I take the time to abide]. It seems like the more I give, the more I have time for."

we face." An American colleague confirms, "[My abiding] is my lifeline; it keeps me going. It keeps me focused. I wouldn't stay in missions if I didn't have that." The leader of the AGWM team on the Comoros Islands agrees: "Abiding gives us more staying power, the ability to remain in the context longer, the ability to see things differently . . . We keep our eyes not on what is seen, but what is unseen." This research finds that abiding gives missionaries content, energy, creativity, and longevity.

Finding 17

The most common corporate practice of abiding is prayer. In the twenty-three interviews, prayer or prayerwalking was mentioned twenty-one times.[6] The core of team abiding includes a fellowship meal, prayer, worship, and Bible study. Joy and celebration are critical components of corporate abiding. The YWAM team in Sudan commented, "As a team, we have always been marked by laughter. Even in the midst of financial hardship or struggles or persecution. Our team has always been marked by laughter and joy." The AGWM team in Somaliland was intentional to "celebrate victories and walk in confession."

Finding 18

Solitude does not play a prominent role for most leaders of church planting teams (to their regret). Sixteen of twenty-three respondents said they do not practice solitude at all.[7] Nine of the twenty-three expressed a longing either to have regular times of solitude or have them more often. An American working in Somaliland said, "And that is when I am most likely to speak to the Lord and him to me, is when I am in quiet times by myself." An American in Sudan admitted, "Yeah, I don't really get away to abide with Jesus, and I think that's probably a hindrance." A leader in Sudan with twenty-four

6. Responses included: Prayer (17), Worship/Singing (11), Teaching/Bible Study (9), Meal/Fellowship/Peacemaking (7), Confession/Accountability (5), Prayer Walking (4), Waiting on God/Listening (4), Thanksgiving/Celebration (4), Laughter/Fun/Play (3), Discussion/Sharing (3), Vision/Strategy (2), Fasting (2), Memorizing Bible in Local Language (2), Prophetic Words (1).

7. Responses included: "Not enough," "never have," "not usually," "we did not do it our whole marriage," "until now I don't have this time," "it's crucial . . . I've never had retreats," "I wonder how it would be some time, but I'm not good at it," "it's something I'd like to do more of," "the last time I ever did that was [seven years ago] . . . but ever since then until now, I haven't had that and I long for it. I long for it so much," and "I don't. I wish I do."

years of missions experience confessed, "The older I get, the more I realize that a prayer retreat or time away is going to have to become more and more necessary. Time every day is good, but some time carved out to hear from the Lord or recharge the spiritual batteries is really good."

For the few who are intentional about solitude, nature plays a key role. Often times of solitude are linked to times outside. "Solitude helps me," admitted a Brazilian leader. "When I'm in solitude, it's a time to present an idea to Jesus, to think through this desire that I have and to pray about it . . . There are times I go to a coffee shop—just sit there. I bring some of the things I want to present to Jesus . . . There are times where I go to parks." A Dutch woman in Egypt revealed, "I've gone quite a few times to a monastery . . . and it was a place of prayer . . . My husband would set me free to just, sometimes—twice a year or something—take a break; go one night, two days . . . So I love the solitude part, and retreating from daily life is very beneficial." An American male in Khartoum shared, "Solitude does play an important part in my walk . . . running and early morning time by myself. I pretty much have the world to myself between about 3 a.m. and 6 or 7." Another American in Sudan describes the benefits of solitude:

> Probably the best times I've had with Jesus are the more occasional times when I go away for intense or focused times . . . I am quiet. Often it will be going out into nature. I will be out in the woods . . . only take my Bible and some edifying book. I feel like I am communing with God—an unbroken communion. I am in a continual state of listening and worship. It is very helpful for me to have those times.

This finding reveals that though solitude is desired and considered helpful, it is for the most part not practiced.

Finding 19

Legalism is not common to those who are intentional about prolonged abiding times. Legalism and intentionality are not synonymous. A striking lack of legalism is found the more that team leaders abide. The vast majority of respondents described themselves as anti-legalistic. Desire in their experience is the culmination of discipline. Fourteen of the twenty-three team leaders made strong statements that they do not struggle with legalism, while five of the twenty-three said that legalism was a struggle. Five of the group set daily goals compared to nine who set no daily goals. Five of the twenty-three intentionally increase their abiding time, while nine do not. A woman with AGWM working in Sudan stated, "I do abiding because I know that I need to and that my spirit should. But it is not like the way I would when I was younger and I would say, 'I have to do it. It's part of the checklist.' Now it is like . . . I need to do it and want to do it to feed my soul." A mother in Egypt expressed her motivation for abiding in terms of its benefit on her children. "The things I do now are the things I will be able to transfer to my children later . . . That motivates me . . . to love the Lord from all my heart . . . My biggest fear maybe is that my children will not walk with God . . . and I want them to . . . That's a big motivation for me to abide myself, so that they will abide later."

Strikingly, the more dedicated the missionary is to extravagant time with Jesus, the less he or she is bound by legalism. A woman in Egypt espoused a balanced approach: "I don't think it's healthy to beat yourself up and get angry at yourself and belittle yourself if you know your time one day wasn't as great. But that is not a license to say, 'Oh, the Lord is forgiving and gracious,' even though he is." A man in Sudan agreed, "I know the Lord wants quality, not necessarily quantity. He wants focus on him. And I don't typically feel bound up by legalism." A single woman heading to the Arabian Peninsula shared, "I have to remind myself that there is grace in the Lord. In my abiding times, if I don't get the full two hours in that I want, or think that I need, then I just don't give myself a hard time about it." A team leader with AGWM revealed, "My primary means [of avoiding legalism] is the confession issue. Because it is in that, if I get legalistic, I know what happens in my heart. I'm looking down on others and I feel like that is something that God points out to me quickly." This finding reveals that while legalism is on the radar of those who intentionally abide, it is neither a concern nor a source of bondage. One feisty team leader spoke for the majority, "Legalism is not one of the things that has held me captive."

Finding 20

The structure (rigid or flexible) of abiding time and place depends on the personality of the abider. This research discovered that there is no fixed way to have abiding time; some prefer diversity, while some prefer routine. One of the more rigid responders explained his method like this:

> I would have a spreadsheet and I would mark down. I would have goals . . . And I would tick those off every day along with some other things. That sounds legalistic. With my personality, I felt I needed to do that. So I don't call it legalistic, but the

structure helped me to do it and then there was joy in the fact I
was doing it. I wasn't counting minutes or looking at my watch.

This personality was on the extreme end of the continuum, while some
appreciated a moderate approach. One YWAM leader in Sudan revealed,
"I don't like diversity much, nor do I seek it out much. So I just keep going
back to reading Scripture, praying, and journaling." A more free-spirited individual clarified, "I don't like to be so set in what I have to do every day. You
know, some days I don't play my guitar, and, you know, pray that way. Other
days I might pace and pray. I don't like to do the same thing." An Egyptian
man explained, "I . . . do not have anything very restricted or rigorous. I believe personally that God doesn't use guilt to motivate us to sit with him . . .
I like to be more spontaneous in my relationship with God." An American
in Sudan observed, "I don't watch the clock and I guess I do expect some
minimums from myself, but no, I don't like the idea of having boundaries
set on that." A Sudanese woman agreed, "It is good if you organize your
time and stuff. But when I do that, I didn't do it by law." Essentially, there
is no proscribed way to abide in Jesus as concerns rigid repetition versus a
fluid, varied approach. The style of abiding tends to reflect the personality
of the abider. Style is not to be confused with content, as an earlier finding
revealed the primacy of the Bible and prayer in the abiding process.

Finding 21

Suffering improves the quality and quantity of abiding. Trial leads to desperation and dependency, which in turn leads to spending more time with
Jesus and greater intimacy with him—an intimacy that can include fric-
tion. There is a usual progression from desperation to discipline to desire to
delight.[8] Sometimes the devil uses trials to draw believers away from Jesus.
A season of dryness is common when abiding falters.[9] Fourteen of the responders reported that trouble leads to more abiding time, while six said

---

8. "[Difficulty] has increased my abiding, and my sweetness of abiding—which is
kind of a scary statement to say—because you're more desperate; you're beyond yourself. So when you just really don't know what to do about something, you're going to
run to the Lord more quickly."

9. An Egyptian Arab leader explained, "One of the difficult things when you keep
asking for something and it never happen for years. There's definitely a conflict between
my feeling and my thinking or belief . . . but even in my good days, sometimes I don't
read the Bible and spend this one hour, the time alone with him. But I'm still having
good relation with him but without this piece. Because as I said before, living with him
is not measured by how long I read the Bible and how long I pray."

that it leads to less. Sixteen of the interviewees said trouble leads to more intimacy with Jesus. One team leader who was expelled from Libya says,

> [Getting kicked out of Libya was] a time of crying out to God in despair, I guess. But then also really feeling that he is carrying you through, that you are at the end of your rope, that you can't do anything anymore, that you don't understand, BUT he is present! I think you feel so needy that you just can't survive without God . . . so you spend more time and then you survive . . . and also with the children when they have these big issues, then you go back to prayer more; like I can't solve this, only God can.

A Brazilian team leader explained, "[Difficulty] has affected me to bring me closer to him . . . Challenges and difficulties in life are not the best tool taken away [by] God. Usually the challenges bring me closer." A Sudanese mother professed, "I pray more [in times of difficulty] because I feel like now there is no one who understands me—just Jesus. He understands me and he feels by me and by what I feel." An Egyptian father warned, "When you have secret police kidnapping your child . . . , you can't do anything. You can try everything you can do to change that, and you trust in him." Over and again, respondents underlined the sweetness of suffering. A young American with YWAM exhorts,

> I think suffering comes hand in hand with the sweetest times with Jesus. Last year when we looked at disappointment and struggles, I would say still my times of abiding in Jesus [have] been my lifeline or the thing[s] that [have] kept us growing . . . I don't want to seek out suffering. It's intimately intertwined with Jesus, but never do I want to choose suffering . . . Suffering strips [some of our crutches] away and pushes us, pushes me to Jesus.

An American father in Sudan shares this testimony:

> The first year that I was in Sudan, my middle son was having a problem with dreams that were almost satanic. And that drove me to my knees and so it certainly increased my abiding time . . . And also praying in tongues . . . I allowed the Spirit to do that. And it wasn't a forced thing. It almost came out naturally . . . I think in that particular time I felt the Holy Spirit so much more closely. Also I shared with teammates, and I think it was the fellowship that really touched me. The fellowship grew as a result of that, particularly with certain teammates that I shared with. And [my wife] and I grew together.

An AGWM team leader in Comoros expressed his journey like this:

> The last three years have been the best season, and that came directly from following probably the season I had the worst suffering and worst difficulty. And again, one of those things of just seeing through the suffering Jesus not showing up in this big miraculous way and relieving it, but in just slowly keeping his presence ever with me, drawing me closer to him and drawing me back—slowly putting out any thoughts [of discouragement], helping to usher those out. And then after that time, I feel like in some ways he's just opened up heaven and the times have been so sweet.

An American woman in Sudan struggled for years with the pain of barrenness, in addition to the stress of living as God's creation in the Muslim world (women in the Muslim world are often objectified, marginalized, silenced, and disempowered). She explains the link between trial and abiding in these terms:

> This place of desperation—I mean, I don't know how many times I've said to the Lord, "You've got to show up because I can't go on another minute." There's just such a correlation [between pain, desperation, and intimacy with Jesus], between understanding aspects of God's character ... and I really feel like it's been a beautiful thing that God gave me a glimpse of his heart for the lost and the desperation he has, crying for his own children. And I feel like it's an honor that I've had to catch this glimpse of God's heart, because I don't think I would have seen it [without going through pain and desperation].

Trials and sufferings come in many different packages. Often fear was something that those under pressure had to fight. Fear came to be seen as an aid. An American woman in Somaliland explains, "Well, yeah, the fear led to the dependency and then when God answered and HE CAME, then I was more intimate. You know, because he's there, but apparently I had not been seeking him in the same way because there was not the dependency. I was seeking him; I felt the need for him in my life, and so that increased ... I sought him. He answered. That is the way it goes."

This research showed that difficulty does not always lead to sweetness. An Egyptian leader shared, "When you have a difficulty, you complain ... even [when one] of our children have difficulty, they complain. I don't feel bad when they complain to me. But I feel it's good, healthy, that there is a place for them to speak, and to express themselves freely without restrictions, or without structure, or without choosing their words." This man expressed that it was freeing to take his complaints and disappointments to God. Venting to the Lord is a fairly common recourse for his troubled servants. A woman in Sudan with AGWM confesses,

> You can make the Scriptures say whatever you want sometimes. Like, if you are reading the Psalms, it's like, 'Yes, smite them!' you know? But you know in your heart that's not what it's all about. So it's just like sometimes you vent and Jesus is gracious to me and listens to my venting. And he always brings me back to center, I think, with my abiding and puts me back on track.

A refreshing aspect of those who have gone through trial leading to abiding in Jesus is their candor. A single American woman admitted, "In [times of trial], the hardest thing during my abiding time is to praise and worship." Another American revealed, "I think often [trouble] probably leads to less [abiding time], but a lot more honest [time]. I think in certain seasons of suffering . . . it's been probably some of my most honest times with the Lord, but it's also been some of the most difficult as far as continuing with Bible reading and prayer . . . those activities are a lot harder just to do." A troubled woman in Sudan expresses,

> [Disappointment] really shook something really deep in me . . . I was a bit like Peter, thinking I could handle whatever he brought my way and I was going to follow him until I died. And then it was something so simple for me to not get what I wanted and all of a sudden I wondered if God really is who he said he is. And again, even with that experience, I feel like it was just another step of God deepening my relationship with him, of just recognition of my humanness and how dependent I am on his grace—and it turns out it isn't about me.

A Swedish woman whose husband was imprisoned in Sudan a few months after this interview commented, "If you are disappointed . . . , it is a great danger to become bitter and angry and dwell on disappointed feelings. Sadness or danger maybe will, a bit more, draw you to Jesus. Disappointment, not as much." A Sudanese man underlined the reality that disappointment can make one withdraw from intimate times with the Lord. "Sometimes some problems happened [and I stopped abiding]. There was a low point in my spirit, but again, our Lord did not leave me. He encouraged me and pushed me by some testimony, and I came back to continuously strong praying." One of the most illustrative comments came from a Lebanese mother in Sudan that is worth quoting at length:

I had times when I . . . misunderstood the Lord. I struggled and it felt like the Lord was a harsh master, rather than a Father for a while. That affected my abiding. It took a very long time for the Lord to straighten that lie in my mind. It was at times that I would just open my Bible to read or spend time with the Lord and I would just look at the page and then close it. Yeah, it was very hard at times . . . at times like this I thought God does not exist.

I was here in Sudan. [My son] was very young, and [my husband] went for five weeks, and both children had malaria. [My daughter] had pneumonia with her malaria. So I was totally alone. We didn't have a team at the time. [My daughter] would not sleep at night very well, and the doctor . . . told me, "Watch her breathing at night. If her breath comes very fast, take her to the hospital or she'll die." So I would just start to fall asleep and wake up wanting to look at her breathing. That happened for several nights. During the day, [my son] was—I told you, he was not a happy child at all. He would cry and scream all the time. Every time [my daughter] would take a nap in the afternoon, I would say, "Oh, it's my turn to rest." [My son] would want to wake her up, so I don't go to bed. It was chaotic. [My husband] was not there, and one time I prayed . . . "God please allow me to sleep only two hours uninterrupted," and that didn't happen. I was like, "God, please help [my son] fall asleep so I can sleep, too," and God did not answer my prayer. I literally held my Bible on the ground [and] . . . I was like, "I believed in a lie." [My son] that night, he said, "Mama, are you gonna pray for me before we sleep? Are we gonna have a Bible story?" I said, "No. No Bible story and no praying tonight." He was shocked. He fell asleep and I lay down in my bed.

Something very weird happened. The presence of God filled the room. Jesus told me: "You are mine, and you will always be mine, and I love you." He didn't rebuke me. He didn't say, "Whoa, you horrible Lebanese coming to be a missionary." He didn't. He didn't tell me, "Why, you of little faith!" He didn't. He rebuked the disciples in the ship. He didn't rebuke me. He just told me how much he loves me.

Oh, how can you respond to that kind of love, except with more love? And I said, "Lord God, I love you and I'm sorry." I didn't feel like he waited for me to say sorry. I really didn't feel like he's waiting for me to repent. He engulfed me. And that night we had the most wonderful sleep—all three of us. And I woke up thinking, "What a wonderful God we have!" And I, you know, we think Peter was horrible to deny Jesus. Look at me! It just made me so compassionate towards people who are troubled, or sometimes it made me . . . it made me not legalistic anymore. I think I was [legalistic] until then because of the upbringing and walking with God, and you know, you think you're so holy, so good, so doing the right thing. You know, and I was like, "No, I'm not that." It's only because of Jesus that we're anything.

This finding (that suffering ultimately deepens both quality and quantity of abiding) is thematically very strong in the interviews. A conclusive majority of those interviewed bore witness to the certainty of suffering and trial and its effective result of drawing them closer to Jesus. This process is not without pain. A woman working with Frontiers explains,

> It's been kind of a painful season, even over the last, let's say nine years, where there's been at least an element of surrender to the Lord every day with my hopes and my dreams and my expectations . . . I really feel there has been something beautiful that's been happening in me. It looked a lot different than I thought that it would, but this dying-to-self process is an ugly one and it's been really beautiful and I definitely feel like I can say now that I don't understand what God's been doing, but I know it's been good.

A corollary finding on trial and abiding is that reliance on Scripture was the primary means of helping the sufferer to survive. Five different responders specifically mentioned the role of Scripture in navigating suffering. An AGWM representative in Sudan commented, "[Jesus] will provide a thought or a word, something in my life that truly speaks to that thing that I am dealing with. And so, when someone cares that much about you, to speak to you personally and intimately, and you know it's for you, that's pretty strong. That's pretty real."

Another AGWM team leader agrees:

> In Cairo, when the Lord was so sweet, there were times when my spirit was so heavy, I just didn't feel like I could pray anything new or that I could pray anything effectively so it would [be] something short: "Jesus, help me." Or even in Sudan when you feel the weight pressing in. There wasn't like a length of abiding in that. It was short sincere prayers of desperation that happened. But I could see times when I would just try to press through and read Scripture a lot, even if I felt like I couldn't pray. I almost felt like a whiny child sometimes with the way I was praying: "Get me out of this. Help me with this." So I would just read Scripture and try to pray it out loud and that would become my prayer.

A wife and mother in Zanzibar said, "[trial] lately, [has led to] definitely more time [with Jesus] and [to] the importance of standing on Scripture for whatever I am going through." A woman in Somalia exclaims,

> Oh man! [Suffering] increases the abiding time. Fear really was one of the big things in my life in Somalia. I got out the Scriptures, because I had to do something. It had grasped me; I needed to be free. So I started memorizing Scriptures. "The Lord is the light of my life, whom shall I fear." But during those times I learned a lot of Scripture and I prayed a lot, because what can you do otherwise? It was like total dependency.

The Scriptures not only helped leaders survive trials; they also helped them heal from wounds. An IMB leader in Sudan declared, "If I weren't having time with Jesus in prayer or in studying, I don't think that I would get the comfort for the problems and the healing from the hurt that I do get." Reading the Scriptures accomplishes a preparatory role for the discipline and character formation that inevitably come. One leader, who left America with her spouse in her forties after leading several successful ministries, reveals,

> I felt like I knew the Lord and had been reading his word and it had been guiding me, but the process of going to a new land and having everything stripped away and all that I had ever known, all my identity removed, that the Lord still knew me and recreated the identity that he had always known me to be. So during that time of rebuilding, my persona that I thought God saw me as was abolished, and he showed me who I was in him at that time. I thought that was a really sweet thing because I thought I had been giving or creating such a good front for him, he should really be proud of this kid. You know, not giving him a moment's trouble, trying to please him. He's like, "That's not really where it's at." Showing that desperation and leaning in, and him saying, "I loved you like this, as a new child in my sight," was an amazing thing to discover.

This research found a strong link between suffering and improved quantity and quality of abiding. The process was not without pain, but invariably led to greater intimacy with Jesus.

Finding 22

Abiding strengths of other cultures provoke a godly jealousy. A godly jealousy arises when the body of Christ interacts. Missionaries from diverse cultures who interacted with each other observed variant practices in the other. It made them hungry to experience the observed reality. The Global North has learned to pray, rejoice, emote, and suffer from the Global South. The Global South has learned discipline, truth, and organization from the Global North. An American on a multinational team in Cairo observes that

> It's beautiful because there's not a right way to spend time with Jesus . . . so you know when you go to America, the church, you might sing three songs then pray for five minutes then you're gone. In other cultures it could be a three-hour long service, and so it's beautiful to see the way that the Lord moves among the cultures and the peoples.

A Lebanese woman commented about her European friend, "In the most horrible situation, in sickness, she sees Jesus. The sweetness of that spirit." An American woman said of Europeans, "I think I've learned consistency. I've learned gentleness from them. I think about some people that just have a quiet, gentle, and consistent spirit about life." A Brazilian man pointed out that "the idea of solitude, it is not common in Brazil . . . I actually learned more about the importance of keeping the spiritual disciplines, like abiding and solitude . . . through the American culture." A Sudanese Arab male said that from Westerners he learned "organization and the word of God, commitment and the quiet time. Commitment in their words— when they promise their people, they are faithful." Though the majority of respondents were from the Global North, the preponderance of lessons flowed from the Global South.

An American woman said of her African friends, "I've learned praying though, like really taking long amounts of prayer to pray through an issue." A Dutch woman praised the Africans, saying they "taught me joy—being content with having nothing." An American in Sudan said of the Sudanese, "The first night we went to overnight prayer, and it's just eight hours of people just crying out in prayer. I feel like there's something so beautiful, specifically in the African church related to prayer and worship. Again in Latin culture, I love the jovialness of worship." A Swede echoed this observation: "The Sudanese, they laugh, pray, and worship which I think is quite humbling to see." An American working among Somalis in Kenya affirmed, "[The Africans] can pray! They can do all-night *keshas* [all-night prayer meeting], and that is something I wish that I could do more often like them."

A team leader in Egypt observed that her Vietnamese team member "misses people worshiping Jesus even when persecution was there . . . She misses the heart to worship even more boldly or loudly even with the threat of prison, [and] I see that in Somali believers who face pretty serious opposition—that they are just bold."

An American male in Sudan appreciated the liberality of African spirituality when contrasted to the rigidity of many North American expressions. "[African spirituality] is so much more emotional. It's less clinical or intellectual. It becomes much more spiritual, emotional, connected to the world around us . . . in a very positive sense, in a healthy, building-up type of emotional way. Connecting the spiritual with the practical feeling of life in a positive way."

An American noted that the "Sudanese . . . seem to be much more vocal than I had been, and that would make me comfortable about praying out loud and praying in tongues. And then . . . they impacted me with the simplicity of their prayers, the new believers, and the sweetness of it." This sweet fervor, the zeal of African corporate abiding made a profound impact on the more staid missionaries from the Global North. An American man in Sudan notes,

> [Abiding] is not something just for spiritual types, but it is something normal, it's a very normal expression for God's people. [African] fervor is not something for a certain personality type. To see the exuberance in the African church, the zeal that they have has challenged my analytical spirituality or my contemplative spirituality. Coming from a pretty conservative church background, it has definitely freed me up to be more expressive or louder than I would have been anyways. It freed me up to be louder and more emotional in worship.

One American woman spent years in East Africa before moving to Sudan, and she observed, "In Kenya and Tanzania there is power in abiding. There it was very simple. It was total submission and they relied on the Lord for everything; it was power." A Lebanese woman in Sudan said of her Sudanese friend, "You know when she lost her child (and I know she suffered and I know her abiding times with the Lord at times she struggled), but she knew that God is good. And she knew in her sorrow if she turns to him, he's the answer. And that made me jealous to be able to do that all the time."

Godly jealousy is a repeated theme when multicultural teams interact.[10] An American woman with AGWM in Sudan soberly stated, "I think

10. An American YWAM missionary relates what he learned from working with a multicultural team: We say one of our

the whole cross-cultural experience just redefined everything about me. Everything about my life has been redefined, including my abiding—how I perceive who the Lord is and what he is in my life and who he is and what is my point of even being on the mission field." Ongoing multicultural interaction tends to expose the missionaries to one another's strengths. This is most clearly put by an American team leader in Somaliland: "We have been around many Europeans, Africans, and now [my friend] from Peru. [She] makes me jealous in her walk with the Lord ... because she has a greater intimacy than I do. I think it is a good jealousy." When missionaries observed the abiding strengths of other cultures, it fostered a godly jealousy to know Jesus in new ways.

This research also found that Muslims teach missionaries about discipline, priority, and community in the positive sense. Missionaries among Muslims noted that Islam seems to foster the positives of dedication, discipline, respect, community, and a priority on prayer and fasting.[11] Con-

greatest blessings here in Sudan has been that we did not come to a primarily Western team. Our team was a few Arabs and a bunch of Sudanese. When we came in our first few years as, particularly here in North Sudan and things were very difficult for us as a young, married couple and trying to adjust and not having a lot of Western relationships to lean on. And going through hard times and struggling, we would look at our Sudanese guys who are living in displacement camps. Living on a tenth of what we live on. They still come into the meetings and laugh and pray and exude the fruit of the Spirit. And we look at them and say, 'Where does that come from?' Earthly blessings, they have nothing. And when you look at sufferings, they have got it ten times worse than we do. Real sufferings, not just they don't have television, they don't have AC. They have got kids dying because of [lack of] health care. They have family living without jobs. All kinds of things. Actually that is one of our greatest blessings, walking in intimacy with the Sudanese brothers and sisters. And actually that got us through the first couple years when we had too much self-pity for ourselves, and that would give us a dose of perspective. You know they have got things ten times worse or a hundred times worse than what we have, and they exude the fruit of the Spirit ten times more than we do. I think that's been one of our greatest blessings getting to see that walked out, and to have those relationships on a continual basis.

11. A Finnish woman in Sudan commented, "We have the tendency, having God almost like a grandfather ... [Muslims helped me see] God—how mighty he is." A team leader in Khartoum who ran a school said, "[Muslims] are consistent in the time

versely, the legalism and formalism in Islam also teaches missionaries to be thankful for the joy and liberty found in Christian worship. A Sudanese Arab woman pointed out that Muslims "don't have hope, but they have time and they pray." A Sudanese man who runs an outreach to Muslims observes that they are "honest in their time, in prayer time. Even morning, very early morning, they run to the mosque wearing their robes. Not in the house, to the mosque. This means they are faithful people . . . , this really touched me." A YWAM team leader said he learned consistency from Muslims, adding, "I mean it is true that many Muslims are nominal, just like many Christians are nominal, but the ones that are seeking to serve God and are consistent in their prayer life, I long for that. You know like, could I put consistent prayer in my life five times a day? That's what I envy in their spiritual lives." Another missionary in Sudan admires Muslims for their intentionality: "I think the sheer discipline of what they are doing and how many times they do it per day. To see some of the ladies actually say, 'Excuse me, I have to go pray.' Have I ever done that? 'I'm sorry. I have an appointment with Jesus. I need to go now.' And to see their willingness to adhere to what they believe is their truth."

The dry legalism of Islam, however, also impacted missionaries. The AGWM team leader in the Comoros explains,

> One thing I love: watching Muslims worship. I love the fact that ours is so much more intimate. And it makes me appreciate that even more. Another thing would be, I find myself in some way gravitating towards that set routine, and five times a day the prayer call goes off and you go pray. And for the more serious Muslims nothing trumps that. You put away visitors, you put away work—everything stops because it's time to worship. And so there's some sense that I'm really drawn to that. Like, alright, here are my set times in the day—visitors, I'll be back in a little while; family, I'll be back in a while; work, whatever. These are my times with Jesus and nothing trumps that.

An American in Sudan observed, "As Christians, we tend to look at Muslims and respect their discipline and effort. It's helped me [realize] the importance of private prayer where nobody notices. But I also do recognize in the kingdom of God that communal prayer is good. It's part of what God's people do. I respect that." It was not only outward ritual that impacted

------

that they give, the priority that they give. It doesn't matter where they are or what is happening. That's the priority of the moment; that's the priority of the day. They don't mind asking you to wait while they go to prayer."

missionaries among Muslims. The slow, steady oppression of Muslim contexts caused a single woman living in Egypt to reflect:

> I think being in the Muslim context really forced me . . . I mean, gave me a new purpose for my abiding time. Because before it was more—it was more on a routine . . . but in the Muslim world it is like I knew I couldn't survive a day without abiding in the Lord. Just the spiritual environment—I knew I wouldn't last long if I didn't abide with him.

If anyone understands the ethos of Islam, it would be Muslim background believers (MBBs) who have been saved out of that religious context. MBBs also have impacted workers in the Muslim context. A Syrian Christian remarked, "[MBBs are] fiery people! They are coming thirsty. They are very interested in the word of God. When they come, they do not doubt like the past. They find everything in the Messiah, and they come hungry, and they find the heavenly food." This research found that when varied races of Christian workers come together in a mission context, encountering one another's spirituality and abiding praxis provokes a godly jealousy.

Finding 23

Corporate abiding is a living demonstration that missionaries not only need Jesus, but they also need each other. There are several key things that happen in corporate abiding that do not normally happen in individual abiding—namely laughter, gifts of the Spirit, loud worship, and perspective. This research discovered important differences between personal and corporate abiding. The abiding distinctions are not value based (what happens corporately is not more important than what happens privately), but function based. Important aspects of abiding are most fully experienced in a corporate setting. The leader of a YWAM team in Sudan explains the importance of corporate joy:

> What has always marked our team is laughter. I feel it's almost like laughing at Satan. Because here in this dark place—full of suffering, full of poverty, full of Islam—when you have a group of believers together from different tribes, different nationalities and there is laughter, which is an expression of the Holy Spirit, those have been the sweetest times. Because I feel like it's just mocking everything Satan can do to us, to them, to the body of Christ, because there is still joy coming up in the desert.

Along with joy, other charismatic gifts benefit the church body more than the individual. An AGWM team leader in Sudan points out the obvious: "[There are] more gifts of the Spirit used amongst the team [than in personal abiding times]." A woman from a separate team in Sudan concurs: "[In corporate abiding] there are different spiritual manifestations, like words of wisdom or words of knowledge and tongues and interpretation when we abide together." Something profound about the verbal corporate expression of praise and worship invigorates the soul. This research found that it is critical for team members to come together and actively and loudly praise the Lord. One woman admitted, "I don't think I am as animated personally as I am in a group. I don't think [my personal abiding is] at the fervor that I feel when it's corporate worship." A man in the Comoros revealed, "I would sing a lot more loudly when I'm with people." A woman in Somaliland agreed, "I love to sing out, you know, in a corporate setting, where there is more than just your voice." A Swedish woman in Sudan affirmed the benefit of a unified approach: "We sing more [corporately] . . . and I enjoy it when I worship together in song . . . it's meaningful."

In a group setting there is room for all kinds of expressions. One woman in Zanzibar humorously reported, "I don't play the guitar because I don't know how. But I play the egg [percussion shaker]." This verbal and voluminous corporate abiding is spiritually essential in Islamic lands because missionaries are bombarded by lies. Singing, praising, and shouting truth are ways missionaries maintain resistance against the lies of Islam.

It is not only volume in corporate abiding settings that is an encouragement; it is also the perspective and wisdom gained from belonging to one another. An American team leader stated, "[Worship] is so much more intimate with Jesus when we are doing it in a group as opposed to if I'm doing it solo in my abiding time . . . [praying] for each other, what sticks out (from the text or message) and things like that you just don't get by yourself." A European mother of four shared, "You get input from other people which gives you more aspects of thinking of what is happening in their lives and how they see the Bible passage." The American leader of an IMB team affirmed, "The dialogue (prayer is a dialogue with Christ) with other believers—there's more input and it's enhanced." Missionaries working in hostile contexts need each other. They need to hear each other sing, pray, praise, and respond to Jesus. Corporate abiding offers aspects of encouragement and sustenance different (though complementary) to individual abiding.

An essential (and often overlooked) component of corporate abiding is the food shared during communal meals. A male from America, whose team shared one communal meal a week, states:

> When we've had our team meetings . . . , I've just sensed the one-
> ness of the group, the oneness in Christ, and the oneness in pur-
> pose. The fact that sometimes I haven't known these people that
> long, but just being in the body like that, is more meaningful
> than having had maybe a ten-year friendship with somebody. I
> think that's been the sweetest time.

A Swede who is married to a Canadian and works in a largely Sudanese team linked food directly to abiding: "Sharing food together is a very
good way of being together . . . abiding with Jesus." An American female
team leader in Sudan comments,

> I love food to have abiding time because you're sitting around
> the table. We always have our team sit around the table. Now,
> even at the other houses, everyone—that is how we start our
> time. It's like the family dinner, and if you don't have the family
> dinner and take advantage of that five o'clock meal, you're go-
> ing to miss out. You're never going to have it happen again. So
> we take time and linger over the table, we bring up our day, we
> transition, and we get comfortable again with each other. Then
> we do our transition into more time in the literature, where we
> just sit and relax. But food breaks down a lot of barriers and it
> gives a good setting.

A male team leader communicated that "[the breaking of bread] . . .
is integral . . . it's a natural thing that people do and it breaks down barriers
when you eat together." A female leader humorously added, "You have to
have food—and chocolate!" The role of communal meals in corporate abiding is valuable and effective in building unity and rapport.

Finding 24

Abiding gives humbled and dependent leaders the content of what they
share with others and leads to a prominent role for the word doing the work
of mission. Even those with leadership gifts and experience prior to arriving
in an Islamic context were overwhelmed at the challenges and mysteries
of leading cross-culturally. Missional leadership humbled them and made
them dependent on Jesus. The leader of a large Business As Mission (BAM)
project in Sudan confessed, "I can't be the leader that I am, or be in this
position without the Lord's help." An engineer with decades of experience
teaching in the U.S. before arriving on the field said,

[Abiding has] certainly strengthened me in terms of knowing the word better . . . even sensing how I need to pray . . . Having spent time with [Jesus], it's more likely to pour out of me in a positive manner. It's more likely that they'd sense Him in me and that it's not an academic exercise. It's not; "Take this, learn this, you'll be okay." It's true sharing.

A gifted woman who founded several ministries to women shared, "[Abiding] . . . makes my core stronger, my internal core stronger, and my resilience towards some spiritual oppression or things that come toward me, and also to be able to impart some wisdom that I would not have had, had I not abided." A teacher in a large international school mentioned, "I feel any great idea I've had in leadership has always come from him." Capable leaders continually referred to the critical role abiding played in helping them survive and impart help to others. One YWAM leader from a Lutheran background explained, "[Abiding] has given me some root and level of integrity to be able to lead . . . some lifeline, some foundation. I wouldn't have anything to give if there wasn't abiding in Jesus. I mean, from the call to make disciples to the ability to make disciples, abiding is crucial." Interestingly, many of these leaders expressed a link between their study of the Scriptures and God's empowerment to disciple others. A missionary in Zanzibar testified, "Learning the Scriptures [has helped me disciple others]." A leader in Cairo shared a similar sentiment: "Spending time with Jesus we learn about his heart, reading the Scripture and learning how he did things . . . I mean that's our model, not just reading the latest leadership book. But he is our model, so we have to spend time with him to know where he's leading us." A Christian Sudanese Arab affirmed, "If I don't abide in him, I can't help others with new teaching. When I change to a new strong teaching, immediately there is an effect." The Bible has formed the basis of what leaders share with their teams and with the lost. A Portuguese leader reports:

When I share, like on the team days, most of the sharing is things that I get from my quiet time. I would read a text, think about it. I would say most of my preaching is from my quiet time . . . [In evangelism] I would use Bible verses and most of them I learned in my quiet time . . . [In discipleship, the Bible] empowered me in terms of knowing about God's will. I would say the content that I use was formed and given to me from my abiding with Jesus.

This research found that abiding gives humbled and dependent leaders the content of what they share with others and leads to a primacy of the word doing the work.

Finding 25

Abiding gives overwhelmed leaders what they do not naturally have. Even the most naturally gifted leaders find that they are not equipped for every development they face in pressurized and foreign contexts. What individual leaders lack varies according to their personalities and backgrounds. An awareness of how much they do not have (in leadership capacity) drove leaders to abide more (they sensed their great dependency) as they discovered God provided the leadership ability required.[12] A woman with Frontiers expressed, "When I am abiding with Jesus, I have a lot more capacity to handle interpersonal relationships with our team." A man with AGWM testified that abiding affected his leadership capacity, in that "the Lord has also given me compassion and a desire to, how do I say, desire to not allow strivings or ambitions of people, even on the team, to interfere with kingdom aspects, so keeping us aligned to his mind."

Whether the need was for information, inspiration, or energy, the findings revealed that leaders saw abiding as providing what they lacked. A leader in Sudan mentioned, "When I am abiding, I mean my cup feels full and it feels even exciting and engaging to go out and be with other people—whether that's discipling or sharing with my neighbors." A Christian Arab woman in Sudan summarizes the feeling of the majority succinctly:

> Nothing works well enough [without abiding]. It just looks like an activity—unless it comes from the spring of life. So if I'm not abiding, many things can go well and people can think I'm so successful, but I know . . . I was able to be very successful in ministry at times when I was not really fully abiding—but I don't know the fruits.

Finding 26

The most common fruit of the Spirit experienced by the respondents as a result of abiding were peace, joy, and patience. In the interviews it was common for "peace and joy" to be mentioned in tandem—and they increased with an increase in abiding time: joy (9), peace (9), and patience (7) were referenced significantly more than others—love (3), gentleness (2),

---

12. Leaders interviewed offered a range of leadership help they felt God provided through abiding, which included "servant" and "better listener," "wisdom," "I'm not so afraid," "appreciation for other people . . . nudges and promptings from the Spirit . . . bigger scope in prayer," "confidence, faith, wisdom, authority," "humility and compassion," "ability to grant grace . . . , boldness . . . , inspiration," "guidance," "energy."

forgiveness (2), wisdom (1), giving (1), flexibility (1), faith (1), and kindness (1). The common sentiment was that fruit resulted from being in the presence of Jesus. A Syrian believer commented, "If you are in the Messiah, you don't leave him again, but I bear fruit when I am close to him. But I know I am in him even if I don't bear fruit . . . when I serve with obedience as he has called me." A Lebanese believer added, "When Jesus is abiding in me, the little things that will be very frustrating are small." A Sudanese Christian commented on how abiding helped her overcome the criticism she faces from Muslim colleagues. "After I have my life with Jesus, I feel that I love them more [. . .] and I can forgive them for anything they say to us." An American woman in Sudan agreed. "I am not a very loving person, and I just feel like when I am spending time in the Lord's presence, it gives me a different perspective on who people are."

The common theme in the research is that abiding in and with Jesus is the source of fruit. An Arab working in Sudan asserts, "When I go with the Lord in the place that he has prepared there, there is fruit . . . [The Lord gave me a lot of joy] because of a lot of fruit. Without me doing anything, we saw fruit. I feel that it is not me, but the Lord. He makes the fruit." Conversely, when leaders were asked the effect of not abiding, it was clear that a lack of abiding led directly to acts of the flesh. An American team leader in Sudan revealed, "It is such a high-stress environment that if I don't have my times of abiding, I am very quick to snap at people, whether it be my own family or my Sudanese friends I am interacting with. Whereas if I have times of abiding, I feel like there is more love and peace and joy within me to operate out of." A male AGWM missionary in Khartoum underlined:

> Abiding is the process of telling the Lord you realize that you are empty and you need him and that he is the source. And until you get out of the way and tell him that through those activities and express through your words and through prayer, in my experience, that's where the filling comes—is when you allow it to come and you get out of the way and tell the Lord that you need him.

Research discovered that fruit (character and souls) directly results from team leaders abiding in Jesus. The most common evidences of that fruit were joy, patience, and peace. It is noteworthy that neither love nor faith was the most common result of abiding.

Finding 27

For Western missionaries, there is no significant connection between dreams and intimacy with Jesus. It is more common for non-Western missionaries to experience intimacy with Jesus through dreams. Most of the missionaries who experienced intimacy with Jesus in dreams are female. One respondent mentioned a dream that was centered on intimacy with Jesus, but her response appears to be an anomaly. A couple respondents mentioned dreams sometimes lead to warnings and prayer or praise, while another mentioned God will sometimes give creative ideas in a dream. But there was no consistent response regarding dreams and intimacy or abiding. Several respondents encountered dreams where God granted direction and information. An American woman in Sudan said, "I don't think I'm a person who has a lot of dreams or visions in particular . . . but when I have had a vision or picture from the Lord, it is very intimate. I feel like a tangible way even of the Lord just reminding me of his presence and who he is. It's definitely a very intimate, personal thing." A Lebanese mother said, "I imagine Jesus is dancing with me . . . especially when I [pray] for joy. It just brought so much joy to my heart."

It is worthwhile to note that in the process of coming to Jesus, many Muslims have spiritually impacting dreams—often of him. A hypothesis that merits further research is that dreams are often used to give Muslims the assurance of God's presence. Muslims believe that God is omnipotent and do not need signs and wonders to convince them of his power. However, Muslims standing on the threshold of faith know they cross over into Christ at great cost. They long for assurance that God will be with them in the looming persecution. The God of the Koran is transcendent, but not intimate or loving. Muslims wanting to come to Jesus often long for his compelling assurance of ongoing presence.

Finding 28

The primary effect of abiding on church planting strategy is guidance (peace and direction) on what to do and what not to do, who to be and who not to be. The research indicates that prayer is the starting point for strategy. A Dutch woman declared that what is required is "lots of prayer, and then God starts working." An American man pointed out the link between the Spirit (leading through prayer) and the planning when he mentioned, "I tend to see strategy as something that has coalesced from spiritual things into your mind." The AGWM team leader in the Comoros described abiding times as "feeling like something has led one way or another as far as what to say to someone or how, what next to disciple someone in or wisdom for a certain heart for people." A Swedish team leader clarified, "We wouldn't have moved forward in planting churches if we didn't feel the peace and the sense that the Lord was leading and guiding." An American leader of a church planting team in Sudan expressed, "Without [strategic] training, I just continue to go to the Lord's word, trying to understand how it was done by the Lord and His apostles and using that as my model." The united theme emerging from the experience of the team leaders pointed to the critical role that abiding in Jesus played in strategic clarity and the creative process. A female leader with Frontiers mentioned, "I feel like there are a lot of ideas that come out of times with the Lord, even specific words . . . spoken into our ministry." Another woman, based in Egypt, described the union of abiding and planning: "It's a combination of cognizant strategy and approach. But then we can't get too bogged down in that and not let the Holy Spirit lead us. We have to have both . . . We can't just pray that the Lord will lead us and not make a well-informed decision about something God's given us the knowledge [about] already."

Leaders generally did not feel they had the insight to plan or create strategy with their own intellect. An AGWM leader in Sudan explained: "We were not clever enough to think about how he would open the doors. So if we maintain our hearts and keep our hearts right before him . . . , be quick to hear his voice and obey it, and to know that right away and better than we ever have before, [then it] is going to make a big difference in how he leads." Abiding offered guidance, clarity, and direction to the strategic planning process, but it never removed or replaced it. This research found that direction from the Spirit and intentional strategy go hand in hand, and that abiding informs planning.

Abiding also gives believers God's heart for those they are trying to reach. As believers spend time with Jesus, their spirits increasingly yield to him. In a missionary age bent toward strategy and methods, one theme emerged from this research: the necessity of simplifying mission to the basics of love and discipleship. A team leader testified that abiding in Jesus helps keep the task simple and the motivation pure. Abiding helps him have "a greater heart for people, and that heart helps drive church planting." In order to love and disciple others, a Sudanese leader clarified that he himself needs to be intimate with Jesus. "I disciple leaders and I cannot disciple them if I am not deep in Jesus. Any action is reciprocal. I am a blessing to them and they are a blessing to me. I abide with them and them with me." A woman in Somaliland affirmed that abiding helped her husband and her maintain God's perspective for the often treacherous people they work to reach. "Trying to form [every decision], trying to take care of people, we would always go to the Lord with it." A YWAM leader expressed the limitation of strategy: "I have all these books, teachings, and strategies over here, whereas my abiding with Christ says, 'Sometimes we just need to love God and love people and the fruit will come out of that. Our abiding needs to come first and our strategy needs to come out of that.'"

A common concern among leaders of church planting teams is the limitations of strategy and the possibility of magnifying method over character. One AGWM leader admitted, "I have wrestled at times if I am just offering people my knowledge as opposed to my intimacy with the Lord . . . I have abided in him and found him to be faithful and that he loves me. On that basis I can very much communicate to others." A Dutch leader in Cairo came to a startling realization about discipleship. "Maybe you should search your heart and see if you are such a disciple that God wants reproduced . . . Maybe he's not giving you fruit because you are not worth being copied." Abiding plays a key role in the strategic process as the source of guidance and direction as well as reminding believers that mission must be character driven.

Finding 29

Abiding is taught by mentors and by Jesus. Practically every responder had multiple inputs (people and tools) into their practice of abiding. The type of mentor would vary—pastors, parents, friends, even charismatic nuns[13]—but most all had someone discipling and holding them accountable in abiding, as well as having books, cassettes, seminars, and conferences, which also played a role.

Accountability plays a huge part in people being consistent in their abiding journey.[14] A Sudanese leader mentioned of his mentor, "He was like Paul to me. I learned a lot from him and he taught me from his experience. In leadership, in praying . . . and I learned a lot from him, but it was not enough. I brought cassettes of teaching from the Bible." A Finnish mother of four pointed out that there was a plurality of influences in her life. "It's several people during all of these years. It's not one single person or one single

13. "And I never heard about the Holy Spirit before. First time I heard about the Holy Spirit was from Catholic nuns, and the first to see them practicing the gifts, the supernatural gifts of the Spirit, was also when I had prayer meetings with these nuns."

14. A Dutch woman in Cairo mentioned, "I would like to be asked how you are really doing in your spiritual life, because just an outside accountability somehow helps."

book. It's not all my time in the Bible school." A common theme emerged that leaders had been taught to abide by other mentors and experiences.

A corollary finding was that leaders of church planting teams felt that Jesus was teaching them to abide. One way he teaches leaders to abide is by just helping them do it (press through). Then he speaks to them from his word and woos them with his person. One AGWM leader affirmed that Jesus "shapes [my abiding time] largely by what he brings into my mind or heart that morning." An AGWM leader in Somaliland expressed in a more detail how Jesus taught her to abide:

> [Jesus taught me to abide] by getting out all the time, going off and talking to the Father, asking us to abide in him, constantly showing us that even though we're on this world we should be constantly with our minds somewhere else . . . by saying he doesn't say anything the Father doesn't tell him to say, by filling the Psalms with psalms and a ton of prayers, by teaching his people to [pray constantly].

A Swedish leader agreed: "I see Jesus talking through the Bible." She found that the biblical example of Jesus in the Scriptures modeled for her what she should do. One YWAM leader sensed the wooing initiative of Jesus in the process. "Jesus called me to [abiding] or kind of has been in the midst of it." An AGWM leader in Sudan expressed the initiative Jesus takes for abiding in these terms:

> Abiding is an inter-relationship with Jesus. There's more give and take; there's more communication, more intimacy in that relationship . . . Once you try [abiding], Jesus takes over and he draws you into it, and then you are like "Yeah! I got to do that more, that was cool and I like that." And it is the dear friend that's for love that you go out and say, "Oh, I have to spend more time with him!"

Jesus taking the initiative to abide and to teach leaders to linger with him both rewards and fulfills. A Frontiers leader shares, "I have been blessed so many times by his presence and just by being able to be in such an intimate relationship. I mean I'm still just blown away that somehow when I meet with him, it feels that I'm the only one and it's just so deep and personal. So, of course, I want to keep going back to that." A Lebanese leader summarizes Jesus' initiative:

> God takes you with him. It seems like he pulls you into that place . . . where you just want to be with him. Even in a busy day, I feel this . . . attraction. It's not from us; it's from him. He pulls you.

> Abiding is like . . . riding a ship with God and allowing him to maneuver it the way he wants, and trusting in storms and good weather and hurricanes and sunny skies that he is taking you somewhere and you are just enjoying sweet fellowship, regardless of what is happening on the outside, alone with the Lord.

Leaders of church-planting teams in Northeast Muslim Africa were mentored to abide. This research found there were multiple mentors (both human and other resources) and that Jesus himself takes the initiative for the leaders' abiding.

7

Findings From Corporate Abiding Praxis of Teams

Q METHODOLOGY DOES NOT typically lead to findings independently of other social science methods and demographic data. Without the triangulation, Q methodology by itself would not have led to most of the findings in this research. What is unique about Q methodology is that it allows shared subjectivity to be discovered through the process of Factor Analysis. Subjectivity of individuals can be revealed through interviews or even the individual Q-sort, but only Q methodology allows statistical analysis to identify the factors that underlie shared subjectivity.

Just as looking at an individual's sort helps to understand his or her subjectivity, Q methodology allows the researcher to understand the character of shared views through statistical analysis of the ranked statements. The correlation of those viewpoints with age, gender, experience, number of disciples, or nationality can be viewed either formally or informally. An informal review is typical of Q methodology ("these results appear to indicate . . ."), but a formal finding is valid if verified by accompanying field research.

It is of importance to note that Q methodology findings can primarily be related only to the particular team leaders studied. The spiritual and geo-political context of these leaders is unique and may or may not indicate transferable principles. This study focused on a relatively small sampling (twenty-seven) of evangelical team leaders in a Muslim context. Despite the small sampling, the range of nationalities, ages, length of experience, and mission agencies present a strong argument for the findings that are generally true and agreed upon in this sample of leaders to be applicable to other church-planting team leaders in similar contexts. To apply Q findings to the generalized public (beyond team leaders in Muslim contexts) or to state the findings in general terms is difficult. The findings below are restricted to the team leaders identified unless clearly indicated otherwise.

Q-SORT 1: CORPORATE ABIDING PRACTICE

Two Q-sort surveys were administered. The first one (Q-sort 1 or QS1) probed into the corporate abiding practice of church planting teams in Northeast Muslim Africa.

Identification of Factor

After participants sorted the forty-eight statements[1] onto a grid, their sort was entered into a computer program that ordered the responses according to a -4 to +4 variance from neutral.[2] A factor extraction program was run (PQMethod—a standard software for Q methodology)[3] and then factors were rotated both manually (investigative) and then automatically.[4] After factor extraction and rotation, factors were automatically pre-flagged to discover if any factors had a noticeable amount of shared values. The Q-sorts related to practice were factor analyzed, and two factors emerged that captured the shared views of twenty-two respondents. A Varimax rotation was conducted on Factors 1 and 5 that proved Factor 5 was not serviceable as it represented primarily the view of one unique respondent. Factor 5 was retained in the study as a control and was used as a cross referent to Factor 1 at the end of the analysis.

---

1. These statements collectively are called a concourse. A concourse "is no more or less than the overall population of statements for final Q set sampled. In other words, concourse is to Q set what population is to person sample (or P set)." Watts and Stenner, *Doing Q Methodological Research*, 34.

2. For QS1 the mean deviation was 0.042 and the standard deviation was 1.989. Both deviations are well within the norm. The only reason the mean deviation was as high as it was (0.042) is because the odd number of statements in the Q-sort necessitated a grid imbalanced to the positive end by one box.

3. More information about PQMethod can be found at http://schmolck.userweb.mwn.de/qmethod/pqmanual.htm (accessed January 21, 2014).

4. "In factor rotation, these same loadings [factor loadings expressed as correlations] take on a spatial or geometric function. They are used as coordinates and hence as a means of mapping the relative positions, or viewpoints, of all the Q-sorts in a study." Watts and Stenner, *Doing Q Methodological Research*, 114. The computer program also provides an unrotated factor matrix that supplies initial Eigen values.

Description of Factor

Factor 1 statistically represents those who made reading of Scripture, praying in orderly fashion, sharing what God is doing in their personal lives and church-planting work, and praying for Muslims their most common practices—with Scripture and ordered prayer the most common of all these practices. Factor 1 is distinguished by a strong agreement on the practice of sharing and praying in an ordered way, indicating a structured and pastoral approach. Factor 1 also held in common that midday meetings, worship by CD, prophesy, words of rebuke, foot washing, tongues and interpretation, and praying in the Spirit together were infrequently practiced. The lack of practice is not necessarily indicative of a lack of value.

Factor 1 can thus be summarized as those who shared a common devotion and frequent practice of Scripture reading and ordered prayer.[5] They do not often practice the prophetic or ecstatic gifts. Their praxis can be summarized as "Scripture Solid," in that they read the Bible and pray in loving and ordered steadiness. The Scripture Solid factor (Factor 1) is organized around the common values of reading Scripture, ordered prayer, corporate praise of Jesus, sharing what God has done in their personal lives and church planting ministry, and affirming one another. These abiding practices were most valued by the Scripture Solid factor.

What those in the Scripture Solid factor did not value were words of rebuke, weeping, meetings in midday or morning, or worship by CD or tape. Of note in negative distinguishing statements for the Scripture Solid factor were praying in the Spirit, tongues and interpretation, weeping, and words of rebuke. These four factors were the least valued by Scripture Solid factor members. The research clearly shows that the Scripture Solid factor values the Scripture, ordered prayer, and corporate praise of Jesus while not valuing the ecstatic means of prayer and body ministry.

Demographics of Scripture Solid

Of the Scripture Solid set, eight were female and thirteen were male. This does not indicate that men marginally tend to prefer more structured prayer or a more ordered approach to prayer than women. The variance is not large enough from the sampling. Ten women filled out QS1, and eight of them

5. Factors need to have an identity/title that is user friendly for the reader of the research that is derived not only from what is held in common with each other, but also by how they are dissimilar. Handles for the various factors are derived by both what they have in common internally and by contrast and similarity with other factors.

preferred more structured prayer with the eleven (of seventeen) men. In terms of percentage, 80 percent of women preferred a more structured prayer system compared to 65 percent of men.

The Scripture Solid set included Korean, Arab, English, Portuguese, German, Sudanese, and American team leaders of multicultural teams. Those at variance from within the same sort were American or European. (The Scripture Spirited foil was also American). This indicates that a spectrum of nationalities, including the Global South, have both a devotion to the Scripture and a common praxis of ordered prayer.

There was strong representation in the Scripture Solid factor of non-Pentecostal (though evangelical) mission agencies and churches, which included the Korean Presbyterians, Evangelical Presbyterians, Antioch Ministries International, Vineyard, Southern Baptist, Lutheran, and Mennonite. Of interest, however, is that more than half of the Scripture Solid factor included AGWM missionaries and team leaders.

Summary of Q-Sort 1

The common factor that best represents the practice of the majority of leaders of church-planting teams in Muslim Northeast Africa is that of Scripture Solid. In their practice, these leaders guide their teams to a focus on the Scriptures and ordered, systematic prayer.

Q-SORT 2: CORPORATE ABIDING VALUES

This section examines the second Q-sort survey that centered on the values of the church-planting teams in Northeast Muslim Africa.

Identification of Factors

One addition to the data of Q-sort 2 (QS2) was a sort comprised of Factor 1 from QS1. This factor of Scripture Solid was consolidated into one sort (made possible by the combined factor Q-sort values for each statement that were arranged by factor arrays on QS1) and titled QSP-F1. This sort then became one of twenty-eight sorts submitted to the computer analysis of QS2. This is standard procedure in Q methodology—second order factor analysis.

A principle components analysis was run, and then factors were rotated automatically. This Varimax rotation indicated significant loadings[6] of 6 (Factor 1), 5 (Factor 2), and 12 (Factor 3), a strong indicator of a three-factor solution. Of the three factors, Factor 1 included as a member of its sort QSP-F1 with a 0.85 correlation.[7] The Q Analyze program was then conducted on the three factors identified. It is important to note that QS2 focused on what team leaders valued in corporate abiding, which may or may not align with what they led their teams to practice.

Description of Factors

Three distinct value streams emerged from the data analysis and have been organized into three factors. These factors can be described as follows: Factor 1 as Scripture Solid, Factor 2 as Scripture Spirited, and Factor 3 as Scripture Sacramental.

Factor 1: Scripture Solid

Factor 1 of QS2 is very similar to Factor 1 of QS1 and can be thus similarly titled "Scripture Solid." The Scripture Solid factor is characterized (as noted above) by the common values of reading Scripture, ordered prayer, corporate praise of Jesus, sharing what God has done in personal lives and church-planting ministry, and affirming one another. What those in the Scripture Solid factor did not value were words of rebuke, weeping, meetings in midday or morning, or worship by CD or tape. Of note in negative distinguishing statements for the Scripture Solid factor were praying in the Spirit, tongues and interpretation, weeping, and words of rebuke. The research clearly shows that the Scripture Solid factor values the Scripture, ordered prayer, and corporate praise of Jesus while not valuing the ecstatic means of prayer and body ministry.

---

6. "Loadings" are correlations between a factor and an individual sort. A "loading" is not the same as a "defining" sort.

7. It is important to note that Factor 1 from QS1 has been labeled QSP-F1 and has been inserted into QS2 as one representative sort. This indicates that Factor 1 in QS1 is very similar to Factor 1 in QS2 (correlation to 0.85). QSP-F1 is sort number 28 in QS2.

Factor 2: Scripture Spirited

Factor 2 organized around the common values of reading Scripture, corporate praise of Jesus, prayer (including ecstatic prayer, such as praying in chorus, praying in the Spirit, and praying Scripture), and upbeat worship. These abiding practices were most valued by Factor 2. What those in Factor 2 did not value were details about meetings, a rigid and segmented approach to team life, feet washing, dancing, or unusual physical manifestations of the Holy Spirit. Two of the main things that distinguish Factor 2 from Factor 1 are that Factor 2 highly values the verbal, corporate praise of Jesus and the confession of sin to one another much more than Factor 1 does.[8] Factor 2 also values praying for individual Muslim friends, testimony, the formal taking of prayer requests, and separate meetings for leadership much less than Factor 1.

What emerges as the defining characteristic of Factor 2 is that, while they are absolutely devoted to Scripture (much as Factor 1), they are also very open to the gifts of the Spirit—primarily in corporate ecstatic prayer, such as praying in the Spirit, tongues and interpretation, and the corporate verbal exaltation of Jesus. While they value ecstatic prayer, they do not value excess of emotion or unusual manifestations of the Spirit. Further, they are more egalitarian in their approach to team than Factor 1. Factor 2 blends a devotion to Scripture with a high value of ecstatic prayer and thus can be titled Scripture Spirited.

Factor 3: Scripture Sacramental

Factor 3 organized around the common values of praying for Muslim friends, reading and praying Scripture, confession, corporate praise, communal fasts, and communion. Factor 3 did not value unusual manifestations of the Spirit, worship without instruments or by CD, or dancing. What distinguished Factor 3 from Factors 1 and 2 was its embrace of sacramental abiding: confession, communion, and communal fasts were valued much higher by Factor 3 than by Factors 1 or 2.[9] Factor 3 differed significantly

8. In the analysis of Distinguishing Statements for Factor 2 (available in the appendix), Factor 2 had Z score of (+1.61) concerning "Praying in Chorus." Factor 1, by contrast, had a Z score of (-0.03). This represents a significant difference in value orientation towards this statement. A Z score is a standard score reflecting distance from the mean. Z = 1 is one standard deviation from the mean.

9. Z scores were as follows: confessing—F1 (-0.26), F2 (0.58), F3 (1.39); communion—F1 (-0.30), F2 (0.26), F3 (1.00); and communal fasts—F1 (-0.15), F2 (0.40), F3 (1.95).

with Factors 1 and 2 concerning worship, not valuing upbeat singing, slow singing, and singing without instruments or by CD. Factor 3 differed with Factor 2 on corporate praise—not valuing the verbal aspect of communal praise. Factor 3 does not seem to value worship (in the singing sense) as highly as either of the other two factors. Factor 3 had a much more ambivalent approach to ecstatic prayer than did Factor 1. Aspects like prophecy, words of rebuke, and exhortation were neither embraced nor rejected.

Factor 3 holds Scripture and prayer as highly valued, but they also highly value a sacramental and communal approach to abiding that has traces of hierarchy. Factor 3 seems to be more tolerant of the spiritual gifts than Factor 1, but not as frequent to move in them as Factor 2. The approach of Factor 3 to corporate abiding can best be titled "Scripture Sacramental."

Table 8.1: Summary Descriptors of Factors

Q-Sort 2	Valued	Not-Valued	Character Description
FACTOR 1	Reading Scripture Ordered Prayer Sharing (Personal/ Church Planting) Affirmation	Praying in the Spirit Tongues and Interpretation Weeping Words of Rebuke Weird Manifestations of the Holy Spirit	Scripture Solid
FACTOR 2	Reading Scripture Corporate Praise Ecstatic Prayer Upbeat Worship	Details of Meetings Rigid/Segmented Team Life Feet Washing Dancing Weird Manifestations of the Holy Spirit	Scripture Spirited
FACTOR 3	Scripture Prayer Communion Confession Communal Fasts	Worship Without Instruments Fixed Meeting times Weird Manifestations of the Holy Spirit Dancing	Scripture Sacramental

The higher the correlation between factors, the more difficult it is to define differences, and thus uniqueness. These three factors are highly intercorrelated (anything over 0.3 considered high). While it makes differentiation more challenging, these correlations are within the range of both acceptability and possible interpretation.[10] What makes three factors so similar is shared devotion to the Scripture and prayer as the primary essen-

10. The correlation between Factors 1 and 3 is the highest (0.66), while the correlation between Factors 1 and 2, and 2 and 3 is similar at 0.60 and 0.58, respectively.

tials of corporate abiding. What makes the factors distinct is the approach to prayer (ordered versus ecstatic) and community (individual versus corporate practice of select disciplines).

The demographics of the individual respondents whose sorts contributed to each of these factors complement the findings of the Q-sort. The Scripture Spirited tended to be the most homogeneous (in terms of culture and agency affiliation), while all factors had a representative gender balance, comparable years of ministry experience, and average age. Scripture Spirited also has by far the most Muslim friends being evangelized or pre-discipled. Scripture Solid averaged the most years in ministry and the most MBBs in current discipleship meetings. The Scripture Sacramental group was the most diverse culturally and had the highest percentage of men. They also averaged the longest tenure in the Muslim world. Both the Scripture Solid and Scripture Sacramental averaged longer service in the Muslim world than the Scripture Spirited, which partially explains why those two factors have made more disciples (on average) than the Scripture Spirited.

Table 8.2: Demographic Profiles of Scripture Solid, Scripture Spirited, and Scripture Sacramental

	Factor 1 Scripture Solid	Factor 2 Scripture Spirited	Factor 3 Scripture Sacramental
Average Age	39	40	44
% Male/Female	40/60	40/60	75/20
% Nationality: American Sudanese Others: Dutch, Korean, Egyptian, Brazilian, Swiss	80/American 20/Sudanese	100/American	42/American 58/Others
% Married	100	100	100
Countries of Service	Tanzania Sudan Egypt	Sudan Kenya Tanzania	Sudan Somaliland Djibouti Morocco India Egypt
Mission Agency	AGWM IMB YWAM STAY ON	AGWM	AGWM Frontiers AIM YWAM GMS

% Believe in Baptism in Holy Spirit as Subsequent to Salvation (Yes–No)	60–40	100–0	83–17
Avg. Years in Ministry	19	18	16
Avg. Years in Muslim World	8	4	11
Avg. Years Leading Church-Planting Team	7	2	5
Avg. Team Size	14	7	8
Avg. # of Nationalities on Team	4	2	3
Avg. MBBs Discipled in Past	15	1	15
Avg. MBBs Discipling Now	6	<1	1
Avg. Close Muslim Friends	4	14	11
Avg. Muslims Pre-discipling	5	25	11

FINDINGS

By contrast and similarity, the different factors can be used to define each other. When two findings are juxtaposed with each other, they shed light on each other. Z scores help to quantify similarity and dissimilarity. A Z score is a standard score reflecting distance from the mean. $Z = 1$ is one standard deviation from the mean. For example, Scripture Solid does not value praying in the Spirit (Z score of -1.593 on the descending array of differences between factors scale), while Scripture Spirited valued praying in the Spirit at +1.121 for a difference of -2.714. The variance in this case is substantial as Scripture Solid had a negative value assigned to praying in the Spirit while Scripture Spirit valued it positively. Differences also arise when both factors negatively value a statement. Though neither Scripture Solid (-1.365) nor Scripture Spirited (-0.087) had a positive value for tongues and interpretation, the variance (-1.279) is still notable and indicates the Scripture Solid factor felt much more negatively about it than the Scripture Spirited factor. A more accurate indication emerges from the contrast of what one factor valued positively with the negative evaluation of the other factor. Scripture Spirited factor valued corporate prayer, whether by chorus or in the Spirit (tongues). Scripture Solid factor did not value praying in chorus (-0.030) and valued praying in the Spirit even less (-1.593). Of interest is that the Scripture Spirited factor was entirely comprised of American sorts, all of whom were from AGWM.

Scripture Solid differed from both Scripture Spirited and Scripture Sacramental in that it had a very ordered approach to prayer. Scripture

Spirited and Scripture Sacramental also approach prayer very differently. Scripture Solid team leaders value corporate abiding that is centered on Scripture and prayer with the prayer being organized, structured, orderly, and intentional. Scripture Spirited team leaders value corporate abiding that is centered on Scripture and prayer with the prayer being ecstatic, verbal, extemporaneous, and informal. Scripture Sacramental team leaders value corporate abiding that is centered on Scripture and prayer with that prayer being communal, interactive, reverent, tolerant, and eclectic.

Table 8.3: Summary of Findings From the Corporate Abiding Praxis of Teams

1	From those surveyed, there are three general expressions of value for corporate abiding. They can be generally titled: Scripture Solid, Scripture Spirited, and Scripture Sacramental. All three expressions place the highest value on Scripture, but experience prayer and community worship differently.
2	Scripture (reading of, study of, prayer of) and prayer (for unreached friends and peoples) are clearly the highest values in abiding for all surveyed varieties of church-planting teams in Muslim Northeast Africa.
3	Among those surveyed, the more difficult the situation, the more abiding practice aligns with abiding value.
4	The most common expression of corporate abiding among those surveyed is Scripture Sacramental. This expression is inclusive of a majority who view ecstatic prayer as a value and do not quench the corporate expression of prayer or the manifesting of spiritual gifts.
5	The corporate abiding of those studied varies most significantly in its approach to prayer, not in its approach to Scripture. If teams are not intentional about the practice of ecstatic prayer, the practice recedes and ceases.
6	The more nationalities and the longer tenure present in a church-planting team, the more likely the corporate abiding will be of the Scripture Solid variety.
7	The Scripture Spirited form of corporate abiding tends to be found among those who have less experience on the field and have led fewer Muslims to Christ.
8	The Scripture Spirited teams surveyed tend to have less longevity on the field compared to the Scripture Solid and Scripture Sacramental teams, and tend to make fewer disciples.
9	According to the survey sample, the Scripture Spirited approach is not enough by itself. It needs collaboration with dissimilar but complementary colleagues. Pentecostals cannot reach Muslims by themselves; they must work with other expressions of the body of Christ.
10	Among those surveyed, a Scripture Sacramental approach appears to combine the strengths of Scripture Solid and Scripture Spirited.

Finding 1

From those surveyed, there are three general expressions of value for corporate abiding. They can be generally titled: Scripture Solid, Scripture Spirited, and Scripture Sacramental. All three expressions place the highest value on Scripture, but they experience prayer and community worship differently. In the analysis of a Q-sort survey, the most indicative findings are the variances in dissimilarities (as opposed to similarities). What is most common to all three factors (Scripture and prayer) is indicated by the root word "Scripture" in each factor's description. Scripture and prayer ranked in the top five of each factor's value and registered no dissonance or divergence when factors were compared to each other. A commitment to Scripture and prayer is the unifying element of all expressions of value concerning corporate abiding.

Finding 2

Scripture (reading, studying, or praying of) and prayer (for unreached friends and peoples) are the clear highest value in abiding for all surveyed varieties of church-planting teams in Muslim Northeast Africa. As mentioned earlier in this chapter, QSP-F1 [Q-sort representing Factor 1 of QS1 (Practice)] correlates extremely closely (0.85) to Factor 1 of QS2 (Values). This proximity infers that practice and values are not too dissimilar. The implication (verified primarily by the testimonies of team leaders during semi-structured interviews) is that the more difficult things become in context, the more practice and values line up. Those things of less value tend to be jettisoned in times of pressure, while the abiding practices of higher value are retained. This finding does not strictly emerge from the Q-sort, but is buttressed by a similar finding from the semi-structured interviews: difficulty helps team leaders abide in Jesus.

Finding 3

Among those surveyed, the more difficult the situation, the more abiding practice aligns with abiding value. In the second Q-sort process, Scripture Solid registered six defining sorts, Scripture Spirited registered five defining sorts, and Scripture Sacramental registered twelve defining sorts. A result of twelve defining sorts is significant and indicates that the majority of the team leaders in the study aligned themselves with the Scripture Sacramental view of corporate abiding. Demographically it should be noted that 58 percent (seven of twelve) of the defining sorts in the Scripture Sacramental category were AGWM missionaries (Pentecostals in belief and praxis). Dissimilar to Scripture Solid responses, the Scripture Sacramental responses viewed ecstatic prayer positively with Z scores of +0.199 for praying for words of wisdom/knowledge, +0.375 for prophecy, +0.511 for praying in the Spirit, and +1.301 for corporate, verbal exaltation and praise of Jesus. The Scripture Sacrament felt negatively (did not value) unusual manifestations of the Spirit, giving it a Z score of -1.538.

Finding 4

The most common expression of corporate abiding among those surveyed is Scripture Sacramental. This expression is inclusive of a majority who view ecstatic prayer as a value and do not quench the corporate expression of prayer or the manifesting of spiritual gifts. A review of the demographics of the Scripture Solid factor contrasted with the Scripture Spirited factor reveals that Scripture Solid has a higher ratio of different agencies (4:1), different nationalities (2:1), and larger team size (2:1) than the Scripture Spirited set. The accommodation of other perspectives demands an approach to abiding acceptable to a broad range of tastes and backgrounds. The longer that a team functions as a multinational team, the larger the team becomes and the more nationalities are represented. In this case it becomes more pressing to have a lower common denominator for prayer. This serves as a caution for AGWM teams pursuing multinational participation. Unless the agencies seeking to partner with AGWM share a common perspective on ecstatic prayer, the likely result will be more formal, structured, and staid varieties of prayer.

Finding 5

The corporate abiding of those studied varies most significantly in its approach to prayer, not in its approach to Scripture. If teams are not intentional about the practice of ecstatic prayer, the practice recedes and ceases. The Scripture Spirited team leaders averaged four years of ministry experience in the Muslim world compared to an eight-year average for the Scripture Solid and an eleven-year average for the Scripture Sacramental leaders. Possibly as a consequence of this fact, the Scripture Spirited team leaders recorded discipling fewer MBBs—only one on average—compared to Scripture Solid leaders discipling fifteen and Scripture Sacramental fifteen. Currently Scripture Spirited team leaders are discipling fewer MBBs than either Scripture Solid or Scripture Sacramental. What team leaders of the

Scripture Spirited set do well, however, is make Muslim friends, witness to them, and pre-disciple those who are at all responsive.

Finding 6

The more nationalities and the longer tenure present in a church-planting team, the more likely the corporate abiding will be of Scripture Solid variety (see Table 8.2 above). Of note, a higher percentage of Scripture Spirited team leaders believe in the baptism in the Holy Spirit as subsequent to salvation; this may be the reason why they are on average doing more witnessing to Muslim friends.

These findings raise the question as to why Scripture Spirited leaders seem to be better at witnessing than discipleship. This question merits further study. It could be that these leaders have not been on the field long enough to move to the discipleship phase or that an orientation of prayer based on ecstatic experience somehow undermines long-term commitment and unrewarded labor. Alternatively, it may be that those who now abide in a Scripture Solid manner were at one time in the Scripture Spirited camp but have, for whatever reason, embraced a Scripture Solid approach. The answers to this question are beyond the scope of this study.

Finding 7

The Scripture Spirited form of corporate abiding tends to be found among those who have less experience on the field and have led fewer Muslims to Christ. Q-sort methodology has the capacity to produce distinguishing statements for the different factors. It is noteworthy that statements that lend themselves to long-term stability and endurance distinguish the Scripture Solid factor. For example, those aligning with the Scripture Solid factor value sharing personal testimonies of what God is doing in their lives. They take specific prayer requests for team members' needs. They meet in the evening, which is more conducive for young families than early morning, and welcome children into their meetings. Those aligning with the Scripture Spirited and Scripture Sacramental factors shared none of these values, yet these values obviously contribute to long-term stability and endurance. Scripture Solid teams averaged eight years on the field, which is four more than Scripture Spirited teams, but three years less than Scripture Sacramental teams (who averaged eleven).

Scripture Sacramental teams demographically include more variety than Scripture Spirited teams; they are more diverse in multiple indices.

Their distinguishing statements reveal that they value confession and repentance (+1.39 Z score compared to +0.58 for the Scripture Spirited and -0.26 for the Scripture Solid), communion (+1.00 to +0.26 for the Scripture Spirited and -0.30 for the Scripture Solid), communal fasts (+0.95 to -0.40 for the Scripture Spirited and -0.15 for the Scripture Solid), and even prophecy (+0.38 to—0.64 for the Scripture Spirited and -0.73 for the Scripture Solid) much more than either other factor.

All of these statements indicate a high value on community. The Scripture Sacramental factor cherishes the symbolic sacraments of the body of Christ—hence its title—and derives from communal sacraments strength to endure and persevere. What negatively distinguishes the Scripture Spirited factor, by comparison, is that they do not testify to each other what God is doing corporately, pray for Muslim friends specifically, or solicit prayer requests from each other to the extent the other factors do.

When the above data is cross-referenced with the demographic data, it is important to observe that on average Scripture Solid team leaders and Scripture Sacramental team leaders have both discipled fifteen MBBs. By contrast, Scripture Spirited team leaders have discipled only one MBB. An obvious link to longevity and discipleship is revealed by these data, yet the minimal variance in tenure does not account for the maximum discrepancy in the number of disciples. The implication of the finding is that Scripture Spirited members do not make disciples as well as Scripture Solid or Scripture Sacramental for the primary reason that they are not as steady over the long-term. Initial zeal and loudly voiced passion do not automatically translate into longevity or disciples that make disciples.

Finding 8

The Scripture Spirited teams surveyed tend to have less longevity on the field compared to the Scripture Solid and Scripture Sacramental teams and tend to make fewer disciples. A Scripture Spirited approach distinguishes itself positively through a commitment to praying in chorus. This verbal prayer and attending exaltation of Jesus is critical in Muslim contexts. However, passion evidently is not enough to carry a leader or a team year after year in difficult contexts. The Scripture Solid camp is comprised mainly of evangelicals who do not embrace ecstatic prayer or gifts. The Scripture Sacramental camp is comprised of Pentecostals and non-Pentecostals. The evidence points to the reality that Pentecostals can neither flourish nor endure if they will not partner with, and learn from, non-Pentecostals.

Finding 9

According to the survey sample, the Scripture Spirited approach is not enough by itself. It needs collaboration with dissimilar but complementary colleagues. Pentecostals cannot reach Muslims by themselves; they must work with other expressions of the body of Christ. According to value orientation, both the Scripture Solid camp and the Scripture Spirited camp agree on the centrality of Scripture and prayer in corporate abiding values. They differ on the nature of prayer. Scripture Solid abiders have a more organized and controlled approach to prayer that is warm in its embrace and support of team members. Scripture Spirited abiders have a more ecstatic approach to prayer that is corporate in its passion, but verges on impersonal in its application. The Scripture Sacramental abiders seem to embrace and unite the strengths of the other two factors.

Any difference of Z score over 1 between statements in a factor is statistically significant depending on the standard error of the study. The standard of error is impacted by the number of statements and number of people involved in the study. Anything twice the standard error has a 95 percent chance of being significant. The Scripture Sacramental factor scored praying for Muslim friends, reading Scripture, praying Scripture, praying for Muslim peoples, confession, church planting testimony, and corporate exaltation of Jesus well over +1.0. In addition, they had positive Z scores for words of exhortation, affirming one another, praying in the Spirit, prophecy, praying for words of wisdom/knowledge, communion, and communal fasts. Scripture Sacramental leaders are in favor of the ecstatic gifts and prayers (a Scripture Spirited strength) as well as in favor of individual concern and dedication to the team members (a Scripture Solid strength).

Finding 10

Among those surveyed, a Scripture Sacramental approach appears to combine the strengths of Scripture Solid and Scripture Spirited.

SUMMARY OF FINDINGS FROM Q METHODOLOGY

Q methodology does not usually lead to findings independent of other social science methods and demographic data. These findings were triangulated with the other research methods in this research and with the pertinent demographical data. Q methodology findings can primarily be related only to the particular sample studied unless clearly indicated otherwise.

Scripture and prayer make up the most commonly shared values for corporate abiding according to the leaders of church-planting team in Muslim Northeast Africa. While there is broad agreement on Scripture, there are three different broad categories of understanding how prayer and community interact in the abiding journey. These three categories can be described as Scripture Solid, Scripture Spirited, and Scripture Sacramental.

8

Findings on Impact of Leaders' Abiding on Teams

TWENTY TEAM MEMBERS FROM seven teams in five countries were interviewed to determine how their team leaders' abiding impacted them. One research reality is that some of those surveyed are from the same team. The twenty responses are spread evenly among seven different teams in five different countries. However, there is enough of a balanced sampling to ensure that the results are not unrepresentative. Further, multiple responses from one team serve as an internal control preserving the bias of one representative of that team from dominating the feedback. These responses are connected to Research Question 3, which investigates the abiding praxis of team leaders of church planting teams. Specifically, these responses indicate the impact of team leaders' abiding on their team members.

Of the twenty interviewed, ten said they perceived their team leaders to spend a moderate amount of time with Jesus daily; three said they perceived their team leader to spend an extravagant amount of time; two said "much time"; two said they perceived their leader to spend little time with Jesus daily; and three said they did not know. Concerning whether they had observed growth in the abiding praxis of their team leader, eight responded that they were unsure, four said "greatly," four said "quite a bit," and three said "a little." Only one said there was no observable growth in the abiding of their leader. When asked what they felt was the most important aspect of their leaders' abiding praxis, twelve of the twenty mentioned the Bible or the Bible and prayer, two mentioned worship, and six stated they did not know.

Following are eleven findings from these interviews. These findings are not arranged in order of importance, but according to the sequence of questions in the remotely administered interview.

Table 9.1: Summary of Findings From Impact of Leaders' Abiding on Their Teams

1	Scripture (being read or prayed) plays the dominant role in corporate abiding.
2	Corporate, verbal exaltation is hugely important in Muslim contexts.
3	Structured prayer is more common than ecstatic prayer.
4	Though time of meeting varies, it is standard to make team meetings required, and it is important not to vary the schedule of meetings in times of crisis.
5	Team members feel strongly that the most important things their team did in corporate abiding were reading and praying Scripture, intercessory prayer, and worship.
6	Team members differ with team leaders on the importance of fellowship, games, business, and logistics.
7	Food (a communal meal) is an essential part of corporate abiding, while fasting and Scripture memorization are not.
8	Team leaders are perceived as relatively strong in abiding but weaker at teaching their team members to abide.
9	Team leaders were perceived to value character as the most important factor in determining whether or not to invite new team members onto the team. Competency was the least important factor.
10	Team members strongly perceive that abiding is more important to their team leaders than ministry activities.
11	Team leaders communicated the priority of abiding either by its practice or by its absence.

FINDING 1

Scripture (read or prayed) plays the dominant role in corporate abiding. Team members were asked to rank seven elements of "Scripture and prophetic words" according to their importance in their teams' corporate practice of abiding. The highest ranked element was given a score of seven, the second a score of six, and so on, down to one point for the lowest ranked element.

Opportunity was also given for respondents to indicate which elements were never practiced in their corporate abiding. "Reading Scripture" was by far the most common practice of abiding in the corporate setting.

Scripture was also often prayed and, thus, the most repeated spiritual functions of teams involved the Scripture, either in the studying or praying of the word of God. Of note was the fact that the majority of surveys indicated that tongues and interpretation never occurred in their team. Team members found the clear study and articulation of Scripture more important than tongues and interpretation or the other gifts of the Spirit.

Table 9.2: Ranked Elements of Corporate Abiding

Element	Average (Maximum 7)
Reading Scripture	6.55
Praying Scripture	5.65
Affirming One Another	4.90
Words of Exhortation	4.50
Prophecy	2.65
Words of Rebuke	1.90
Tongues and Interpretation	1.85

Table 9.3: Elements of Corporate Abiding Never Practiced by Team

Element	Times Mentioned (20 Surveys)
Tongues and Interpretation	12
Prophesy	8
Words of Rebuke	8
Praying Scripture	1

FINDING 2

Corporate, verbal exaltation is hugely important in Muslim contexts. Team members were asked to rank seventeen elements of "Praise and Body Ministry" according to their importance in their teams' corporate practice of abiding. The highest ranked element was given a score of seventeen, the second a score of sixteen, and so forth, down to one point for the lowest ranked element. Opportunity was also given for respondents to indicate which elements were never practiced in their corporate abiding.

Analysis of this finding indicates worship (whether up-tempo or reflective) and praise (corporate, verbal exaltation) of Jesus are critically important, for they not only encourage the worshiper, they also combat spiritual forces of darkness. In Muslim contexts, the deity of Jesus is under continual assault. As a result, it is essential for teams to fight the anti-Christ spirit of Islam through intentional, verbal, passionate praise and worship.

Table 9.4: Ranked Elements of Praise and Body Ministry

Element	Average
Reflective, Slow Singing	14.10
Corporate, Verbal Exaltation of Jesus	13.70
Worship with Guitar or Keyboard	13.25
Upbeat Singing	12.90
Testimonies about Church Planting Work	12.65
Sharing Personal Testimonies	12.20
Silent Listening	12.05
Worship Without Instruments	11.50
Worship by CD/Tape	8.75
Confessing	8.25
Laughing	6.75
Weeping	6.20
Communion	6.05
Communal Fasts	4.90
Feet Washing	3.55
Unusual Physical Manifestation of the Spirit	3.25
Dancing	2.95

Table 9.5: Elements of Praise and Body Ministry Never Practiced by Team

Element	Times Mentioned (20 Surveys)
Dancing	16
Feet Washing	14
Unusual Manifestations of the Holy Spirit	14
Communal Fasts	10
Communion	9
Laughing	7
Weeping	6
Worship by CD	4
Confessing	2
Worship by Guitar or Keyboard	1

Silent Listening	1
Sharing Personal Testimonies	1
Upbeat Singing	1
Worship Without Instruments	1
Corporate, Verbal Exaltation of Jesus	1

Table 9.5 reveals that dancing, feet washing, and unusual manifestations of the Spirit were never experienced by 75 percent of the respondents in their teams. It further notes that half of those interviewed experienced neither communion nor fasting in the corporate setting.

FINDING 3

Structured prayer is more common than ecstatic prayer. Team members were asked to rank eleven elements of "Prayer" according to their importance in their teams' corporate practice of abiding. The highest ranked element was given a score of eleven, the second a score of ten, and so forth down to one point for the lowest ranked element. Opportunity was also given for respondents to indicate which elements were never practiced in their corporate abiding.

More than 30 percent of the responses mentioned that their teams do not pray in the Spirit. Almost 50 percent of the teams interviewed were not AGWM, so a 30 percent figure indicates that non-Pentecostal teams also pray in the Spirit. More than 50 percent of the teams, however, did not practice the spiritual abiding of waiting on the Spirit for specific words or encouragement (whether for an individual person or for a general encouragement). This finding indicates that teams are generally more comfortable with structured prayer than extemporaneous prayer.

Table 9.6: Ranked Elements of Prayer

Element	Average
Praying in Turns (around the room)	9.05
Praying for Muslim Friends	8.25
Praying for Muslim Peoples	8.00
Praying in Turns (whoever feels led)	7.80
Taking Prayer Requests	7.75
Praying in Chorus (everyone out loud)	6.35
Praying Silently	5.65

Praying in Small Groups	5.30
Praying in the Spirit	3.00
Providing Solitude for Team Members to Pray Privately	2.95
Praying for a Word for Others	1.90

Table 9.7: Elements of Prayer Never Practiced by Team

Element	Times Mentioned (20 Surveys)
Praying for a Word for Others	11
Praying in the Spirit	6
Providing Solitude for Team Members	4
Praying in Chorus (everyone out loud)	3
Praying in Small Groups	1
Praying in Turns (around the room)	1
Praying in Turns (whoever feels led)	1

FINDING 4

Though time of meeting varies, it is standard to make team meetings required, and it is important not to vary schedule of meetings in times of crisis. Team members were asked to rank thirteen elements of "Meeting" according to their importance in their teams' corporate practice of abiding. The highest ranked element was given a score of thirteen, the second a score of twelve, and so forth, down to one point for the lowest ranked element. Opportunity was also given for respondents to indicate which elements were never practiced in their corporate abiding.

The highest ranked response indicated the importance of all team members being present during team meetings. There was some variance as to when those meetings should be and if children should attend, but the majority of responders felt the most important aspect of meetings was that all attended. The findings also showed that team members do not want to meet more or less often in times of crisis. This finding indicates both that teams find it unhelpful to stop meeting during pressured times and unnecessary to meet more often under pressure. A steady rhythm of team meetings seems to have a stabilizing and calming effect on team members. Meetings do not increase in times of crisis, nor are core leadership meetings frequent (for spiritual or strategy purposes).

Table 9.8: Ranked Elements of Meetings

Element	Average
Meetings Are Required of All Team Members	11.25
Meetings in the Evening	10.45
Meetings in the Morning	10.15
Meetings in the Middle of the Day	7.85
Children Are Present	7.25
Strategy Decisions Linked to Prayer Meetings	6.80
Meeting Times Are Open-Ended (no fixed ending time)	6.35
Separate Meetings for Strategy	5.95
Meetings Are Optional for One Spouse If There Are Children	5.65
A Core Leadership Team Meets for Spiritual Reasons	5.05
Meetings on a Tight Schedule	4.90
A Core Leadership Team Meets for Strategic Reasons	4.85
Meetings More Often (For Spiritual Needs) in Crisis	4.50

Table 9.9: Elements of Meetings Never Practiced by Teams

Element	Times Mentioned (20 Surveys)
Meetings on a Tight Schedule	6
Strategy Decisions Linked to Prayer Meetings	5
Meetings Optional for Spouse with Children	5
Separate Meetings for Strategy	3
Meetings More Often (for spiritual needs) in Crisis	3
Meetings in the Middle of the Day	3
A Core Leadership Team Meets for Strategic Reasons	2
A Core Leadership Team Meets for Spiritual Reasons	2
Meeting Times Are Open-Ended	2
Meetings in the Evenings	1

FINDING 5

Team members strongly feel that the most important things their team did in corporate abiding were reading and praying Scripture, intercessory prayer, and worship. Team members were asked to list the three abiding practices most important to them. These statements were gathered and divided by twenty (total number of respondents) to ascertain the percentage of mention. As the question was open-ended, answers were very specific. The second stage was to group the specific answers into general categories and to divide again by twenty to gain the percentage of overall mention. When this was done, it was discovered that an absolute majority of respondents had three essential elements in common: reading and praying Scripture (80 percent), prayer (70 percent), and worship (60 percent). This finding suggests that team members consider the most important activities of a team to be spiritual, not strategic, business, or logistical. Though practical options were suggested for consideration, the dramatic absence of practical issues considered to be important by team members is noteworthy. The implication is not that team members consider strategy or practical matters unimportant, but that they consider Scripture, prayer, and worship as their primary strategy.

Table 9.10: Most Important Abiding Practices to Team Members

Specific Elements	%	Mentioned
Worship	60	12
Prayer	50	10
Reading Scripture	45	9
Praying Scripture	35	7
Corporate Verbal Exaltation of Jesus	20	4
Affirming One Another	15	3
Quiet Listening	10	2
Fellowship	10	2
Sharing What God Is Doing in Church Planting Team	10	2
Prayer for People Groups	10	2
Sharing What God Is Doing in Your Life	5	1
Strategy Meetings Linked to Prayer	5	1
Praying in Turns	5	1
Specific Words of Knowledge or Insight	5	1
Words of Exhortation	5	1
Meetings in the Morning	5	1
Confession	5	1
Praying for Muslim Friends	5	1
General Elements	%	Mentioned
Reading or Praying Scripture	80	16
Prayer (all forms)	70	14

Worship	60	12
Fellowship and Affirming One Another	25	5
Corporate Verbal Exaltation of Jesus	20	4
Sharing Church Planting or Personal Testimonies	15	3
Quiet Listening	10	2
Specific Words of Knowledge/Insight/Exhortation	10	2
Confession	5	1
Strategy Meetings Linked to Prayer	5	1
Meetings in the Morning	5	1

FINDING 6

Team members differ with team leaders on the importance of fellowship, games, business, and logistics. Team members were asked to rank seven elements of "Team Meetings" according to their perception of what their team leader felt was important for their team. The highest ranked element was given a score of seven, the second a score of six, and so forth, down to one point for the lowest ranked element. Opportunity was given for respondents to indicate if there were other elements that were practiced in their team meetings that were not suggested by the survey question.

Table 9.11: Most Important Elements of Team Meeting According to What Team Members Thought Team Leader Valued

What the Team Leader Thought Most Important	
Elements	Average
Missiology and Methodology	4.55
Fellowship and Games	4.30
Strategy	3.75
Business and Logistics	3.60
Language and Culture	3.40
Other	1.70
What the Team Member Thought Most Important	
Elements	Average
Abiding in Jesus	6.95
Fellowship and Games	4.65
Missiology and Methodology	4.50

Strategy	3.65
Language and Culture	3.35
Business and Logistics	3.10
Other	1.80

What Team Spent Most Time Doing (19 Surveys)	
Elements	Average
Abiding in Jesus	7
Fellowship and Games	7
Business and Logistics	2
Language and Culture	1
Missiology and Methodology	1
Other	1

Team members believed that team leaders valued abiding as most important. However, an equal number of respondents said their teams spent the most time in fellowship and games as said their teams prioritized abiding. This finding speaks to the importance of teams having fun and fellowship together. Abiding is considered by team members to include fellowship and fun. Team leaders tend to focus on the spiritual (formal) aspects of abiding, followed by business details and logistics. Team members prefer to focus on the formal spiritual aspects of abiding, followed by fun and fellowship. Team members also mentioned four categories of "Other" that included an equal distribution of all the elements of a team meeting: sharing food together, worship, and sharing testimonies of ministry, followed by encouragement from the word.

Table 9.12: Difference Between What Team Members Thought Was Important to Their Team Leaders and What Team Members Considered Important

	Team Leader	Team Member	Difference
Elements	Average	Average	
Fellowship and Games	4.65	4.30	+0.35
Abiding in Jesus	6.95	6.70	+0.25
Other	1.80	1.70	+0.10
Missiology and Methodology	4.50	4.55	−0.05
Language and Culture	3.35	3.40	−0.05
Strategy	3.65	3.75	−0.10
Business and Logistics	3.10	3.60	−0.50

Fellowship and games were more important to the team member than they perceived it was to their team leaders by a divergence of +0.35. This means essentially that the team members wished for more fellowship and games than the team leader provided. Conversely, the team members differed with the team leaders by -0.5 on the issue of business and logistics. This means that team members did not consider time spent on business and logistics as important as their leaders did—at least based on their perception of their leaders.

FINDING 7

Food (a communal meal) is an essential part of corporate abiding, while fasting and Scripture memorization are not. Team members were asked to select abiding activities their team participated in from a presorted list. This list emerged from the semi-structured interview process conducted on these team members' leaders. Of special note, all respondents (seven different teams from five different countries) mentioned food and Bible study. One hundred percent included these aspects of team life. As a point of concern, it should also be noted that less than 40 percent of respondents indicated that their team fasts together, and less than 30 percent indicated that Scripture memorization is a part of their corporate abiding praxis.

Table 9.13: Further Abiding Activities of Teams

Element	Mentions	Percentage
Share Meals	20	100
Bible Teaching (Study)	20	100
Practice Accountability	17	85
Prayer over Business as Mission (BAM) Platform	15	75
Prayer Walking	14	56
Fasting	8	40
Memorizing Scripture	6	30
Other (Worship)	4	20

FINDING 8

Team leaders are perceived as relatively strong in abiding but weaker at teaching their team members to abide. Statistically, team leaders' abiding was reported as positively impacting church planting and corporate abiding. It is clear that team leaders across the board have been intentional about prioritizing their lives around abiding and also encouraging their team members to abide. There is one apparent area of weakness, however. While most team leaders seemed to model abiding to their team members (65 percent of respondents felt abiding had been modeled to them), they do not intentionally teach their team members to abide. Only 40 percent of respondents felt that their team leader had been proactive in teaching them to abide.

Table 9.14: Team Leader's (TL) Impact on Abiding

	Agree	Neutral	Disagree	Strongly Disagree	% Agree
TL Abiding Positively Impacted Church Planting Team	9	3	0	0	85
TL Abiding Impacted Team Members' Abiding	8	5	1	0	70
TL Modeled Abiding to Team Members	5	7	0	0	65
TL Taught Team Members to Abide	5	7	4	1	40
TL Led Team to Corporately Abide	9	3	0	0	85
TL Prioritized Abiding Personally	8	5	0	0	75
TL Encouraged Team Members to Prioritize Abiding	4	2	2	0	80

FINDING 9

Team leaders were perceived to value character as the most important factor in determining whether or not to invite new team members onto the team. Competency was the least important factor. Character and calling emerge as the strongest factors team leaders consider when determining who they will invite to join their team. The implication is that if a leader can verify a prospective team member is genuinely called of God and has godly character, competency is less essential and can be added through the process of time and training. A further assumption warranting further research is that the best team members are not necessarily the most gifted ones; rather, they are the ones with the most integrity. Rather than looking for people to fulfill certain jobs or roles, team leaders tend to look for people who share a common calling and have godly character. Competencies are then developed, instilled, and refined along the way.

Table 9.15: Team Leaders' Criteria for Selection of Team Members

Elements	Averages
Character	3.85
Calling	3.75
Maturity	2.85
Competency	2.85
Other	1.70
Other Elements	
Willingness to Serve	2
Flexibility	1
Agency Just Assigned	1
Availability	1
Personal Connection	1

FINDING 10

Team members strongly perceive that abiding is more important to their team leader than ministry activities. When asked if abiding was more important than, equal to, or less important than ministry activities for their team leaders, twelve respondents said more important (60 percent), seven said equal (35 percent), and one said less important (5 percent). This finding indicates that of the teams surveyed, a strong priority on abiding exists—and abiding is considered more important than ministry activity.

FINDING 11

Team leaders communicated the priority of abiding either by its practice or by its absence. This research showed that team leaders have an important role to play in encouraging their team members concerning the priority of abiding in Jesus. When team members were asked what their leaders had taught them about abiding, responses ranged from the simplistic "[Abiding] is essential" to the pragmatic "Abiding in Jesus works. We must depend on him for all things" to the superlative "Before all things our time with Jesus is the most precious." It should be pointed out that the theoretical importance of abiding being communicated is not synonymous with teaching how to practically abide. An earlier finding found that team leaders are weak in teaching the "how" of abiding, even as this finding shows that they do well in communicating the "theory" of abiding. A twenty-six-year-old team member in Sudan commented that her leader taught her, "Abiding in Jesus must be the first priority in our lives. No matter how busy our schedule, we must take that time to be with Jesus. We so desperately need time with him to be refreshed, to be filled anew with his Spirit, to be emboldened, to hear his voice, and to be gradually transformed to be more and more like him."

Team leaders did an exceptional job of communicating the priority of abiding. A twenty-four-year-old male in Tanzania said, "I [have learned that I] have room to grow and that I can continue to abide in Jesus regardless of how busy I become." Team leaders consistently taught their team members that abiding is critically important and should have the priority of schedule. As a twenty-seven-year-old female team member in the Comoros put it: "[Abiding] keeps us from endlessly striving [and leads us] to trusting and walking and partnering with Jesus."

Among the team members, there was some insignificant variation in understanding about abiding as related to the question of its essence. A thirty-four-year-old male viewed abiding as "a necessary part of my daily life and ministry. The more I abide, the more I can demonstrate Jesus to those I am working among, as well as grow and develop personally in my walk with God." This team member felt that "[abiding] is critical to the longevity of one's ministry and their satisfaction with wherever they are in life." In this view, abiding is expressed as a part of the whole. A twenty-seven-year-old woman in Sudan stated that "abiding in Jesus is the most important component of ministry, and without it nothing should be attempted." Another team member in Sudan espoused, "Abiding (while being the priority in ministry) is all about relationship with Jesus—knowing him, loving him, receiving from him." In this collective understanding, abiding is an important—the most important—aspect of ministry. It is the first among many aspects.

A twenty-nine-year-old team member in Egypt articulated a refined view of abiding: "[Abiding in Jesus] is the only critical thing we do. If we don't do this, then we aren't really doing anything. Everything we do here flows out of this." In his view, abiding is even more important than the most important component of ministry, for abiding is the foundation and source of all ministry.

A female team member in Egypt agreed. "When we abide in Jesus, we will bear much fruit. The Spirit will help us in every area—our relationships, witnessing, decisions, culture, emotions, etc. to give glory to Jesus." In this view, abiding impacts every area of one's being and serving and is not limited to merely being the most important component of one's ministry.

Some responses indicated not all communication of the priority of abiding was done positively. A thirty-three-year-old European remarked, "What [my team leader] did was good, but abiding is more and should include seeking refilling of the Holy Spirit." In this team member's view, there is a difference between a disciplined devotional life and having a regular hungry longing for, and lingering in, the presence of Jesus. An American said of the same team leaders, "[Their abiding] should be done more frequently or it should be communicated more what they are learning from that time." These team members did not feel that their team leaders lived a deep abiding, yet wished that they would.

Team members tended to recognize abiding is not purely mystical, and that collaboration and effort is required on the believer's part. A female team member from a Baptist background in Sudan quipped, "It is not always lollipops and candy canes. You must give of yourself in abiding and it will never return void." An AGWM woman in Sudan reflected, "Jesus is worth the effort we give him. It is a work in progress. We are always reevaluating how to be with Jesus more."

Though there was some variance in experience, all team members indicated that their leaders had impressed on them the theoretical value and importance of abiding.

9

Integration of Social Science Findings

FINDINGS

EACH OF THESE THREE research methods produced findings that were triangulated with each other and with demographic information provided by the participants. The synthesized findings are listed thematically in twenty-six categories below.

Table 10.1: Summary of Integration of Social Science Findings

1	Scripture and prayer are the heart of both personal and corporate abiding.
2	Scripture is supreme in personal abiding and is the unifying element in corporate abiding.
3	Prayer is the most common corporate practice of abiding.
4	All team leaders spent a daily block of time abiding.
5	Team leaders incorporate listening as an integral part of abiding.
6	Music enriches both fixed and continual abiding.
7	Suffering and pressure are vital contributors to the maturing and deepening of personal abiding.
8	Outside activity keeps lines of communication open with Jesus.
9	Those who abide in Jesus experience steady growth in the depth and length of their abiding time.
10	Jesus takes the initiative for the abiding of his disciples.

11	Abiding in Jesus increases team leaders' effectiveness, giving them energy, creativity, longevity, and content for ministry.
12	Solitude does not play a prominent role in the abiding of most leaders of church-planting teams.
13	Legalism is not commonly embraced by those who are intentional about prolonged abiding times.
14	Abiding strengths of other cultures provoke a godly jealousy.
15	The most common fruits of the Spirit experienced as a result of abiding by the respondents were peace, joy, and patience.
16	For Western missionaries, no significant connection exists between dreams and intimacy with Jesus.
17	Abiding's primary impact on the church-planting strategy of team leaders is guidance.
18	From those surveyed, three primary expressions of corporate abiding emerged.
19	Scripture Solid corporate abiders share a commitment to Scripture and prayer as the foundation of their corporate abiding. They highly value ordered prayer—systematically praying for one another, their Muslim friends, and Muslim peoples in general. They are very pastoral, relational, and family oriented. Compared to their high value of Scripture and ordered prayer, Scripture Solid corporate abiders place less value on corporate praise of Jesus, praying in the Spirit, prophecy, or speaking in tongues with interpretation.
20	Scripture Sacramental corporate abiders have a commitment to Scripture and prayer as the foundation of their corporate abiding. They tend to employ inclusive corporate prayer with elements of both order (systematic and individual) and ecstatic (exuberant, corporate praise, praying in the Spirit) styles. Scripture Sacramental abiders are very intentional about Body aspects of worship, such as communion, confession, and corporate fasts.
21	Scripture Spirited abiders have a commitment to Scripture and prayer as the foundation of their corporate abiding. They tend toward ecstatic prayer: praying in chorus, corporate exaltation of Jesus, praying in the Spirit, tongues and interpretations, prophecy, words of exhortation and rebuke, and waiting on God for specific words for the group or individuals in the group.
22	It is standard across all teams to make team meetings required, though meeting times vary. It is important not to vary schedule of meetings in times of crisis. Church planting teams have different types of meetings that respond to a variety of strategic and spiritual needs.
23	Team members differ with team leaders on the importance of four key variables: fellowship, games, business, and logistics.

24	Team leaders communicated the priority of abiding either by its practice or by its absence.
25	Food (a communal meal) is a common and essential part of corporate abiding, while communal fasting and communal Scripture memorization are uncommon.
26	Team members perceived that team leaders valued character as the most important factor in determining whether or not to invite new team members onto the team. Competency was the least important factor according to the perception of the team members surveyed.

Finding 1

Scripture and prayer are the heart of both personal and corporate abiding. During the personal daily rhythm of spending time with Jesus, Bible reading and prayer were the most common elements of abiding—every respondent mentioned them. The most common corporate practices are based on the Scripture and ordered prayer. Scripture (reading, study, and prayer of) and prayer (for unreached friends and peoples) are clearly of highest value in abiding for all teams. Team members strongly feel that the most important things their teams did in corporate abiding were reading and praying Scripture, intercessory prayer, and worship.

Finding 2

Scripture is supreme in personal abiding and is the unifying element in corporate abiding. The Bible is the central discipline for personal abiding. This finding does not contradict Finding 1. Rather, it clarifies that while the Bible and prayer are the most essential components of abiding, prayer tends to flow from the Scripture and be guided by the Scripture. Scripture (being read or prayed) plays the dominant role in corporate abiding. Scripture dominance does not necessarily mean that the most time is spent on Scripture. Rather, Scripture informs and guides all other aspects of abiding.

Finding 3

Prayer is the most common corporate practice of abiding. It is difficult to separate the value of prayer and Scripture as (1) the difference between them according to those surveyed is minimal, and (2) prayer and Scripture are often employed together. In the factor analysis, Scripture and prayer ranked in the top five activity (of forty-eight) for each factor. The most common activity of the church-planting teams is to pray together.

The corporate abiding of those surveyed varies most significantly in their approach to prayer, not in their approach to Scripture. Respondents varied considerably in their approach to prayer. The "ordered prayer" practitioners were more structured and methodical (taking requests, praying one at a time, not praying in chorus, not praying in the Spirit, not open to prophecy or prophetic words). In contrast, the "ecstatic prayer" practitioners were more passionate in prayer (praying in the Spirit, praying in chorus, praying for specific words to share with the group or one another, embracing tongues and interpretation in prayer, and not being so intentional about taking prayer requests or praying in turn). A higher percentage of women than men (80 to 65 percent) prefer ordered prayer over ecstatic prayer. Women are sometimes stereotyped as more emotional in their approach to prayer than men are. This research indicates the opposite: a higher percentage of women preferred ordered prayer (both more structured and personal) than men did. One effect of ordered prayer is that it is more personal, pastoral, and intimate (via the solicitation of personal views, needs, feelings, and requests).

Team leaders from the Global South do not vary significantly in their corporate devotion to Scripture nor, interestingly, to ordered corporate prayer. Majority world missionaries (Global South missionaries) are sometimes characterized as being less attentive to the Scriptures and more open to ecstatic prayer. This research showed that team leaders from the Global South hold a devotion to Scripture as their essential starting point and to ordered prayer as a corporate form of intercession proportionate to their colleagues from the West.

Statistically, there is little difference between the Pentecostal[1] missionaries from around the world and other evangelical missionaries surveyed concerning the practice of ecstatic prayer in corporate abiding.[2] Both are equally infrequent in their practice of ecstatic prayer, even though Pentecostal missionaries indicated that they value it. In this finding, value and praxis do not align. This is not to say that ecstatic prayer does not happen

1. Those that believe the doctrine of subsequence, that there are ongoing experiences and fillings of the Holy Spirit post-conversion.

2. On a scale of 1 to 9, Pentecostals averaged a score of 2.91 concerning the practice of tongues and interpretation compared to 2.40 for non-Pentecostals. Any score less than 4.5 indicates a practice not often performed. On praying in the Spirit, Pentecostals averaged 3.39 and non-Pentecostals averaged 2.80. All these scores are below the marker for frequent practice. On the same point scale (over 4.5 indicating a practice that is valued), Pentecostals scored 4.22 on tongues and interpretation (not really valued) and 5.00 on collective prayer in the Spirit (marginally valued).

(either in evangelical or AGWM teams), but according to team members, whatever the professed value of the team leaders concerning ecstatic prayer, structured prayer is more common than ecstatic prayer.

Finding 4

All team leaders spent a daily block of time abiding. The average block of time spent abiding in Jesus is just over one hour a day (sixty-four minutes). The most common framework for lingering with Jesus is an extended block of time in the morning. However, stages of life and circumstances require flexibility.

Finding 5

Team leaders incorporate listening as an integral part of abiding. For team leaders, abiding is two-way communication (Jesus and the disciple), requiring quiet times of reflection and intentional waiting for Jesus to speak.

Finding 6

Music enriches both fixed and continual abiding. Worship (listening to music, playing guitar, singing in the local language, praise, etc.) is a strong common denominator for those who daily abide in Jesus. It is common for personal abiding times to be enhanced and lengthened through music. Music plays a vital part in ongoing abiding (all-day communion). One of the key ways that team leaders experienced the presence of Jesus throughout the day was through the reminder of worship music, both played and sung.

Finding 7

Suffering and pressure are vital contributors to the maturing and deepening of one's personal abiding praxis. Contexts of pressure and overwhelming lostness focus continual attention on Jesus. The oppression experienced in Muslim lands, the frustration associated with being unable to bring one Muslim to Jesus (let alone a people group), the unending difficulties and practical roadblocks to effective evangelism all serve to drive team leaders to a place of being desperate for Jesus, both for his presence and his help.

Abiding is sweetest when life is hardest or about to become harder. Jesus prepared team leaders for trials by drawing them close to himself before it began. He made himself most real to team leaders when they went through pain, anguish, and suffering. Team leaders felt most intimate with Jesus when they endured great sorrow and difficulty.

Suffering improves the quality and quantity of abiding. Not only did the research of this sample of team leaders show that suffering improved intimacy with Christ, it also revealed that in suffering, team leaders spent more time with him. It was suffering that taught team leaders to linger with Jesus, to give him extravagant time.

Among those surveyed, the more difficult the situation, the more their abiding practice aligned with their abiding values. The praxis of team leaders was shown to diverge from what they valued (they did not do what they said was most important to them). Suffering served as a teacher, reminding those leaders to practice what they valued. In times of pressure and suffering, what is not valued drops away and what is valued is embraced and employed.

Finding 8

Outside activity keeps lines of communication open with Jesus. God's creation through nature and exercise helped team leaders experience his ongoing presence.

Finding 9

Those who abide in Jesus experience steady growth in the depth and length of their abiding time. Those who daily spend extravagant time with Jesus are not satisfied or complacent. They want more of Jesus, specifically to hear his voice and to be intimate with him.

Finding 10

Jesus takes the initiative for the abiding of his disciples. Jesus invites, befriends, guides, and becomes the source of mission. The impetus to abide does not rest solely on the disciple, for Jesus delights to woo disciples to himself. Team leaders who comprehend his initiative do not pressure themselves to abide, but rejoice in responding to Jesus. Abiding becomes a delight, not just a discipline.

Both mentors and Jesus teach abiding. Most team leaders had a mentor who modeled abiding for them. Team leaders also felt that through the years Jesus gently taught them how to abide in him. Leaders cannot assume that team members will know how to abide or actually will abide just because they were exhorted to do so. Team members need to be mentored in how to abide. According to team members, team leaders do a poor job of teaching their team members to abide. Team members strongly observed that abiding was important to their team leaders, and even that their leaders had exhorted them to abide. Yet team members frequently commented that their leaders had not taught or mentored them in what abiding looks like practically.

Finding 11

Abiding in Jesus increases team leaders' effectiveness, giving them energy, creativity, longevity, and content for ministry. When team leaders stop abiding, even for short periods, this has a negative effect on their attitude and tolerance for difficulty. When team leaders stop abiding over longer periods, they lose the capacity to persevere in difficult contexts. The result is often a termination of church-planting ministry.

Abiding gives humbled and dependent leaders the content of what they share with others and leads to a primacy of the word doing the work. Team leaders who abide discover that much of what they say comes directly from their daily intimacy with Jesus. Jesus speaks through them from that intimate place of union and companionship. Often abiding quickens the Scripture and makes it fresh to the speaker in the immediacy of unexpected or overwhelming need. Abiding gives overwhelmed leaders what they do not naturally have. Team leaders commonly feel they do not have the capacity or energy to do what is required. The team leaders who have learned to abide discovered divine resources, energy, and capacity to fulfill their responsibilities.

Finding 12

Solitude does not play a prominent role in the abiding of most leaders of church planting teams. Most team leaders surveyed do not take time away for personal spiritual retreats, though they wish that they did.

Finding 13

Legalism is not commonly embraced by those who are intentional about prolonged abiding times. Many team leaders experienced a progression from desperation to discipline, from discipline to desire, and from desire to delight. Team leaders who delight in abiding have a spirited and free devotion, characterized as regular but not bound. The structure (rigid or flexible) of abiding time and place varies according to the personality of the leader.

Finding 14

Abiding strengths of other cultures provoke a godly jealousy. Team leaders were envious of the strengths (in abiding) they saw in those from other cultures. This envy produced a desire to grow in that aspect of abiding.

Corporate abiding is a living demonstration that believers not only need Jesus; they also need each other. Corporate abiding differs in several ways from individual abiding. There are several key aspects of corporate abiding that do not normally happen in individual abiding: (1) laughter (communal joy, not necessarily an unusual manifestation of the Holy Spirit); (2) gifts of the Spirit (prophecy, tongues, and interpretation, etc.); loud worship (singing, praises are louder and fuller in chorus); and perspective (whether through testimony or discussion of Scriptural text, multiple perspectives always enhance understanding).

Though personal and corporate abiding have some similar components, neither one is incomplete without the other.

Finding 15

The most common fruit of the Spirit experienced as a result of abiding by the respondents were peace, joy, and patience. Noticeably absent was love. This is not because love is unimportant. Conceivably it is because in strict Muslim contexts, peace, joy, and patience tend to be what is most needed. Peace overcomes fear, joy overcomes depression, and patience overcomes resistance.

Finding 16

For Western missionaries, no significant connection exists between dreams and intimacy with Jesus.[3] It is more common for non-Western missionaries to experience intimacy with Jesus through dreams. A majority of the missionaries who experienced intimacy with Jesus in dreams are female.

Finding 17

Abiding's primary impact on the church-planting strategy of team leaders is guidance. This guidance (peace and direction) directs team leaders on what to do and what not to do, who to be and who not to be. The result of intimacy with Jesus is assurance regarding the way forward.

Finding 18

From those surveyed, three primary expressions of corporate abiding emerged. The three expressions can generally be titled: Scripture Solid, Scripture Spirited, and Scripture Sacramental. All three expressions place the highest value on Scripture, but experience prayer and community worship differently. The corporate abiding of those surveyed varies most significantly in its approach to prayer, not in its approach to Scripture.

Finding 19

Scripture Solid corporate abiders share a commitment to Scripture and prayer as the foundation of their corporate abiding. They highly value ordered prayer—systematically praying for one another, their Muslim friends, and Muslim peoples in general. They are very pastoral, relational, and family oriented. Compared to their high value of Scripture and ordered prayer, Scripture Solid corporate abiders hold less value for corporate praise of Jesus, praying in the Spirit, prophecy, or speaking in tongues with interpretation.

---

3. In other research and reporting, dreams have been shown to play a significant role in the conversion of Muslims. Because Muslims already believe in the omnipotence of God, these dreams are often not related to power issues, but to intimacy. Muslim seekers tend to be convinced of God's power and are more in need of his assurance. They need to know that God will be with them if they take the drastic step of following him. This research did not probe dreams in the conversion process of Muslims, but did look into the role of dreams among church planters.

Those who shared a Scripture Solid perspective on corporate abiding tend to last longer on the field and have on average made more disciples than Scripture Spirited abiders. The Scripture Solid abiders have fewer Muslim friends and fewer Muslims they are witnessing to than those who share a Scripture Spirited perspective. According to the survey sample, the more nationalities and the longer tenure on a church-planting team, the more likely the corporate abiding will be of the Scripture Solid variety. Length of service on the field tends to temper enthusiasm and passion, and leads to a more eclectic approach to prayer that prioritizes inclusion and non-offensive terms and actions.

Finding 20

Scripture Sacramental corporate abiders have a commitment to Scripture and prayer as the foundation of their corporate abiding. They tend to employ inclusive corporate prayer with elements of both order (systematic and individual) and ecstatic (exuberant, corporate praise, praying in the Spirit) styles. Scripture Sacramental abiders are very intentional about body aspects of worship, such as communion, confession, and corporate fasts.[4] The most common expression of corporate abiding among those surveyed is Scripture Sacramental. This expression is inclusive of a majority who view ecstatic prayer as a value and do not quench the corporate expression of prayer or the manifesting of spiritual gifts. They pray in the Spirit and are open to prophecy. A Scripture Sacramental approach appears to combine the best corporate aspects of the Scripture Solid (individualized prayer and pastoral care) and Scripture Spirited (passion, corporate exhortation) approaches.

A Chi-square test was performed to ensure that no statistically significant difference was observable when comparing the corporate abiding values of Pentecostals and non-Pentecostals. The X2 value of 4.685 was less than the degree of freedom (df) table value of 5.99. Therefore the study can assert that frequencies in the table do not differ significantly when examined by the Pentecostal variable. In fact there is no significant difference in values of abiding when Pentecostals are compared with non-Pentecostals.[5]

---

4. Earlier in the research (see page 189), it was noted that fasting was more valued than practiced. Scripture Sacramental abiders tend to be more regular in their fasting (communally at least) than Scripture Solid or Scripture Spirited abiders.

5. There were, however, only a small number of non-Pentecostals in the study.

Finding 21

Scripture Spirited abiders have a commitment to Scripture and prayer as the foundation of their corporate abiding. They tend toward ecstatic prayer: praying in chorus, corporate exaltation of Jesus, praying in the Spirit, tongues and interpretations, prophecy, words of exhortation and rebuke, and waiting on God for specific words for the group or individuals in the group.

The Scripture Spirited tends to be exclusive. In the sample surveyed, all were from one Pentecostal mission agency. The Scripture Spirited form of corporate abiding tends to be led by those who have less experience on the field and have led fewer Muslims to Christ than either the Scripture Solid or Scripture Sacramental group. The Scripture Spirited teams tend toward less longevity on the field compared to the Scripture Solid and Scripture Sacramental teams. Largely as a result of this, they tend to make fewer disciples. Scripture Spirited teams have more passion and volume, but less staying power and pastoral care than the other forms of abiders. According to the survey sample, the Scripture Spirited approach is not adequate by itself; it needs collaboration with dissimilar but complementary colleagues. This finding suggests that Pentecostals cannot reach Muslim peoples effectively by themselves. They may be more effective when working with other like-minded expressions of the body of Christ

Finding 22

It is standard across all teams to make team meetings required, though meeting times vary. It is important not to vary schedule of meetings in times of crisis. Church-planting teams have different types of meetings that respond to a variety of strategic and spiritual needs.

Finding 23

Team members differ with team leaders on the importance of four key variables: fellowship, games, business, and logistics. Team members feel that times of fellowship, relationship, and games are more important than meetings for business, details, or logistics. While team members felt planning meetings were important, they valued them less than team leaders did. Team members strongly perceived that abiding is more important to their team leaders than ministry activities.

Finding 24

Team leaders communicated the priority of abiding either by its practice or by its absence. While the vast majority of team leaders communicated to their team members that abiding is important, some validated their verbal proclamation by living it. Others undermined their abiding exhortations by not evidencing what they espoused.

Finding 25

Food (a communal meal) is a common and essential part of corporate abiding, while communal fasting and communal Scripture memorization are uncommon.

Finding 26

Team members perceived that team leaders valued character as the most important factor in determining whether or not to invite new team members onto the team. Competency was the least important factor according to the perception of the team members surveyed.

SUMMARY

In summation, this research employed varied social science methods to probe the personal abiding of team leaders of church planting teams in Muslim Northeast Africa. It also probed how leaders led their teams in corporate abiding. Each of these three research methods produced findings that were triangulated with one another and with demographic information provided by the participants. The most significant findings of this section are as follows: First, Scripture and prayer form the heart of both personal and corporate abiding irrespective of age, gender, nationality, experience, or denominational background. Second, Scripture is the unifying element in multi-cultural and multi-agency abiding. Third, prayer is the most common corporate practice of abiding but also the point of distinction. There are three general groups of missionary leaders: Scripture Solid, Scripture Spirited, and Scripture Sacramental. The essential difference is the praxis (or lack thereof) of ecstatic, corporate prayer. The Scripture Sacramental approach appears to combine the best corporate aspects of the Scripture Solid (individualized prayer and pastoral care) and the Scripture Spirited (passion, corporate exhortation) approaches. Fourth, abiding value and abiding praxis do not align across the board until suffering, pressure, or difficulty force them to do so. Fifth, those with less experience on the field tend to lead the Scripture Spirited form of corporate abiding. They are zealous in evangelism but evangelize and disciple fewer Muslims to Christ than either the Scripture Solid and Scripture Sacramental groups. Scripture Spirited teams have more passion and volume but less staying power. They provide less pastoral care for their own than the other forms of abiders. Critically, this research suggests that the Scripture Spirited approach benefits from collaboration with dissimilar but complementary colleagues. This finding suggests that Pentecostals can reach Muslim peoples most effectively while working with (and/or learning from) other like-minded expressions of the body of Christ.

The most critical finding of this research is that abiding in Jesus is not only the preparation for the work of fruitful mission, but it is the most basic element of fruitful mission. Abiding in Jesus is indeed the foundation for making disciples. The missionaries that learn to abide in Jesus make disciples, and their disciples abide and make more disciples (John 15:16).

SECTION 4

Synthesis of Findings

THIS SECTION SYNTHESIZES THE findings of this book in order to draw conclusions about the operationalization of abiding and to speculate on how abiding leads to disciples. The following chapter will present a spiritual theory of discipleship and make recommendations for further research. The research is based in an epistemological sequence of biblical exegesis, historical reference, social science research, and theory development from these synthesized findings.

10

Theory Development

THE RESEARCH IS BASED on biblical exegesis, historical review, and social science findings. This chapter will briefly review the components of the research. It will then develop abiding theory.

REVIEW OF EXEGETICAL FINDINGS

An exegetical summary of John 15:1–17 can be found on page 55 above. In short, abiding in Jesus is both a discipline and a state. The discipline of abiding involves lavishing extravagant time on Jesus on a daily basis. This discipline is centered on the word of God (Bible) and prayer, but is also personalized according to context and season of life. The state of abiding is the all-day, all-night-long constant intimacy with Jesus, characterized by quick and joyful obedience.

Abiding is the first priority of the disciple and the chief methodology of the disciple's mission. Without abiding in Jesus as described above, the disciple is powerless to make other enduring disciples. With abiding, the disciple is welcomed into a friendship with God and a loving interdependence on other disciples, which empowers the ongoing (and difficult) work of discipleship.

REVIEW OF HISTORICAL FINDINGS

The abiding praxis of the seven missionaries researched (Daniel Comboni, Samuel Zwemer, Oswald Chambers, Temple Gairdner, Douglas Thornton,

Lillian Trasher, and Lilias Trotter) show evidence of all aspects of the definition of abiding as exegeted in Section 2 (see page 90). All communed with
Jesus in dedicated blocks of time. All dedicated blocks of time to lavish extravagant attention on Jesus. All spent the majority of those blocks of time in
the word and prayer. All disciplined themselves and their followers to spend
time with Jesus (and experienced suffering in the process). All engaged others in a communal celebration and interaction with Jesus. All found time
with Jesus to be the strategy, not just empowerment for the strategy. As a
result, all seven produced disciples, and in turn their disciples reproduced.
History attests to their lasting impact on missions.

REVIEW OF SOCIAL SCIENCE FINDINGS

Semi-structured interviews, Q-Sort methodology, and a remotely administered electronic survey probed the abiding praxis of the team leaders of
church planting teams in Egypt and Northern Sudan. The primary findings
were as follows:

1. Scripture and prayer form the heart of both personal and corporate
   abiding irrespective of age, gender, nationality, experience, or denominational background.

2. Scripture is the unifying element in multi-cultural and multi-agency
   abiding.

3. Prayer is the most common corporate practice of abiding but also the
   point of distinction. There are three general groups of missionary leaders: Scripture Solid, Scripture Spirited, and Scripture Sacramental. The
   essential difference is the praxis (or lack thereof) of ecstatic, corporate
   prayer. The Scripture Sacramental approach appears to combine the
   best corporate aspects of the Scripture Solid (individualized prayer
   and pastoral care) and the Scripture Spirited (passion, corporate exhortation) approaches.

4. Abiding value and abiding praxis do not align across the board until
   suffering, pressure, or difficulty force them to do so.

5. Those with less experience on the field tend to lead the Scripture
   Spirited form of corporate abiding. They are zealous in evangelism
   but evangelize and disciple fewer Muslims to Christ than either the
   Scripture Solid and Scripture Sacramental groups. Scripture Spirited
   teams have more passion and volume but less staying power. They provide less pastoral care for their own than the other forms of abiders.

Critically, this research suggests that the Scripture Spirited approach benefits from collaboration with dissimilar but complementary colleagues. This finding suggests that Pentecostals can reach Muslim peoples most effectively while working with (and/or learning from) other like-minded expressions of the body of Christ.

The most critical finding of this research is that abiding in Jesus is not only preparation for the work of fruitful mission, but it is the most basic element of fruitful mission. It is possible to be in Christ and not abide (John 15:6). Abiding in Jesus is indeed the foundation for making disciples. The missionaries that learn to abide in Jesus make disciples, and their disciples abide and make more disciples (John 15:16).

CONCLUSION FROM SYNTHESIZED FINDINGS

An integration and synthesis of the above leads to these conclusions:

1. Jesus promised fruit to those who abide in him. Abiding is more than being "in Christ," as John 15:6 points out that there are branches who do not abide.

2. John 15 defines fruit as disciples.

3. Missionary praxis (historical and contemporary) affirms abiding both as always being in the presence of Jesus and as spending extravagant daily blocks of time with Jesus. Abiding can thus be described as lavishing extravagant daily time on Jesus. The discipline of abiding requires disciples to spend daily blocks of time with Jesus. The state of abiding requires disciples to continually commune with Jesus.[1] Neither the discipline nor the state of abiding is effective without the other.

4. The historical praxis of exemplary missionaries and the current abiding praxis of current missionaries to Muslims in Egypt and North Sudan affirm that Scripture and prayer are the heart of abiding at both the personal and corporate level. Scripture is the starting place for abiding and informs the content of prayer. Prayer is the most common expression of corporate abiding. Scripture tends to unite disparate missionary approaches while prayer tends to distinguish them. The missionary body of Christ has an easier time agreeing on Scripture than it does on prayer as some church-planting teams embrace ecstatic

---

1. Interestingly, music is a primary aid to helping missionaries abide all day long. Worship music and personal singing help missionaries remain (abide) in the presence of Jesus over time.

prayer (speaking in tongues, prophecy, exuberant praise, gifts of the Spirit) and some do not. Corporate prayer (prayer meetings that unite the body of Christ) tends to exclude ecstatic prayer.

5. Two critical components of personal abiding notable for their absence are regular solitude/retreats and the practice of ecstatic prayer. The absence of these practices has a detrimental effect on the individual.

6. Abiding requires both intentionality and discipline, and is learned. The missionaries studied (past and present) were notable for making disciples who learned to abide. Someone taught them to abide in Jesus. Missionaries who abide are disciplined and intentional, yet their abiding is not sustained by their effort alone. Jesus takes initiative for abiding as well, wooing his disciples to himself. Abiding is often a response to the invitation of Jesus to be with him. Christians from other cultures also teach/invite missionaries to abide by displaying an aspect of abiding hereto not experienced. When missionaries observe a vibrant aspect of abiding in a colleague from another culture, it provokes a godly jealousy in them and they begin to desire that experience.

Difficulty and suffering also teach missionaries to abide and improves both the quantity and quality of abiding. Personal suffering is a normal part of the abiding life and should be expected and embraced. The exemplary missionaries in this research endured great personal suffering and loss. When missionaries encounter difficulty, their values and praxis of abiding align. What is unimportant or ineffective falls away and what is potent is employed. When missionaries do not know what to do or how to resist an evil attack, they begin praying in the Spirit. When missionaries suffer, they are so broken and wounded they run to Jesus and are forced to linger with him as no one else can help them. This compelled abiding is good for making disciples because intense time with Jesus makes disciples more like him. Missionaries should welcome suffering, for the result (via improved abiding and if they suffer well) is ultimately more disciples. The longer missionaries serve, the more trouble they encounter; and the more trouble they encounter, the more they turn to Jesus for help and learn to abide in him. Abiding becomes increasingly important as missionaries mature and begin to experience results in their ministry.[2] Abiding fosters abiding.

---

2. Unfortunately, missionary success often inhibits abiding as responsibilities and opportunities accumulate and compete for the missionary's time. Ironically, if a missionary is not careful, the fruit that resulted from abiding can be lost due to a cessation of abiding.

7. Abiding is for both individuals and corporate groups and is transcultural. There are components of corporate abiding not common to personal abiding: laughter and joy; gifts of the Spirit; exuberant, loud, vocal praise; and broader perspective. It is not enough to have regular personal abiding. Church-planting teams must also have regular corporate abiding times and learn to linger together in the presence of Jesus.

8. The most effective (i.e., sustained disciple-making) church-planting teams (in evangelism and discipleship) among Muslims are Scripture Sacramental teams (teams that embrace both the word and the everyday activity of the Holy Spirit). Three essential components characterize Scripture Sacramental teams: (a) they devote themselves to Scripture as the base of their belief, witness, prayer, and strategy; (b) they employ both systematic (organized, pastoral) and ecstatic (tongues, prophecy, corporate praise, and spiritual gifts) prayer; and (c) they take a communal approach to body life. They take communion together often, confess privately and publicly their sin, and undertake corporate fasts together.

9. John's teaching on abiding links to a missional hermeneutic of empowerment by the Holy Spirit. The context of John 13–17 centers on Jesus sending his disciples to do mission in the power of the Holy Spirit. Thus, the disciple's first activity in mission is to abide (as abiding positions disciples to be filled and refilled with the Spirit). Abiding empowers and prepares disciples for mission activity.

10. Abiding empowers; it does not preclude other mission activities. Abiding is the first activity of the missionary, not the only one. Missionaries must still learn language and culture, serve the recipient people, witness verbally of the death and resurrection of Jesus, etc. Abiding does not replace or remove sound missionary praxis.

11. Abiding is not just preparation and empowerment for mission; it is the primary work of mission. Abiding both informs and constitutes strategy. Missionaries do not abide only to access the energy, wisdom, creativity, and power to do mission. Missionaries abide because there is a mystical component to abiding, and when missionaries linger with Jesus, the Spirit does something in the unseen realms that is more effective than human activity. When missionaries abide, they are at spiritual war; when missionaries abide, they are fighting. Abiding is not passive mission; it is active advance in the heavens. Prayer is not just preparation or empowerment for missions; prayer is the primary

work of mission. Therefore, it is strategic to abide and strategic to assign the prime working hours of the day to abiding, as missionaries accomplish more through abiding than even study, evangelism, discipleship, and the overt (and necessary) exercise of mission.

12. The fundamental assumptions that provoke the activity of abiding are: (1) the inability of the missionary to make disciples in his or her own strength or by means or methods apart from spirituality, and (2) the unflinching desire of God for the missionary to make disciples. These two assumptions (the desperation of the missionary and the determination of God) combine to lead the missionary to abide. Desperation leads to discipline, which leads to desire, which leads to delight.

13. According to the social science research among leaders of church-planting teams, legalism has no legitimate place in true abiding and is uncommon among those who spend extended daily time with Jesus. Abiding in the morning (for a time tithe—over two hours) were common practices of missionaries in history who made many disciples.

14. It is possible for missionaries to make disciples posthumously. Missionaries that learned to abide and either wrote about their spiritual journey or were written about have impacted as many (or more) after their death than while they lived.

THEORY

The theory that this research was designed to produce is a descriptive mid-range theory that proposes abstract application to the biblical connection between abiding and fruitfulness described in John 15:1–17 across the missiological spectrum.

The result of this research is a theory of spirituality that posits that missionaries who serve among the Muslim peoples of Egypt and Northern Sudan and abide by continually communing with Jesus and by lavishing extravagant daily time on Jesus make disciples. The state of abiding requires missionaries (and all followers of Christ) to commune with Jesus continually. The discipline of abiding requires missionaries to spend daily blocks of time with Jesus. Neither the state of abiding nor the discipline of abiding is fruitful without the other. Abiding should be both the first priority of the missionary and the base corporate methodology for mission.

CHALLENGES TO ABIDING MISSION THEORY

There are two immediate challenges to abiding theory. The first is framed by the question: "What about those that abide and do not make disciples?" The second challenge is, "What about those who do not abide yet make disciples?" If abiding theory is to be universal, these two objections must be addressed.

The first challenge (those who abide and do not make disciples) betrays two assumptions: (1) that a disciple equates to a new believer and (2) that a disciple must be made in the lifetime of the discipler. Samuel Zwemer provides a response to both assumptions. He is not known to have led one Muslim to Jesus, yet he is called "The Apostle to Islam" for his groundbreaking work in the Arabian Peninsula and Egypt. Zwemer discipled countless missionaries both in his lifetime and after his passing through his speaking and writing. A disciple can be a believer who is helped along in mission; he does not have to be a convert. Disciples can be made long after the death of the missionary. Zwemer discipled many missionaries—some of them long after he died.

The second challenge (those who do not abide yet make disciples) does not take seriously that abiding produces disciples who abide (John 15:16). John's view of a disciple links directly to Jesus and to his mission. The disciple or missionary cannot reproduce other than himself. Thus, if a missionary does not abide, he cannot produce in his own strength disciples that abide. Missionaries who do not abide may indeed produce disciples, but they generally are disciples who do not abide. A Christian Arab woman in Sudan summarizes this principle:

> Nothing works well enough [without abiding]. It just looks like an activity, unless it comes from the spring of life. So if I'm not abiding, many things can go well, and people can think I'm so successful, but I know ... I was able to be very successful in ministry at times when I was not really fully abiding, but I don't know the fruits.

God's sovereignty can overrule the norm (missionaries have to abide in order to produce disciples who abide), but essentially disciples that abide do so because the one who discipled them knew how to abide.

OPERATIONALIZING ABIDING MISSION THEORY

Abiding mission theory posits that missionaries who serve among the Muslim peoples of Egypt and Northern Sudan and abide by continually communing with Jesus and by lavishing extravagant daily time on Jesus make disciples. The following examines the mechanisms of how abiding translates to disciples. The nine mechanisms explained below are: (1) abiding produces disciples by keeping Jesus at the center, (2) abiding produces disciples by keeping the abider connected to and dependent on the Spirit, (3) abiding produces disciples by beginning the fight in the heavens, (4) abiding produces disciples by slowing the missionary down and breeding peace, (5) abiding produces disciples by empowering longevity, (6) abiding produces disciples by providing missionary content, (7) abiding produces disciples by redeeming suffering, (8) abiding produces disciples by correcting and refining missionary strategy, and (9) corporate abiding produces disciples by exposing missionaries to the wider body of Christ.

Abiding Produces Disciples by Keeping Jesus at the Center

When a person spends a lot of time with Jesus, he or she becomes increasingly like him. The thick presence of Jesus is like an aroma or light surrounding the missionary. When a missionary abides in Jesus, the presence of Jesus can be felt when others are near him or her, even before he or she speaks. When a missionary abides in Jesus, his or her goodness is God-sourced and thus potent and effectual. Abiding makes a missionary like Jesus, and when one disciples he does not pass on carnal traits but Christlike ones. Jesus becomes the model for what a missionary does and how he or she does it, and the missionary learns this model by abiding. The person who is continually with Jesus cannot help talking about him or acting like him. The missionary that abides evangelizes more and has more opportunities for disciple making. Abiding keeps mission God-centered; mission becomes more about evangelism and less about projects and service ministries.

When Jesus is at the center, the missionary realizes he or she is dispensable or replaceable. The missionary who spends extended time abiding has to spend less time in meetings and ministry. As the missionary abides, he or she finds that mission continues fine (often better) without constant intervention. This realization makes the discipler more aware of his or her dispensability and thus more comfortable to delegate and quicker to do so, as he or she realizes it is Jesus who does the work anyway. Early delegation and trust is critical for the production of disciples, for it gives them frequent opportunity to exercise their own faith.

Abiding Produces Disciples by Keeping the Abider Connected and Dependent on the Spirit

Missionaries testify that without abiding they have nothing to give. Abiding connects missionaries with the Holy Spirit and grants a renewed energy, freshness, passion, and power. The Ephesians 5 refilling of the Spirit is in the context of "evil days." Thus, when times are difficult, missionaries can be replenished by waiting on the Spirit for renewal. A Christian Arab in Cairo stated that abiding gives creativity, and this creativity is sourced in the creativity of the Spirit. The Spirit supplies the content of the message and also shapes the character of the messenger. Abiding allows time for the Spirit to fashion missionaries into vessels worth being copied, vessels that can be trusted to duplicate themselves. Abiding positions the missionary to be shaped and refined by the Holy Spirit, and a Spirit-empowered missionary is more potent in making disciples than a self-powered one.

Abiding Produces Disciples by Beginning the Fight in the Heavens

Prayer is the real work of missions. Oswald Chambers believed "we must go into heaven backwards; that we must grow into some definite things by praying not by seeing."[3] Missionaries begin and sustain the fight for disciples by praying for them. When missionaries fight for souls in prayer, it gives them compassion for those souls and thus urgency and compulsion when they are physically with them. When missionaries pray in the Spirit, it ignites a fire within their souls as they pray the will of God and it launches weapons of war in the spirit realm. Abiding is not passive missions; it is active warfare. More happens at the spirit/unseen level to bring the lost to Jesus than happens at the physical/seen level. Abiding is war at the Spirit level.

When missionaries abide in Jesus and his words abide in them (John 15:7), it leads to answered prayer. Missionaries pray souls into the kingdom. Missionaries pray disciples into the kingdom before they talk them into the kingdom. It is the Spirit who convicts of sin, and it is the prayers of the missionary band (those on the ground and those providing covering prayer) that lead to disciples. The real fight for disciples is not in the streets or the marketplace—it is in the abiding place. When missionaries take time to intercede for disciples, they are more effective in finding and growing them.

3. Chambers, *Prayer*, 59.

Abiding Produces Disciples by Slowing the Missionary Down and Breeding Peace

To spend extravagant daily time with Jesus functionally requires the missionary to slow down. There are limited hours in a day. When a missionary spends more than two hours with Jesus daily, there are fewer practical things a missionary can do on a daily basis. This forces the missionary to prioritize and focus on what is truly important; it also gives God time to work. When a missionary is not available to "solve" problems or answer questions, it allows others to learn to depend on God for themselves. This self-limitation (from others) in order to spend time with Jesus also increases the opportunities for the missionary to listen to what the Spirit speaks. Without the discipline of abiding (lavishing extravagant daily time on Jesus), missionaries often are too busy to hear what God is saying, and without hearing the nuances of the Spirit, they are less effective in discipleship. Abiding also teaches the missionary to stop striving and stressing. Rather than rushing to fix a problem or a person, the missionary goes to Jesus and asks Jesus to solve the issue.

Abiding thus produces disciples because it breeds peace and calm in the disciple maker. The abider does not tend to overreact or make poor or quick decisions about others. The abider waits on Jesus for instructions on how to handle difficult people or complex discipleship matters rather than making hasty judgments or inopportune interventions. Abiding is antithetical to rushing and fosters wisdom. Rather than reacting, the abider lingers in the presence of Jesus and is often inspired by the Spirit on how to be proactive or who to engage in witness or mentoring. A missionary to Sudan testified that abiding increases her internal core and resilience and enables her to impart wisdom "I would not have had, had I not abided." Because abiding slows down the pace of life for the missionary, he or she makes fewer relational mistakes and has greater Spirit-provided counsel in the discipleship making process. There is an atmosphere of peace around the missionary who takes time to abide in Jesus. The measured, peaceful missionary tends to be a steady missionary, and a steady missionary attracts those who are in need of stability or who are appreciative of the counsel steadiness affords.

Abiding Produces Disciples by Empowering Longevity

Without longevity it is difficult to make disciples. Disciples are made over time with extended life-on-life encounters. The average tenure of service for missionaries to the Muslim world according to Vision 5:9 is seven years and declining. It often takes missionaries two terms (usually eight years) to learn the local language fluently, adjust to the culture, develop relationships, and earn a right to be respected and heard. Missionaries usually do not come into their most productive years of service until they have been in the field for over eight years. Yet most missionaries do not stay that long. The detrimental effect on disciple making is self-evident—if missionaries are not present, it is difficult to make disciples.

Abiding provides a rhythm of rest and renewal that gives missionaries the practical and spiritual stamina to remain on the field for the long haul. When a missionary has regular Sabbaths, times of retreat and solitude, and practices extended daily time in the presence of Jesus, he or she is fortified with the emotional capacity to continue plodding. At a very practical level, missionaries who abide tend to live more structured and organized lives, including the seemingly minor but critical component of being early to bed and early to rise. To lavish two-plus hours per day on Jesus inevitably means that one needs to either get up early or be disciplined enough in a daily calendar to carve out the requisite time to linger with Jesus.

The structure necessary for an abiding lifestyle orders all aspects of life (sleep patterns, exercise habits, and diet) and therefore keeps missionaries healthier (spiritually, emotionally, and physically). Abiding fundamentally contributes to missionary health, and missionary health often determines missionary longevity. When missionaries stay longer on the field, they make more disciples, and the ratio of return (disciples made) often increases with maturity and experience.

Abiding Produces Disciples by Providing Missionary Content

Missionaries who dedicated themselves to lavishing extravagant time on Jesus framed that time of lingering primarily around the Bible. A single American woman working with Arabs commented that the word directed both the content of her prayers and their direction. Reading the Bible showed her who to pray for. Missionaries who linger in the word on a daily basis have fresh content to minister. They find their daily reading is what they pray over disciples or seekers in the course of the day. Missionaries find that what they read that morning is what they share that afternoon. Those who abide do not feel they are repeating stale truths; rather they feel they offer fresh bread cooked that morning in prayer and reflection on the word.

The preparation of abiding allows the missionary to be spontaneous, in season with a word, an exhortation, or a prayer that is applicable and current. This freshness of content empowers the missionary in the disciple making process. Further, abiding gives missionaries the vital supply of faith to call other men and women into discipleship. J. Christy Wilson wrote of the role prayer played in giving Zwemer influence over other men: "Never did his faith stumble at the power of God to do the impossible . . . through prayer and service he was used to call out and equip bands of men and women for the most difficult mission fields."[4] It was his abiding time that made him a mighty discipler of men and women.

Abiding Produces Disciples by Redeeming Suffering

When missionaries suffer, their abiding values align with their praxis. What is essential becomes the very thing the missionary does most often—and usually this is related to primal, ecstatic prayer. Suffering aligns abiding praxis and values. It aligns what the missionary values with what is important to God. Suffering compels missionaries to cling to Jesus. In doing so, they understand his heart better and are thus better qualified to represent him. Jesus becomes more real to missionaries when they share in his sufferings,[5] and thus becomes more real to the pagans or converts observing them—further empowering the missionaries to make disciples. When missionaries suffer well, they become a living example to others. Not all missionaries suffer well, and suffering has destroyed as many as it has refined. Abiding faithfully in times of peace and prosperity prepare the missionary to emerge from suffering more like Jesus (better) not more exposed as carnal (bitter). Missionaries who abide do not easily falter under pressure; their witness is turbo-charged and effectual in making disciples.

The implication of this reality (suffering well gives missionaries a platform for discipleship) is simple and staggering. Missionaries should both want to abide in Jesus and joyfully embrace the suffering he ordains for them. When missionaries suffer well, the result is disciples. An Egyptian serving with YWAM in Sudan said that joy is

> Almost like laughing at Satan. Because here in this dark place, full of suffering, full of poverty, full of Islam, when you have a group of believers together from different tribes, different nationalities, and there is laughter, which is an expression of the Holy Spirit, those have been the sweetest times, because I feel like it's just mocking everything Satan can do to us . . . to the body of Christ, because there is still joy coming up in the desert.

4. Wilson, *Apostle to Islam*, 241.

5. Suffering for Jesus is different than suffering for foolish or evil actions. The suffering mentioned in this section refers to suffering for Jesus and the gospel.

Jesus clearly warns the disciple who bears disciples that painful divine allowances (pruning) will assist the suffering servant to produce more disciples. This understanding is underlined in John 15:13 when Jesus reminds the disciple that great love is a suffering love—a love that will lay down one's life for others.

Intimacy with Jesus demands suffering with him. This union of purpose, this sharing of sufferings, is what elevates the disciple from servanthood to friendship (John 15:15). When missionaries suffer, it makes them more approachable and more dependent on Jesus. When a disciple (or a seeker) sees a missionary in pain, agony, vulnerability, sickness, and weakness, his or her heart opens to the life and message of the missionary in ways that health, strength, and victory cannot provide. When missionaries suffer with Jesus, it takes the edge off their personality and opens the hearts of listeners to the message. Suffering opens the ears of disciples, particularly when missionaries remain on the field during and despite their suffering—a continuance aided by abiding. Disciples are more impressed by sustained missionary presence through trial than by theoretical ideas presented in seasons of peace and prosperity. When missionaries allow suffering to make them sweeter, it opens the hearts of their disciples to the deep truths of the cross.

Abiding Produces Disciples by Correcting and Refining Missionary Strategy

When missionaries lavish extravagant time on Jesus and commune with him all day long, the Spirit speaks to them, calls them, and shows them what to do. Actions, plans, and methods are either refined or refused when submitted to the Holy Spirit for his input. Padwick notes that Temple Gairdner taught that "in prayer all things are explained."[6] When challenges of doctrine or deployment arise, the best thing the missionary can do is to take that challenge to Jesus and wait for the counsel of the Holy Spirit. A missionary teacher in Sudan said, "I feel any great idea I've had in leadership always comes from him." It is abiding (the patience of waiting on Jesus and listening to the Spirit) that both gives and refines strategy.

Continuance in the word reveals what disciples must obey, and obedience keeps disciples in God's love with the surprising benefit of complete joy. This love (of Jesus for us) and joy (of engaging in what missionaries were created for) gives disciples the power to love one another at great cost. When disciples love one another at great cost, they so endear themselves

6. Padwick, *Temple Gairdner of Cairo*, 142.

to the Father that he promotes them from servants to friends, because they understand his character, his means, and his ends. No longer unthinking, unknowing instruments, disciples now share a sympathetic union with the Father and ascend the heights of partnership in mission with the Lord of the Harvest.[7] This strategic impartation results from disciples lavishing extravagant daily time on Jesus.

Strategic discipleship is inspired when missionaries take the time to individually and communally abide in Christ. Rex Andrews declares that when ministers abide they "come to do naturally what God plans for [their] life no matter where [they] are."[8] "The whole reason we pray is to be united into the vision and contemplation of him to whom we pray."[9] As missionaries abide with Jesus they understand the strategy of the Spirit—a strategy centered on making disciples and a strategy uniquely adjusted for personalities and contexts. John's understanding of abiding realizes the Holy Spirit is the executive of mission and that missionaries who abide in Christ will be best positioned to hear and obey God's strategies of discipleship.

Thornton firmly believed that his missionary strategy came directly from his abiding time. He wrote to his fiancée, "Help me to be true to my past convictions, wrought out on my knees, and in the presence of the life and Book of Christ."[10] Trasher's methodology of discipleship centered on a dissemination of the word from which she daily fed. She wrote, "[The children] are getting the Word of God, and sometime, somewhere it will spring up and bear fruit, if not in them, then in their children. The word of God is alive and will not die. We were not asked to give the results; that is for God to do."[11] Trotter's personal prioritization of daily time in the word and prayer informed all her decision-making. "Lilias put the highest priority on spending time completely alone with God, studying his word with a heart open and receptive to his voice—an activity requiring utmost commitment from her, given the many demands on her time."[12] Comboni did not think abiding only informed strategy; he proposed that it was strategy. "They must pray and have faith, and pray not just with words but with the fire of faith and charity. This is how the undertaking in Africa was planted. This is how our Religion and all the missions in the world were planted."[13]

---

7. Westcott, *The Gospel According to St. John*, 206.

8. Andrews, *What Are You Here For?*, 3.

9. Foster, *Prayer*, 159.

10. Gairdner, *D. M. Thornton*, 66.

11. AGWM, *Letters From Lillian*, 88.

12. Rockness, *A Passion for the Impossible*, 187.

13. Lozano, *The Spirituality of Daniel Comboni*, 101.

Comboni's point was that all missions in the world were planted by the prayers of faith and love—because of them and by them. Zwemer's "prayer and service" were indistinguishable. He did not see prayer as cursory or even a precursor to the task. He viewed prayer as the main task and all other efforts were supplemental. Wilson notes that he told missionaries to Muslims in China that they "dare not be careless in the matter of intercession. All the plans and organizations suggested will be of no avail and will not result in the conversion of one soul to Christ unless it be accompanied by our prayers in the all-prevailing Name of Jesus Christ our Lord."[14] The great, influential missionaries to Muslims believed that abiding not only gave them insight into disciple-making strategy, but abiding was also the primary way disciples were made.

Contemporary missionaries to Muslims testify that abiding increases capacity, quality, creativity, and opportunity in mission. A team leader in Somaliland stated, "Every time I feel a great sense of the Lord really being with me, then I feel there's more to give and share." An American leader reflecting on his ministry to MBBs in Sudan links his success in discipling to his abiding time. "I attribute the opportunities I had to the abiding time I was doing. I just had more opportunities than I ever had before." An American male with the IMB said, "In the work that we do, relationships are the key to success and I think the relationships are less efficient if I'm not abiding." A single woman who is a teacher in a Muslim-dominated elementary school details how abiding led to effective ministry:

> I definitely see the Lord gave me a lot of creative ideas for my classroom that I was able to share the gospel more with the kids . . . The Lord really gave me creativity, and I really felt like I was really sensitive to the Spirit, too. So during that time [favorite season of abiding], I just remember the Spirit directing me so instantaneously in the classroom, and I think that was a direct result of just the sweet time with Jesus that I spent in the mornings.

An American man pointed out the link between the Spirit (leading through prayer) and planning when he said, "I tend to see strategy as something that has coalesced from spiritual things up into your mind." The sequence (abiding preceding the formation of strategy) is critical. A YWAM leader expressed the limitation of strategy outside of abiding when he commented, "I have all these books and teachings and strategies over here, whereas my abiding with Christ says, 'Sometimes we just need to love God and love people and the fruit will come out of that. Our abiding needs

14. Wilson, *Apostle to Islam*, 156.

to come first and our strategy needs to come out of that.'" One AGWM leader admitted, "I have wrestled at times if I am just offering people my knowledge as opposed to my intimacy with the Lord. I have abided in him and found him to be faithful and that he loves me. On that basis I can very much communicate to others." Abiding empowers discipleship strategies. It clears the mind of the missionary of his or her own goals by his or her own means and allows him or her to hear what Jesus is saying about methods and means.

Corporate Abiding Produces Disciples by Exposing Missionaries to the Wider Body of Christ

John writes his gospel with missiological intent to a multicultural audience. In John 15:16, disciples are appointed to bear disciples wherever they go. "Going away, departing" implies multiple contexts and cultures. In the going (making disciples of everyone, everywhere they go, as in Matthew 28:19–20), the disciples who were made also lavish extravagant time on Jesus. Simplistically, Jesus says that all disciples of his everywhere are to abide. Abiding is transcultural. All peoples apply the basic principles of abiding, making accommodations for context.[15] Critically, when corporate abiding happens in multicultural contexts, discipleship is empowered because varied cultural expressions of abiding reveal various aspects of God. No one culture understands God in isolation. The body of Christ needs all ethnolinguistic members to fully understand God. When missionaries abide in multi-cultural settings, they understand God better. With a fuller understanding of God, they better disciple their followers to understand God.

Mission contexts, especially severe ones such as the Islamic world, demand a corporate multi-lateral approach to prayer and service. Gairdner affirms that Thornton "had the privilege of learning how to think and read and work with as much accuracy as possible by contact with many various minds, whose habit it was never to do things by halves, but to take every step after thorough deliberation and constant prayer."[16] Thornton, not a Pentecostal, was deeply impacted by Egyptian Pentecostals in prayer. He felt better prepared to disciple others on account of his own understanding of prayer being stretched by ecstatic prayer. There is a godly jealousy that arises when the Body of Christ interacts. Missionaries from diverse cultures who interact with each other observe variant practices in the other. It makes

15. For example, the centrality of the word and prayer is transcultural. Yet in oral cultures (with high illiteracy rates), the word may be listened to, not read.

16. Gairdner, *D. M. Thornton*, 167.

them hungry to experience the observed reality. An American woman with AGWM in Sudan soberly stated, "I think the whole cross-cultural experience just redefined everything about me. Everything about my life has been redefined including my abiding—how I perceive who the Lord is and what he is in my life, and who he is and what is my point of even being on the mission field." Ongoing multicultural interaction tends to expose the missionaries to one another's strengths. This is most clearly put by an American team leader in Somaliland: "We have been around many Europeans, Africans, and now [my friend] from Peru. [She] makes me jealous in her walk with the Lord . . . because she has a greater intimacy than I do. I think it is a good jealousy." Team leaders surveyed found that the abiding strengths of other cultures provoked a godly jealousy. Team leaders were envious of the strengths (in abiding) they saw in those from other cultures. This envy produced a desire to grow in that aspect of abiding.

Transcultural abiding empowers discipleship primarily by evoking a godly jealousy for how other cultures experience God. The missionary who corporately abides with believers from other cultures is more sensitive to and capable of contextualizing the methods of abiding he or she models to seekers and disciples.

No one missionary understands all there is to know about Jesus. No one culture or sending body has all the wisdom or fullness of the Spirit. Disciples need exposure to the Body of Christ, to believers of different races, cultures, personalities, and perspectives. When teams abide corporately, some things intrinsic to discipleship happen with more regularity than in one-on-one relationships and interaction: vibrant praise, spiritual gifts, prophetic utterances—all are best exercised in group settings. When missionaries and their disciples abide together, the new disciple or pre-disciple learns to praise, prophesy, and move in the gifts of the Holy Spirit by participation. Lecture cannot teach the disciple to move in the charismatic gifts; the gifts must be experienced. Even when the gifts are misused, it is a discipleship opportunity. New disciples learn body ministry by trial and error, guided by loving mentors.

MYSTERY

Abiding mission theory states that abiding leads to disciple making. The cause (abiding) and effect (disciples made) is promised in John 15, but the promise does not remove the necessity of human activity in the process. There is an empirical side and a speculative side to abiding theory. Empirically, missionaries who prove effective in making disciples tend to do so because they abide. The historical phase of this research found this truth with seven diverse figures from 1880 to 1920. General missiology has yet to identify a missionary who was effective in making disciples (that abide) who did not abide personally (though God could certainly allow this if he chooses). Speculatively, not all missionaries' abiding praxis can be studied in depth, nor the extent of their discipleship known. Therefore, an exhaustive claim to an inviolable formula cannot be made. Abiding theory speculates, based on the preponderance of missionary biographies, the current testimony of the church-planting team leaders interviewed, and the promise of Scripture, that abiding in Jesus leads to disciples. There is an element of mystery in how abiding leads to disciples. There is a counterintuitive aspect to the theory that rests on the promise of God and requires the trust of the missionary. The missionary trusts that by spending more time with God (and, by necessity, less time with people), he or she will be more effective in making disciples.

While admitting that abiding mission theory has a mystical component, it is still important and possible to operationalize the theory by speculating on how abiding leads to the making of disciples.

RECOMMENDATIONS

Given the above examples of the operationalization of abiding mission theory (speculation on how abiding leads to disciples), the following recommendations are presented:

1. Every missionary should tithe his or her time. Every missionary should dedicate two-plus hours of the early morning (before any work begins) to lavish extravagant time in Jesus. This time is to be centered on the word of God and prayer but may include other disciplines.

2. Every missionary should rededicate himself or herself to continual communion with Jesus and to a process whereby he or she learns what that means and how to accomplish it in the power of the Holy Spirit.

3. Missionary couples with young children should make provision for the abiding time of the mother. If it is not possible for both parents to have a daily block of abiding time, parents should rotate days so that both are able to have blocks of abiding time.

4. Church-planting teams should structure team activities and schedule to allow for and to empower abiding times. All team meetings should include time for and begin with corporate abiding. This includes

business meetings, leadership training, seminars, and executive meetings. A tithe of the meeting time minimally should be set aside for corporate abiding and waiting on the Lord for the input of the Holy Spirit.

5. Church-planting teams should be intentional about a Sacramental approach to corporate abiding. A Sacramental approach values both a solid biblical base and ecstatic prayer (spiritual gifts, corporate praise, praying in the spirit). A Sacramental approach is also intentional about frequent communion, communal fasts, and corporate confession.

6. Church-planting teams should vigorously and corporately seek fresh fillings of the Holy Spirit.

7. Business as Mission (BAM) platforms should allow time for staff to abide in the morning before they come to work. For example, this could mean the business opens at 10 a.m. rather than 9 a.m.

8. The first thing missionaries need to teach new converts is how to abide in Jesus. Disciplers need to open their abiding time/praxis to the new disciple and not assume they will figure out how to abide by themselves. Abiding needs to be taught and mentored.

9. The first term of new missionaries should be dedicated to spiritual formation, specifically how to abide in Jesus. This term should be three years long and include the language-learning process but should fundamentally be about spiritual formation and learning both the discipline and state of abiding.

10. Mission agencies should insist and encourage personal abiding to be the first priority of the missionary and the base corporate methodology of the mission. Mission agencies should put as much energy and time into corporate abiding as they do into training and orientation.

The more influence a mission leader has, the more time he or she needs to spend abiding and the less time he or she needs to spend in administration, meetings, and projects. Missionaries need to demand that spiritual leaders abide in Jesus increasingly (and systemically provide the means for them) as their responsibilities increase. The mission will only benefit from leadership that is devoted to lavishing extravagant daily time on Jesus.

ITEMS FOR FURTHER RESEARCH

The result of this research is a theory of spirituality that posits missionaries who serve among the Muslim peoples of Egypt and Northern Sudan and abide by continually communing with Jesus and by lavishing extravagant daily time on Jesus make disciples. The state of abiding requires missionaries (and all followers of Christ) to continually commune with Jesus. The discipline of abiding requires missionaries to spend daily blocks of time with Jesus. From abiding with Jesus comes the empowerment of the Spirit to obey him; therefore, abiding should be both the first priority of the missionary and the base corporate methodology for mission. In order to validate and test this theory, the following items are suggested for further research:

- A testing of the theory by operationalizing the concepts and measuring people's level of abiding (high and low) and how it relates to discipleship

- A testing of the theory by examining the abiding praxis of other sampling groups in other locations and religious environments

- A testing of the theory by research of missionary teams' success in making disciples before and after they adopt the abiding praxis defined in this theory

- An investigation of the mechanisms whereby and the extent to which missional abiding impacts work ethic, relational intelligence, leadership capacity, and endurance in persecution

- An investigation of the process by which abiding breaks down the false dichotomy of "be, not do" and integrates spirituality into activity

Of particular interest to Pentecostal mission would be further research into why Pentecostal practice (in the corporate abiding of Pentecostal teams) does not often match up with Pentecostal values as regards the charismatic gifts. This seemingly negative discovery is weighed against the potentially positive unity possible when Pentecostals pray with other evangelicals. Research is needed to discover how Pentecostals can become more Pentecostal (in their private meetings) and more cooperative (in their corporate meetings) at the same time. Both aspects are critical to Pentecostal mission.

Further research could reveal why Pentecostal missionaries—in their zeal and passion—do not last as long on the field as their evangelical counterparts and why they appear better at evangelism and poorer at discipleship than their colleagues. Research in this vein could reveal what Pentecostal missionaries need to learn from non-Pentecostals and suggest ways for ongoing partnership in mission.

CONCLUSION

The aim of mission is to make disciples of every people group on earth. Disciples are not made or matured in isolation; they must be gathered together in churches. John refers to the making of disciples as "bearing fruit" and records Jesus as promising that missionaries and all followers of Christ will make disciples if they abide in him.

This research into the promise of Jesus is based in an epistemological sequence of biblical exegesis, historical reference, social science research (with synthesized findings), and theory development.

The result of this research is a theory of spirituality (abiding mission) which posits missionaries who serve among the Muslim peoples of Egypt and Northern Sudan and abide by continually communing with Jesus and by lavishing extravagant daily time on Jesus make disciples and thereby plant the church. The state of abiding requires missionaries to continually commune with Jesus. The discipline of abiding requires missionaries to spend daily blocks of time with Jesus. Neither the state of abiding nor the discipline is fruitful without the other. Abiding should therefore be both the first priority of the missionary and the base methodology for mission.

If missionaries are going to plant the church among every ethno-linguistic people on earth, the most important thing they can do is to abide in Jesus. David Shenk's concern about a lack of attention to abiding contributed to the launch of this research. His implication is correct—mission methodologies will come and go, but abiding will abide and make disciples.

Appendix A

Semi-structured Interview Guide (Test)

A Research Project to Evaluate the Abiding Praxis of Leaders of Church Planting Teams in the Context of Muslim North Africa, Primarily Egypt and the Sudan

Introduction and Opening Remarks

QUESTION 1: How much time do you spend with Jesus on a daily basis?
   Additional Question: Can you give me some examples of how you spend that time?
   Clarifying Question: Can you expand a little on this?

QUESTION 2: To what extent would you say you commune with Jesus throughout the day?
   Additional Question: Can you give me some examples of how you continually commune with Jesus?
   Clarifying Question: Can you expand a little on this?

QUESTION 3: How much time do you spend with Jesus on a daily basis now compared to five years ago?
   Additional Question: What do you long for in your walk with Jesus?

Clarifying Questions: How would you like your intimate times with Jesus to change? Can you explain that a bit more?

QUESTION 4: How would you characterize your experience of Jesus' abiding in you?

Additional Question: Can you give me some examples of how this happens?

Clarifying Question: How is this different than your abiding in Jesus?

QUESTION 5: How do you abide differently now than when you were single/younger/without children?

Additional Question: Can you give me some examples of how your abiding praxis has changed over the years?

Clarifying Question: Do you have a favorite season of abiding?

QUESTION 6: What role does the Word of God play in your abiding time?

Additional Question: Are there other spiritual disciplines more central to your approach to abiding than the Word of God and prayer?

Clarifying Question: Can you expand a little on this?

QUESTION 7: How has abiding in Jesus affected your capacity for and quality of mission work?

Additional Question: If you do not abide on a certain day, do you notice any causal effect on your production/effectiveness/accomplishment?

Clarifying Questions: Does abiding in Jesus ever limit you? Has this limitation been positive or negative?

QUESTION 8: How does your team abide corporately?

Additional Question: Can you give me some examples of how you spend that time?

Clarifying Question: Can you expand a little on this?

QUESTION 9: What role does solitude and retreat play in your abiding in Jesus?

Additional Question: Can you give me some examples of how you spend that time?

Clarifying Question: How often and for how long do you retreat or take time away from ministry and/or family for these times?

QUESTION 10: How do you avoid legalism in your spiritual disciplines?

Additional Question: Do you set daily goals/times/places for abiding?

Clarifying Question: Do you intentionally seek to extend your daily time with Jesus?

QUESTION 11: How has suffering, difficulty, trouble, or disappointment affected your abiding in Jesus?

Additional Question: When you have experienced trial, trauma, or stress, has it led you to spend more time with Jesus or less?

Clarifying Questions: Can you expand a little on this? Has difficulty in Jesus led you to greater intimacy with Jesus? How exactly has that happened?

QUESTION 12: What have you learned about abiding from those not from your home culture?

Additional Question: What have you learned about abiding from Muslims?

Clarifying Question: Do you abide differently than those in your home culture after your experiences with multinational team members and Muslim friends and neighbors?

QUESTION 13: What do you do when abiding communally that you do not do when abiding privately and vice versa?

Additional Question: How does your team enjoy the presence of Jesus together?

QUESTION 14: How has abiding in Jesus affected your leadership capacity?

Additional Question: Now that you are a leader, is your abiding praxis different than before?

Clarifying Question: Can you expand a little on this?

Additional Question: Has abiding in Jesus helped you to make disciples?

Clarifying Question: Can you expand a little on this?

QUESTION 15: What fruit of the Spirit emerge as a result of your abiding?

Additional Question: What links (if any) are there to you abiding in Jesus and the demonstration of the fruit of the Spirit?

Clarifying Questions: Does quality or quantity of abiding time have any influence on the display of fruit of the Spirit in your life? In what ways?

QUESTION 16: What impact has your personal abiding time had on your church planting strategy?

Additional Question: Can you give me some examples of how your abiding has impacted your strategy?

Clarifying Question: Can you expand a little on this?

Transition

End of Interview

Appendix B

Semi-structured Interview Guide (Kenya)

A Research Project to Evaluate the Abiding Praxis of Leaders of Church Planting Teams in the context of Muslim North Africa, primarily Egypt and the Sudan

Introduction and Opening Remarks

QUESTION 1: How much time do you spend with Jesus on a daily basis?

    Additional Question: Can you give me some examples of how you spend that time?

    Clarifying Question: Can you expand a little on this?

QUESTION 2: What role does the Word of God play in your abiding time?

    Additional Question: Are there other spiritual disciplines more central to your approach to abiding than the Word of God and prayer?

    Clarifying Question: Can you expand a little on this?

QUESTION 3: To what extent would you say you commune with Jesus throughout the day?

    Additional Question: Can you give me some examples of how you continually commune with Jesus?

Clarifying Question: Can you expand a little on this?

QUESTION 4: How much time do you spend with Jesus on a daily basis now compared to five years ago?

Additional Question: What do you long for in your walk with Jesus?

Clarifying Questions: How would you like your intimate times with Jesus to change? Can you explain that a bit more?

QUESTION 5: How would you characterize your experience of Jesus' abiding in you?

Additional Question: Can you give me some examples of how this happens?

Clarifying Question: How is this different than you abiding in Jesus?

Additional Question: Do you see a link between your favorite season of abiding and greater fruitfulness in ministry—disciples made?

QUESTION 6: How do you abide differently now than when you were single/younger/without children?

Additional Question: Can you give me some examples of how your abiding praxis has changed over the years?

Clarifying Question: Do you have a favorite season of abiding?

QUESTION 7: How has abiding in Jesus affected your capacity for and quality of mission work?

Additional Question: If you do not abide on a certain day, do you notice any causal effect on your production/effectiveness/accomplishment?

Clarifying Questions: Does abiding in Jesus ever limit you? Has this limitation been positive or negative?

QUESTION 8: How does your team abide corporately?

Additional Question: Can you give me some examples of how you spend that time?

Clarifying Question: Can you expand a little on this?

QUESTION 9: What role does solitude and retreat play in your abiding in Jesus?

Additional Question: Can you give me some examples of how you spend that time?

Clarifying Question: How often and for how long do you retreat or take time away from ministry and/or family for these times?

QUESTION 10: How do you avoid legalism in your spiritual disciplines?

Additional Question: Do you set daily goals/times/places for abiding?

Clarifying Question: Do you intentionally seek to extend your daily time with Jesus?

QUESTION 11: How has suffering, difficulty, trouble, or disappointment affected your abiding in Jesus?

Additional Question: When you have experienced trial, trauma, or stress, has it led you to spend more or less time with Jesus?

Clarifying Questions: Can you expand a little on this? Has difficulty in Jesus led you to greater intimacy with Jesus? How exactly has that happened?

QUESTION 12: What have you learned about abiding from those not from your home culture?

Additional Question: What have you learned about abiding from Muslims?

Clarifying Question: Do you abide differently than those in your home culture after your experiences with multinational team members and Muslim friends and neighbors?

QUESTION 13: What do you do when abiding communally that you do not do when abiding privately and vice versa?

Additional Question: How does your team together enjoy the presence of Jesus?

QUESTION 14: How has abiding in Jesus affected your leadership capacity?

Additional Question: Now that you are a leader, is your abiding praxis different than before?

Clarifying Question: Can you expand a little on this?

Additional Question: Has abiding in Jesus helped you to make disciples?

Clarifying Question: Can you expand a little on this?

QUESTION 15: What fruit of the Spirit emerge as a result of your abiding?

Additional Question: What links (if any) are there to you abiding in Jesus and the demonstration of the fruit of the Spirit?

Clarifying Questions: Does quality or quantity of abiding time have any influence on the display of fruit of the Spirit in your life? In what ways?

QUESTION 16: What role have dreams played in your intimacy with Jesus?

Additional Question: How has God given you direction through dreams?

Clarifying Question: How has God drawn you closer to himself through dreams?

QUESTION 17: What impact has your personal abiding time had on your church planting strategy?

Additional Question: Can you give me some examples of how your abiding has impacted your strategy?

Clarifying Question: Can you expand a little on this?

Transition

End of Interview

Appendix C

Semi-structured Interview Guide (Sudan & Egypt)

A Research Project to Evaluate the Abiding Praxis of Leaders of Church Planting Teams in the context of Muslim North Africa, primarily Egypt and the Sudan

Introduction and Opening Remarks

QUESTION 1: How much time do you spend with Jesus on a daily basis?

Additional Question: Can you give me some examples of how you spend that time?

Clarifying Question: Can you expand a little on this?

QUESTION 2: What are the central spiritual disciplines for abiding?

Additional Question: Are there other spiritual disciplines more central to your approach to abiding than the Word of God and prayer?

Clarifying Question: What role does the Word of God play in your abiding time?

QUESTION 3: To what extent would you say you commune with Jesus throughout the day?

Additional Question: Can you give me some examples of how you continually commune with Jesus?

Clarifying Question: Can you expand a little on this?

QUESTION 4: How much time do you spend with Jesus on a daily basis now compared to five years ago?

Additional Question: What do you long for in your walk with Jesus?

Clarifying Questions: How would you like your intimate times with Jesus to change? Can you explain that a bit more?

QUESTION 5: How do you abide differently now than when you were single/younger/without children?

Additional Question: Can you give me some examples of how your abiding praxis has changed over the years?

Clarifying Question: Do you have a favorite season of abiding?

QUESTION 6: How would you characterize your experience of Jesus' abiding in you?

Additional Question: Can you give me some examples of how this happens?

Clarifying Question: How is this different than you abiding in Jesus?

Additional Question: Do you see a link between your favorite season of abiding and greater fruitfulness in ministry—disciples made?

QUESTION 7: How has abiding in Jesus affected your capacity for and quality of mission work?

Additional Question: If you do not abide on a certain day, do you notice any causal effect on your production/effectiveness/accomplishment?

Clarifying Questions: Does abiding in Jesus ever limit you? Has this limitation been positive or negative?

QUESTION 8: How does your team abide corporately?

Additional Question: Can you give me some examples of how you spend that time?

Clarifying Question: Can you expand a little on this?

QUESTION 9: What role does solitude and retreat play in your abiding in Jesus?

Additional Question: Can you give me some examples of how you spend that time?

Clarifying Question: How often and for how long do you retreat or take time away from ministry and/or family for these times?

QUESTION 10: How do you avoid legalism in your spiritual disciplines?

Additional Question: Do you set daily goals/times/places for abiding?

Clarifying Question: Do you intentionally seek to extend your daily time with Jesus?

QUESTION 11: How has suffering, difficulty, trouble, or disappointment affected your abiding in Jesus?

Additional Question: When you have experienced trial, trauma, or stress, has it led you to spend more time with Jesus or less?

Clarifying Questions: Can you expand a little on this? Has difficulty in life led you to greater intimacy with Jesus? How exactly has that happened?

QUESTION 12: What have you learned about abiding from those not from your home culture?

Additional Question: What have you learned about abiding from Muslims?

Clarifying Question: Do you abide differently than those in your home culture after your experiences with multinational team members and Muslim friends and neighbors?

QUESTION 13: What do you do when abiding communally that you do not do when abiding privately and vice versa?

Additional Question: How does your team enjoy the presence of Jesus together?

Clarifying Question: What roles do the following play in your communal abiding: prayer walking, food, accountability, prayer over creative access venues, fasting, memorization of Scripture, and/or Bible teaching/study?

QUESTION 14: How has abiding in Jesus affected your leadership capacity?

Additional Question: Now that you are a leader, is your abiding praxis different than before?

Clarifying Question: Can you expand a little on this?

Additional Questions: Has abiding in Jesus helped you to make disciples? Has abiding helped you in evangelism? How?

Clarifying Question: What does abiding look like for BMBs (believers from a Muslim background)?

QUESTION 15: What fruit of the Spirit emerge as a result of your abiding?

Additional Question: What links (if any) are there to your abiding in Jesus and the demonstration of the fruit of the Spirit?

Clarifying Questions: Does quality or quantity of abiding time have any influence on the display of fruit of the Spirit in your life? In what ways? What links do you see between abiding and being baptized in the Holy Spirit?

QUESTION 16: What role have dreams (when sleeping and/or visions) played in your intimacy with Jesus?

Additional Question: How has God given you direction through dreams?

Clarifying Question: How has God drawn you closer to himself through dreams?

QUESTION 17: What impact has your personal abiding time had on your church planting strategy?

Additional Question: Can you give some examples of how your abiding has impacted your strategy?

Clarifying Question: Can you expand a little on this?

QUESTION 18: Who taught you to abide? Did you learn to abide by yourself or were you mentored in abiding?

Additional Question: Can you give some examples of how your abiding has impacted your strategy?

Clarifying Question: Can you expand a little on this?

Transition

End of Interview

Appendix D

Q-Sort Interview Instructions

Q-Sort of Corporate Abiding Factors in the Context of Multinational Church Planting Teams in North African Islamic Contexts

Question Under Consideration:
"What is important when missionary teams gather to abide in Jesus?"

Verbal Instruction:
Each of the 48 index cards contains a spiritual or practical factor that is sometimes viewed as important when a team leader is leading his or her multinational team to abide in Jesus. Please carefully review these spiritual and practical factors, and:

First sort them into three piles: One pile you do often, one pile you do sometimes, one pile you rarely or never do.

Second, begin to place them on the grid, starting with the card representing what you do most often (one card on the far right of the grid, working vertically downward to fill the columns) and the next card from representing what you never do on the far left of the grid.

Sort the cards according to what you actually do together, not what you would like to do or think would be helpful to do.

After your sorting has been recorded[1], a second sort will be conducted. The same guidelines will be followed, but the second sort will be conducted based on what you think is important to do, and whether you do it or not.

Index Cards (with spiritual and practical factors to sort):

1. Silent listening
2. Reading Scripture
3. Upbeat singing
4. Reflective, slow tempo singing
5. Corporate, verbal, individual exaltation and praise of Jesus
6. Praying in turns (around the room, each one prays)
7. Praying in turns (those who feel led to pray, pray)
8. Taking prayer requests and then praying for the mentioned needs
9. Praying silently
10. Praying Scripture
11. Praying for Muslim (or unsaved) friends
12. Praying for Muslim (or unsaved) peoples
13. Praying in chorus (everybody out loud)
14. Praying in small groups
15. Praying in the Spirit (everybody praying in tongues out loud)
16. Sharing about what God is doing in your personal life
17. Testifying about what God has done in the ministry or church planting work
18. Prophecy
19. Tongues and interpretation
20. Confessing (repenting)
21. Feet washing
22. Weeping
23. Laughing
24. Dancing
25. Unusual physical manifestations of the Holy Spirit

1. Responses will be recorded on the pile sorting data collection sheets

26. Worship is done without instruments

27. Worship is by CD or tape

28. Worship is led by team member with guitar or keyboard

29. Communion

30. Affirming one another

31. Words of exhortation

32. Words of rebuke

33. Communal fasts

34. Praying for "word" (insight) for specific individual and relating that word/image/picture to them

35. Meet in the morning

36. Meet in the evening

37. Meet in the middle of the day

38. Children are present

39. Separate meetings for strategy

40. Strategy meeting linked to prayer meeting decisions

41. Meeting is required of all team members

42. Meeting optional for one spouse if family has children

43. Solitude provided for (members scatter for private times of prayer)

44. Meeting times are on a tight schedule (end at a certain time)

45. Meeting times are open-ended (no fixed ending time)

46. Team meets more often (for spiritual practices) in times of crisis or trouble

47. There is a core leadership team that meets for spiritual reasons

48. There is a core leadership team that meets for strategic reasons

Appendix E

Informed Consent Form—Semi-structured Interviews

Research Project:

A Research Project to Evaluate the Abiding Praxis of Leaders of Church Planting Teams in the North African Islamic Context—Particularly Egypt and the Sudan.

The objective of this phase of my study is to discover how the leaders of church planting teams in North African Islamic contexts abide in Jesus. For this purpose, semi-structured interviews will be conducted with key informants. Interviews will last for about one hour and questions will deal with the abiding praxis of team leaders.

For any information about the project or your rights as a participant, you can contact _____, who is acting as the advisor for this phase of my dissertation project at _____ or email at _____.

I, _____, agree to participate in this project in accordance with the following conditions:

The interview I participate in and the information I disclose will be used solely for the purposes defined by the project. Essentially my participation poses no risks to me.

At any time, I can refuse to answer certain questions, discuss certain topics or even decide to stop the interview without prejudice to myself.

To facilitate the interviewer's job, the interview will be recorded and transcribed.

All interview data will be handled so as to protect my identity. Therefore, no names will be mentioned in any written or verbal presentation of the findings and the information will be coded so as to separate my name from the information I provide during the interview.

Respondent's Signature: _____

Date: _____

Interviewer's Signature: _____

Date: _____

Appendix F

Informed Consent Form—Q-Sort Interview

Research Project:

A Research Project to Evaluate How Leaders of Church Planting Teams in the North African Islamic Context, Particularly Egypt and the Sudan, Lead Their Teams in Communal Abiding

The objective of this phase of my study is to learn about how the leaders of church planting teams in North African Islamic contexts lead their teams to abide in Jesus. For this purpose, a Q-sort survey will be conducted with key informants. The procedure will require about forty-five minutes to one hour per person. The Q-sort will examine participants past experiences and present realities expressed in the perceptions, values, and behaviors related to leading teams into communal abiding with Jesus.

For any information about the project or your rights as a participant, you can contact _____ who is acting as the advisor for this phase of my dissertation research at _____ or email at _____.

I, _____, agree to participate in this project in accordance with the following conditions:

The Q-sort survey I participate in and the information I disclose will be used solely for the purposes defined by the project. Essentially my participation poses no risks to me.

At any time, I can refuse to answer certain questions, discuss certain topics, or even decide to stop the interview without prejudice to myself.

I understand that in order to facilitate the interviewer's job, the interviewer will take notes during the survey.

All Q-sort data will be treated as confidential information so as to protect my identity. Therefore, no names will be mentioned in any written or verbal presentation of the findings and the information will be coded so as to separate my name from the information I provide during the interview.

Respondent's Signature: _____

Date: _____

Interviewer's Signature: _____

Date: _____

Appendix G

Socio-Demographic Participant Form (Kenya)

Semi-structured Interviews and Q-sort Interviews
(To be completed by interviewer)

Participant ID: QS1/QS2/SST _____

Date of interview: _____ Time: _____
am/pm

Interview venue: _____

Age: _____ years

Gender: male/female

Nationality: _____

Ministry title: _____

Place of ministry: _____

Organization / missions agency: _____

Years of ministry experience: _____(years)

Years of missions experience in the Muslim world: _____(years)

Years of experience as leader of a CP team: _____(years)

Number of people on the team: _____(team members)

Nationalities represented on the team: _____

Number of MBBs you have played a role in discipling: _____(disciples)

Number of MBBs you are currently discipling: _____(disciples)

Number of Muslims you have close relationship with: _____(Muslims)

Number of Muslims you are pre-discipling (evangelizing, storying): _____(Muslims)

Completed education: High School/Bachelors/Masters/Doctoral degree

Appendix H

Socio-Demographic Participant Form (Sudan & Egypt)

Semi-structured Interviews and Q-sort Interviews

(To be completed by interviewer)

1. Participant ID: QS1/QS2/SST _____

2. Date of interview: _____

3. Time: _____am/pm

4. Interview venue: _____

5. Age: _____ (years)

6. Gender: male/female

7. Preferred language used during abiding times: _____

8. Nationality: _____

9. Marital status: _____

10. Ministry title: _____

11. Place of ministry: _____

12. Organization / missions agency: _____

13. Denomination: _____

14. Believe baptism of Holy Spirit subsequent to salvation: Yes: ___No:___

15. Years of ministry experience: _____(years)

16. Years of missions experience in the Muslim world: _____(years)

17. Years of experience as leader of a CP team: _____(years)

18. Number of people on the team: _____(team members)

19. Nationalities represented on the team: _____

20. Number of MBBs you have played a role in discipling: _____(disciples)

21. Number of MBBs you are currently discipling: _____(disciples)

22. Number of Muslims you have close relationship with: _____(Muslims)

23. Number of Muslims you are pre-discipling (evangelizing, storying): ___ (Muslims)

24. Completed education: High School/Bachelors/Masters/Doctoral degree

Appendix I

Self-Administered Electronic Survey

SECTION 1: Personal and Background Information

1. Age?
2. Gender?
3. Nationality?
4. Highest degree earned?
    a. High school diploma
    b. Technical training
    c. Associates degree or post-high school diploma
    d. University degree (BA or BS)
    e. Masters degree
    f. Doctoral degree
    g. Other _____
5. Mission agency?
6. Sending church/denomination?
7. Country where you were part of a church planting team?
8. Time on that team?

    _____ years and

    _____ months

9. Time in the Muslim world?

    _____ years and

    _____ months

10. What is your preferred or customary language of prayer (not in reference to praying in tongues)?

11. What is your preferred or customary language for Bible reading for your personal abiding time?

12. Do you believe that the baptism in the Holy Spirit . . .
    a. Happens at salvation
    b. Happens AT salvation and is then repeated
    c. Happens AFTER salvation and is repeated
    d. Other: _____

13. Number of Muslims considered to be good friends:
    a. 0
    b. 1–5
    c. 6–10
    d. 10–25
    e. 25–50
    f. Over 50

14. Number of Muslims with whom you shared enough of the gospel that they could have come to faith in Christ (or did):
    a. 0
    b. 1–5
    c. 6–10
    d. 10–25
    e. 25–50
    f. Over 50

15. Number of Muslims you pre-discipled (pre-conversion)?
    a. 0
    b. 1–5
    c. 6–10
    d. 10–25
    e. 25–50
    f. Over 50

16. Number of Muslims you discipled (post-conversion)?
    a. 0
    b. 1–5
    c. 6–10
    d. 10–25
    e. 25–50
    f. Over 50

17. Number of house churches you helped to start?
    a. 0
    b. 1–5
    c. 6–10

  d. 10–25

  e. 25–50

  f. Over 50

SECTION 2: Impact of Team Leader's Abiding Activities on Team Member

18. As far as you can tell, how much time did your team leader(s) spend in set abiding times with Jesus on a daily basis?

  a. Little (less than 30 minutes)

  b. Moderate (30–60 minutes)

  c. Much (1–2 hours)

  d. Extravagant (more than 2 hours)

  e. I don't know

19. What was the most important aspect of abiding in Jesus for your team leader(s)?

  a. Bible reading

  b. Prayer

  c. Bible reading and prayer combined

  d. Worship

  e. Journaling

  f. Other: _____

  g. I don't know

20. If possible, describe how your team leader(s) walked with Jesus all day long. (If you do not know, just type "not sure.")

21. During the time I was on the team, my team leader(s) grew in his or her abiding time and intimacy with Jesus:

  a. In no noticeable way

  b. A little

  c. Quite a bit

  d. Greatly

22. In John 15, Jesus says, "If you abide in me, and I in you, you will bear much fruit." Describe ways in which you observed Jesus living in and through your team leader(s).

23. Describe a time when your team leader did not do something he or she planned to do as a direct result of abiding in Jesus.

On questions 24–27 rank in order of importance for your team's corporate practice of abiding in Jesus (1 is always most important).

24. Scripture and prophetic words (rank from 1 to 7 with 1 being most important):
    a. Reading Scripture
    b. Praying Scripture
    c. Prophecy
    d. Tongues and interpretation
    e. Affirming one another
    f. Words of exhortation
    g. Words of rebuke

25. Praise and Body Ministry (rank from 1 to 17 with 1 being most important):
    a. Silent listening
    b. Upbeat singing
    c. Reflective, slow tempo singing
    d. Corporate, verbal, exaltation of Jesus
    e. Sharing about what God is doing in your personal life
    f. Testifying about what God has done in the ministry/CP work
    g. Confessing (repenting)
    h. Feet washing
    i. Communion
    j. Communal fasts
    k. Weeping
    l. Laughing
    m. Dancing
    n. Unusual physical manifestations of the Holy Spirit
    o. Worship is done without instruments
    p. Worship is by CD/tape
    q. Worship is led by team member with guitar or keyboard

26. Prayer (rank from 1 to 11 with 1 being most important):
    a. Praying in turns (around the room, each one prays)
    b. Praying in turns (those who feel led to pray, pray)
    c. Taking prayer requests and then praying for the mentioned needs
    d. Praying silently
    e. Praying for Muslim (or unsaved) friends
    f. Praying for Muslim (or unsaved) peoples
    g. Praying in chorus (everybody out loud)
    h. Praying in small groups
    i. Praying in the Spirit (everybody praying in tongues out loud)
    j. Praying for "word" (insight) for specific individual and relating that word/image/picture to them

k. Providing time of solitude (members scatter for private times of prayer)

27. Meetings (rank from 1 to 13 with 1 being most important):
    a. Meet in the morning
    b. Meet in the evening
    c. Meet in the middle of the day
    d. Children are present
    e. Separate meetings for strategy
    f. Strategy meeting linked to prayer meeting decisions
    g. Meeting is required of all team members
    h. Meeting optional for one spouse if family has children
    i. Meeting times are on a tight schedule (end at a certain time)
    j. Meeting times are open ended (no fixed ending time)
    k. Team meets more often (for spiritual practices) in times of crisis or trouble
    l. A core leadership team that meets for spiritual reasons
    m. A core leadership team that meets for strategic reasons

28. Which of the above corporate practices (Questions 24–27) of abiding in Jesus were the three most important for you?
    a.
    b.
    c.

29. What did you perceive to be most important to your team leader(s) during team meetings? Rank from 1 to 7 with 1 being most important:
    a. Abiding in Jesus
    b. Strategy
    c. Fellowship and games
    d. Business and logistics
    e. Missiology and methodology
    f. Language and culture
    g. Other: _____

30. Which of the following did your team (when together) spend the most time doing?
    a. Abiding in Jesus
    b. Strategy
    c. Fellowship and games
    d. Business and logistics
    e. Missiology and methodology
    f. Language and culture
    g. Other: _____

31. List in order of what you perceived to be of most importance (rank from 1 to 7 with 1 being most important:
    a. Abiding in Jesus
    b. Strategy
    c. Fellowship and games
    d. Business and logistics
    e. Missiology and methodology
    f. Language and culture
    g. Other: _____

32. Which of the following did your team do corporately? Tick all that apply.
    a. Prayer walking
    b. Share meals
    c. Practice accountability
    d. Prayer over creative access venues (pray at location of platform)
    e. Fasting
    f. Memorization of Scripture
    g. Bible teaching (study)

33. The abiding in Jesus of your team leader(s) clearly and positively impacted your team's church planting:

    (Likert Scale with progression from "Strongly Disagree" to "Strongly Agree" with a space for "Explain: _____")

34. The abiding in Jesus of your team leader(s) positively impacted your own abiding in Jesus practices:

    (Likert Scale with progression from "Strongly Disagree" to "Strongly Agree" with a space for "Explain: _____")

35. Your team leader(s) modeled abiding in Jesus for you:

    (Likert Scale with progression from "Strongly Disagree" to "Strongly Agree" with a space for "Explain: _____")

36. Your team leader(s) specifically taught you how to abide in Jesus:

    (Likert Scale with progression from "Strongly Disagree" to "Strongly Agree" with a space for "Explain: _____")

37. Your team leader(s) took time to corporately abide in Jesus during team meetings:

    (Likert Scale with progression from "Strongly Disagree" to "Strongly Agree" with a space for "Explain: _____")

38. Your team leader(s) prioritized abiding in Jesus in his or her personal schedule:

    (Likert Scale with progression from "Strongly Disagree" to "Strongly Agree" with a space for "Explain: _____")

39. Your team leader(s) encouraged you to prioritize abiding in Jesus in your personal schedule:

    (Likert Scale with progression from "Strongly Disagree" to "Strongly Agree" with a space for "Explain: _____")

40. What was most important to your team leader(s) when he or she was accepting new team members? List in order of what you perceived to be important (rank from 1 to 5 with 1 being most important):
    a. Character
    b. Competency
    c. Maturity
    d. Calling
    e. Other: _____

41. How important was abiding in Jesus to your team leader(s):
    a. More important than ministry activities
    b. Equal in importance to ministry activities
    c. Less important than ministry activities

42. What have you learned from observing how your team leader(s) abides in Jesus?

Appendix J

14 Critical Aspects of Abiding from John 15:1–17

1. ABIDING IS BOTH REGULAR AND CONTINUAL.[1]

A SPIRITUAL THEOLOGY OF abiding posits that abiding is both a daily set period of extravagant time (regular and disciplined) that is lavished on Jesus and a continual fellowship with him all day long. Abiding is both a discipline (extravagant daily blocks of time with Jesus centered on the word and prayer) and a state (ongoing communion and obedience throughout the day).

The verb μείνατε in the aorist, active, imperative, second person plural sense means, according to Johannes Louw and Eugene Nida, to "remain in the same place over a period of time . . . to stay."[2] Buist M. Fanning says, "The constative aorist [is] used to heighten the urgency of the command and [calls] for customary or general occurrence."[3] According to F. Hauck's article cited by Gerhard Kittel and Gerhard Freidrich, the intransitive use of μένειν means "remain in a place," "tarry," or "dwell."[4] Taken together, abiding is to remain in one place over an extended period of time in habitual

---

1. The regular lavishing of extravagant time with Jesus means the most generous, consistent, and focused investing of the disciple's best time in the most attentive way. Continual means to commune with Jesus all day long and to obey him in all things.

2. Louw and Nida, "μένω," in Greek-English Lexicon,

3. Fanning, Verbal Aspect in New Testament Greek, 369–70.

4. Kittel and Freidrich, "μένω," in Theological Dictionary of the New Testament.

(customary) practice. This regular encounter is linked directly to Jesus, thus abiding first means lavishing extravagant daily time on Jesus. Explicitly, abiding is a continuance with Jesus all day long. Implicitly, abiding calls for fixed and extended daily focused times. Followers of Jesus from around the world and across the centuries prove this premise.

> The Covenant of Time means a commitment to a regular experience of prayer. In his Rule St. Benedict insisted on regularity in prayer because he did not ever want his followers to forget who was in charge . . . Benedict would call for prayer at regular intervals throughout the day—right in the middle of apparently urgent and important work. We, too, will find that a commitment to regular prayer will defeat self-importance and the wiles of the devil . . . The Hebrew pattern was three times a day—morning, afternoon, and evening.[5]

Foster advocates that abiding is regular and disciplined and even localized. "Find a place of focus—a loft, a garden, a spare room, an attic, even a designated chair—somewhere away from the routine of life, out of the path of distractions. Allow this spot to become a sacred 'tent of meeting.'"[6] Bonhoeffer, in his seminary, understood abiding to have a daily rhythm and "emphasized a strict daily routine and the spiritual disciplines."[7] Rex Andrews encouraged a daily period of two hours with the Lord. He writes:

> One value to this Eight-to-Ten Prayer period is that it gives an opportunity for you to develop a basic habit. You need to have a basic habit in which a prayer time is INVIOLABLE, SACRO-SANCT, BELONGS TO GOD. In your ministry there might sometime have to be a re-adjustment of that time; or if you should happen to be working somewhere daily, you might have to change the hours that you pray—but you need to have a habit of spending two hours a day in prayer.[8]

Daily extravagant time lavished on Jesus is integral to abiding. Extravagant time is difficult for some stages of life and professions. In reference to this challenge to mothers with small children, Richard Foster says,

> We must be careful here not to lay impossible burdens on people . . . This time will pass . . . Discover God in your times with your baby. God will become real to you through your baby. The

---

5. Foster, *Prayer*, 72–73.

6. Ibid., 75.

7. Metaxas, *Bonhoeffer*, 267.

8. Andrews, *What Are You Here For?*, 9.

times with your baby are your prayer. You may be able to pray during feeding time—this is especially true for nursing mothers–so sing your prayers to the Lord . . . Once we have made generous latitude for individual differences and schedules, we must firmly discipline ourselves to a regular pattern of prayer. We cannot assume that time will somehow magically appear. We will never have time for prayer—we must make time. On this score we have to be ruthless with our rationalization. We must never, for instance, excuse our prayerlessness under the guise of "always living prayerfully." John Dalrymple rightly observes: "The truth is that we only learn to pray all the time everywhere after we have resolutely set about praying some of the time somewhere."[9]

Abiding balances "a generous latitude for individual differences" and "ruthlessness with our rationalization." Dalrymple's caution is well taken. The all-day communion with Jesus is an incomplete abiding if it is not anchored in specific, regular, focused, and extravagant time. To avoid the "spiritual greed" to which mystics are prone, extravagant time can only be sustained in the context of a healthy life. Healthy prayer comes from a healthy and balanced lifestyle. Foster explains:

Healthy prayer necessitates frequent experiences of the common, earthly, run-of-the-mill variety. Like walks, and talks, and good wholesome laughter. Like work in the yard, and chitchat with neighbors, and washing windows. Like loving our spouse, and playing with our kids, and working with our colleagues. To be spiritually fit to scale the Himalayas of the spirit, we need regular exercise in the hills and valleys of ordinary life.[10]

Abiding is not only extended and regular daily times with Jesus, but also is walking in communion with Jesus all day long.[11] John's use of abiding indicates lengthy daily times with Jesus as well as a continual connection to Him. Essential viticulture reveals that both of these understandings have precedent in the health of the vine. When grapevines are grown, there is a certain minimum period of rest that is essential to their long-term health.

9. Quoted in Foster, *Prayer*, 74.

10. Ibid., x.

11. Regarding Jesus' devotional life, Richard Foster affirms, "He went up to the synagogue on the Sabbath . . . No doubt Jesus embraced the two disciplines of every faithful Jew: recite the Shema twice a day and observe the three hours of prayer—morning, afternoon, and sundown . . . When Jesus told his disciples to abide in him like a branch abides in the vine they instantly understood what he meant, for they had watched for years his abiding with the Father (John 15:1–11)." Foster, *Prayer*, 106, 121.

They do not constantly produce fruit, nor do they constantly grow. A dormant period is necessary for a process of renewal, which leads to effective fruit bearing.

The dormant period, into which the vine now lapses with the shedding of its leaves, is necessary for the production of good grapes. When grapevines are grown in tropical or subtropical regions, which have no winter, they become evergreens. This unaccustomed evergreen habit lures them into fatal inconsistencies—shoots are put forth, flowers are blossom, and fruit ripens all at the same time. The result is a small continuous production of worthless fruit accompanied by a tremendous burst of vegetative activity and an early death. That period of rest is necessary (for some reason). The experience of those who raise grapes in hothouses furthers the point. No matter how high one turns the heat on, hothouse vines resolutely refuse to grow at all once they lapse into their dormant period and have had their minimum period of rest.[12]

In addition to a significant minimum period of rest on a repeated basis, vines also need a minimum period of daily energy production to thrive.

> All organic matter in the vine is ultimately provided by photosynthesis, one of the most significant of all life processes . . . 6 moles of Carbon dioxide, 12 moles of water, and 673,000 calories of [light] energy yield 1 mole of glucose, 6 moles of molecular oxygen, and 6 moles of water . . . From the sugar produced, other compounds found in the vine are metabolized . . . A leaf is light saturated at 2500–5000 foot-candles (ft-c). On a clear day there can be 12,000 ft-c of light. At 125 ft-c the compensation point is reached, where the amount of food manufactured in photosynthesis is just equal to that lost by respiration.[13]

In practical terms (based on a capacity of 2500 ft-c), a leaf must have 125 ft-c to have input match output five percent. Survival based on photosynthesis draws a demand of five percent of the day. For the vine to grow and produce fruit, this percentage must increase. Survival for a vine requires an absolute minimum of five percent of its capacity being effective in the photosynthesis process. Growth and fruit bearing require a higher percentage. A tithe of a disciple's day (144 minutes or 2 hours and 24 minutes) is more than enough time to be renewed. Disciples believe in the tithe principle for their finances, a spiritual theology of abiding proposes that tithing their time involves similar principles.

12. Wagner, *A Wine-Grower's Guide*, 93.

13. Weaver, *Grape Growing*, 29–30.

In the fourth to the sixteenth centuries, breath prayers were common. These prayers were one sentence heart longings that were addressed to the Lord multiple (hundreds) of times a day. Isaac the Syrian said, "When the Spirit has come to reside in someone, that person cannot stop praying, for the Spirit prays without ceasing in him. No matter if he is asleep or awake, prayer is going on in his heart all the time."[14] Brother Lawrence attempted to practice the presence of God all day long. Frank Laubach attempted a

> *Game with Minutes,* in which he sought to see how many min-
> utes in a day he could become conscious of God's presence.
> On New Year's Day 1937 he wrote, "God, I want to give you
> every minute of this year. I shall try to keep you in mind every
> moment of my waking hours." On another occasion he notes,
> "God, after a sleepless night, I open my eyes, laughing, for we
> are together!"[15]

A spiritual theology of abiding suggests that abiding consists of both a daily (regular and extended) period of extravagant communion with Jesus and a conscious interaction with Him all day long.

2. ABIDING IS BOTH A JOURNEY AND A DESTINATION.

Jesus spoke the opening words of his teaching on abiding, ἐγώ εἰμι ἡ ἄμπελος ἡ ἀληθινὴ (John 15:1), to state the parameters for his teaching on abiding and fruit bearing. Jesus is the true grapevine—the only source of life. By declaring himself the true grapevine, "Jesus displaces Israel as the focus of God's plan of salvation."[16]

The grapevine in the intertestamental period also took on national significance. "The emblem on the coins of the Maccabees was the vine . . . It was the very symbol of the nation of Israel."[17] The temple mount also included a graven grapevine—the Golden Vine—clearly visible to all who approached the temple to worship. Jesus, knowing the importance of the imagery of the vine (nationally, religiously, historically, scripturally) and seeing it again (either a literal vineyard, the Golden Vine of the temple mount, or even the fruit of the vine at the Last Supper) redefined its symbolic meaning. Jesus declares that he alone is the source and center of life. John quotes Jesus using

14. Foster, *Prayer,* 119.

15. Ibid., 33.

16. Kostenberger, *John,* 448.

17. Barclay, *The Gospel of John,* 201.

the nominative singular feminine article and adjective ἡ ἀληθινὴ to imply all other vines are false or incomplete sources of life and that only Jesus can truly give life.

Abiding is both a fixed and a continuous event. It is by definition both a journey and a destination. On the one hand, disciples are continually learning to be with Jesus (because disciples are hungry for divine life and all other sources leave them empty) and, on the other hand, disciples are already content to be with Him (because He gives so much life). Disciples are both satisfied and fulfilled in His presence and desperate for more of Him at the same time. Abiding is both a destination and an arrival. "Both spirituality and psychology (as originally conceived) are concerned with the functioning of the human soul/spirit on its journey to wholeness and maturity."[18] Disciples are ever at home, even as they always journey.

> Contemplative prayer keeps us home, rooted and safe, even when we are on the road, moving from place to place, and often surrounded by sounds of violence and war. Contemplative prayer deepens us in the knowledge that we are already free, that we have already found a place to dwell, that we already belong to God, even though everything and everyone around us keep suggesting the opposite.[19]

Abiding is to dwell (remain) and to walk (grow/move) at the same time. Rex Andrews says, "We are . . . to learn to: dwell in His presence, use [our] time to redeem the time, live and walk in the Spirit, live in daily grace, live the inward life of a life turned toward God all the time, and live a faith life."[20] In this sense, disciples are always learning to abide even as they are at rest. "At the micro-level . . . we recycle through the seasons or phases repeatedly . . . The spiritual journey pictorially might be represented as an upward trending, outwardly expanding spiral movement. Hardly ever does spiritual growth and fruit-bearing advance in linear fashion consisting of a series of static states."[21] Nouwen said,

> If there is any focus that the Christian leader of the future will need, it is the discipline of dwelling in the presence of the One who keeps asking us, "Do you love me? Do you love me?" . . . The central question is, Are the leaders of the future really men and women of God, people with an ardent desire to dwell in

18. Demarest, "Reflections," 151.
19. Nouwen, *In the Name of Jesus*, 43.
20. Andrews, *What Are You Here For?*, 31.
21. Demarest, "Reflections," 164–65.

God's presence, to listen to God's voice, to look at God's beauty, to touch God's incarnate Word, and to taste fully of God's infinite goodness?[22]

A spiritual theology of abiding is both at rest and ever moving. To abide is to be completely satisfied with Jesus and insatiably hungry for more of him at the same time.

3. ABIDING IS RECIPROCAL.

The phrase κἀγὼ ἐν ὑμῖν (and I in you) implies that abiding is reciprocal. Disciples not only lavish extravagant daily time on Jesus, but he, in turn, lavishes extravagant daily attention on them. Lussier develops the concept of mutual abiding:

> The Johannine use of the verb to abide introduces us to the Johannine theology of immanence, that is, a remaining in one another that binds together Father, Son, and the Christian believer . . . [The] concept of reciprocal indwelling . . . this indwelling is not the exclusive experience of chosen souls within the Christian community; it is the essential constitutive of all Christian life.[23]

For disciples to abide in Jesus is to have him abide in disciples. Union with Christ implies a reciprocal indwelling, an exchange that forms disciples' character. This reciprocal abiding is modeled in the Trinity. Miroslav Volf states, "[I]nternal abiding and interpenetration of the Trinitarian persons . . . determines the character of both the divine persons and of their unity."[24] Disciples cannot abide in him if he is not, in turn, living in them. As disciples give Jesus extravagant and ongoing attention, he grows in them as they grow in him. Living with Jesus determines character—it makes disciples more like him.

> The command in Ephesians 5 to be filled . . . with the Spirit is . . . a present passive imperative . . . [The] person is not primarily commanded to do something but to allow something to be done or happen to the person. In this case, the verb could be translated as a command to allow yourselves to be acted upon or influenced by another person ("be continuously acted upon or filled by the Holy Spirit") . . . Consequently, the whole of our

22. Nouwen, *In the Name of Jesus*, 42–43.

23. Lussier, *God Is Love*, 36, 38.

24. Volf, *After Our Likeness*, 208.

spiritual life is a kind of openness to another person, an allowing ourselves to be acted upon by the Spirit of God. It involves the practice of watching, sometimes waiting, and listening for the Spirit . . . This is merely the logical, common-sense response to the reality of the Living God having revealed Himself both in His Word and by His Indwelling presence.[25]

This passive nature of abiding is crucial if disciples are to submit to the re-forming acts of the living God within them and to allow his power to trans-form their behavior and perspective. Abiding, then, is not only the active work of consciously daily placing oneself in Christ, but also the submissive yielding to his acts internally as "we both act and are acted upon."[26] Abid-ing has the duality of reciprocation. "In John, these are two sides to the same coin: a person bears fruit only through the union with and abiding in Christ, which means that one bears no fruit apart from that abiding."[27] True union combines the discipline of choosing to give Jesus extravagant daily time and allowing him to constantly enliven mortal bodies through his life and power. Jesus, too, seeks to abide with his disciples.

4. ABIDING IS IDIOSYNCRATIC.

The text of John 15:1–17 mentions three different types of branches. Branches refer to disciples. Disciples are similar in that they all connect to the grapevine, but different in that they have unique responsiveness to the grapevine and different treatments by the vinedresser. Some disciples do not make disciples. Because their hearts are right, God will lift them up (αἴρειν) and nurture them by training them to abide. Some disciples are making disciples. These disciples will go through a "pruning/cleansing" process that will grant them the capacity to bear many disciples (as long as they continue to lavish extravagant daily time on Jesus). Other disciples refuse to lavish extravagant daily time on Jesus and wither (ἐξηράνθη). This withering leads to a falling out (ἐβλήθη) into a place of judgment and marginalization.

Different responses to the grapevine (by disciples) and different treatments of disciples (by Jesus) imply both seasonal and personal flex-ibility. God relates to people both individually and corporately. He interacts uniquely with disciples, even as his character and nature holds some prin-ciples inviolate for all. A spiritual theology of abiding accommodates the breadth of God's ability to interact with His children individually.

25. Coe, "Spiritual Theology," 30.

26. Foster, *Prayer*, 98.

27. Billings, *Union with Christ*, 36.

There is no "one brand fits all" pattern of growth that accommodates every saint in every respect. Since the sovereign God deals
with His children uniquely (within of course, the parameters
of the Gospel), no two saints travel identical paths. With God,
as Friedrich von Hugel (1852–1925) stated, there are no dittos
. . . Movement occurs through flexible seasons rather that fixed
states.[28]

The flexible seasons von Hugel mentions are also applicable to varied personalities. Willett quotes Benedict J. Groeschel while linking the common
journey and the personal experience. "We all take the same journey and
must pass through similar stages and ways. But like travelers across a continent, we have different experiences of the same reality."[29] Willett continues,
"[Each] of us will pass through the same stages in the same order but not
in the same way. There are substantial differences among believers as to
when and how stages are experienced. Spiritual growth may be triggered by
unique life experiences, significant events, and turning points that do not
occur at any predictable or scheduled time."[30]
Abiding, then, is not so much a methodology as a paradigm. Demarest
quotes Phil Zylla as he describes a paradigm as

. . . a set of assumptions, concepts, values, and practices that
constitutes a way of viewing reality for the community that
shares them, especially in an intellectual discipline.
    Paradigms are flexible but settled sets of core convictions
that are derived from living with ambiguity, practicing displacement, and managing complex, and often competing, bodies of
information . . . paradigms have the simplicity that a child could
accept but are layered with deep, symbolic understandings and
function as at the ontological level.[31]

Abiding has the simplicity that a child can accept and the layered (individual interaction) that functions differently for different children of God.
The simplicity of abiding is in its two essential components: extravagant
daily times with Jesus that are fixed and regular and continual communion
with the Lord all day long. The complexity of abiding is how those times
(both fixed and continual) are idiosyncratically experienced. Obedience is
critical to abiding. What Jesus asks of one Christian may be radically different from what he asks of another. Not all missionaries are granted the same

28. Demarest, "Reflections," 166–67.
29. Willett, "A Biblical Model," 100.
30. Ibid., 100.
31. Demarest, "Reflections," 150–51.

fruit (nature or scope), but all missionaries are exhorted to obey, to abide by the injunctions of their Lord.

5. ABIDING IS BASED ON MEDITATION ON THE WORD OF GOD AND PRAYER.

John declares the strategic role of the words of Jesus in the formative and reproductive processes. In light of the promised cleansing ("every branch that bears fruit he cleans"), Jesus explains this cleansing process as ongoing due to the disciple's exposure to his teaching. Those that heed and apply the words of Jesus will continually be prepared and used to bear fruit. In John 15:7, Jesus indicates that the central disciplines to abiding are linked to the word of God and prayer. When Jesus' words abide (dwell extravagantly) in His disciples as a complement to them lavishing extravagant daily time on Jesus, the result is answered prayer.

A noun in the nominative case that is plural and neuter, ῥήματά, refers to "a minimal unit of discourse, often a single word."[32] "This is how we remain in Jesus: by receiving and permanently holding . . . his utterances, the ῥήματά that come from his lips. He in us, and we in him, the medium and bond of his spiritual union being his spoken word."[33] When Jesus' ῥήματά (words) abide in His disciples, they can ask what they desire and have it done—γενήσεται ὑμῖν (literally, "it shall come to pass for you"). Extravagant daily time with Jesus is linked in John 15:7 to extravagant dwelling in Jesus' words and prayer.

While "[Christians] can never dictate the means of God's grace,"[34] they can carefully observe the teaching of Scripture as lived out by the progression of those who have gone ahead of us. "Prayer—secret, fervent, believing prayer—lies at the root of all personal godliness."[35] Those who have dedicated themselves to the Word of God and prayer (Acts 6) bore fruit and those who have not withered. Athanasius warned,

> The presence and love of the Word had called them into being; inevitably, therefore when they lost the knowledge of God, they lost existence with it . . . God . . . also graciously bestowed on them His own life by the grace of the Word . . . The grace of their union with the Word made them capable of escaping from the

32. Louw and Nida, "ῥήματά," in *Greek English Lexicon*.

33. Lenski, *The Interpretation of St. John's Revelation*, 1,040.

34. Foster, *Prayer*, 34.

35. Ibid., 57.

natural law . . . That is to say, the presence of the Word with them
shielded them from natural corruption.[36]

Dietrich Bonhoeffer felt the need for the church to focus on Bible
reading and prayer.

> [He] longed to see a church that had an intimate connection
> with Christ and was dedicated to hearing God's voice and obey-
> ing God's commands, come what may, including the shedding
> of blood. But how could one hear the voice of God, much less
> obey God, when prayer and meditating on the Scriptures were
> not even being taught in German seminaries?[37]

Eric Metaxas includes a letter from Bonhoeffer to Karl Barth (who was
concerned about legalism in the disciplines that Bonhoeffer practiced
and taught), in which Bonhoeffer states: "It is, though, certain that both
theological work and real pastoral fellowship can only grow in a life which
is governed by gathering around the Word morning and evening and by
fixed times of prayer."[38] Demarest notes the Franciscan Bonaventure was
like-minded:

> We cannot rise above ourselves unless a higher power lifts us up.
> No matter how much our interior progress is ordered, nothing
> will come of it unless accompanied by divine aid. Divine aid
> is available to those who seek it from their hearts, humbly and
> devoutly; and this means to sigh for it in this valley of tears,
> through fervent prayer. Prayer, then, is the mother and source
> of the ascent.[39]

Andrew Murray in his reflections on abiding in Christ adds his concurrence
on the central role of Bible reading and prayer.

> It is still and waits in holy silence until all is calm and ready to
> receive the revelation of the divine will and presence. Its reading
> and prayer then become a waiting on God with ear and heart
> open and purged to receive fully only what He says. Abide in
> Christ! Let no one think that he can do this if he does not daily
> have his quiet time, his seasons of meditation and waiting on
> God. In these a habit must be cultivated in which the believer
> goes out into the world and its distractions with the peace of

---

36. Athanasius, *On the Incarnation*, 30.

37. Metaxas, *Bonhoeffer*, 2,010.

38. Ibid., 271.

39. Demarest, "Reflections," 156–57.

God that passes all understanding keeping the heart and mind
(Phil. 4.7).[40]

Foster links the purpose of prayer to abiding. "[Prayer] changes us . . .
The primary purpose of prayer is to bring disciples into such a life of communion with the Father that, by the power of the Spirit, we are increasingly
conformed to the image of the Son."[41] Andrews concurs and establishes the
core of interaction with Jesus as being prayer and Bible-based. He writes,

> The [abiding time] is for Bible and Prayer . . . . You can use that
> Prayer Period in whatever way your heart dictates. But be sure
> that you have asked the Lord to direct your heart, so that your
> heart dictates right! What do I mean by prayer? . . . Waiting
> on the Lord. If you do that, He will put prayers in your heart
> to pray, and you will pray in the Will of God; you will pray in
> the Spirit . . . The [abiding time] is there to help you REDEEM
> YOUR TIME.[42]

Andrews also underlines the importance of Bible reading in the spiritual
formation process as the primary instrument God uses to shape minds.

> I should read the Bible, not to find a text to develop into some
> kind of talk, but just to read the Bible to let the Bible mold my
> mind . . . You need a hunger for the Word, which the Lord can
> utilize to overthrow the devil in your life, who will come against
> you to try to take you away from prayer, and try to get you not
> to be circumspect, and not to use your time, to not redeem your
> time, and to not be hungry for the Word of God. The Lord bless
> you, if you have hunger for the Word of God, Glory to God, then
> you are a divine astronaut—moving IN GOD. Just be hungry for
> God's Word![43]

This combination of prayer and Bible reading as the locus for abiding has
implications on the ministry of disciple making (bearing fruit). Andrews
explains, "If you use your time, redeeming your time, and live the Word of
God, and live a life of prayer—you are bound to be a witness! The fountain
will spring up . . . If you live in the Presence of the Lord, do you think you
have no witness? If you are using your time for God, do you think you have
nothing to say?"[44]

40. Murray, *Abide in Christ*, 148.

41. Foster, *Prayer*, 57.

42. Andrews, *What Are You Here For?*, 10.

43. Ibid., 11.

44. Ibid., 25.

6. ABIDING IS DOING LESS THAT GOD MIGHT DO MORE.

The phrase οὐ δύνασθε ποιεῖν οὐδέν (John 15:5b) is the combination of two verbs. οὐ δύνασθε is the negation of the present indicative second person plural (you are not able) and ποιεῖν is also present tense, active, infinitive (to do), which are combined with the adverb οὐδέν (anything). Apart from lavishing extravagant daily time on Jesus, one "accomplishes nothing, there is no permanent result."[45] ποιεῖν means "to make or to do." John is specifically saying without lavishing extravagant daily time on Jesus, Christians cannot produce disciples; they can't do anything. The only way to produce disciples (that, in turn, produce disciples) is to lavish extravagant daily time on Jesus. Therefore, in order to do more (produce disciples), disciples should undertake fewer activities in their own strength (which ultimately accomplish nothing) and spend more time in the presence of Jesus.

Inherent to abiding is the challenge of giving Jesus extravagant time every day. Practically, this means that there are fewer hours to accomplish the things that must be done. A spiritual theology of abiding is a life of faith, a life that believes God can do more than ministers or missionaries can, a life that believes a person intimate with God can do more in fewer hours than he or she could do with more time and less God. Foster quotes Søren Kierkegaard: "God creates everything out of nothing—and everything which God is to use he first reduces to nothing."[46] Abiding is a reminder that God does not need humans and, similar to the Sabbath, "it has a way of tempering our gnawing need to always get ahead."[47] In applying this principle to leaders, Henri Nouwen said that they "must be rooted in the permanent, intimate relationship with the incarnate Word, Jesus, and they need to find there the source for their words, advice, and guidance."[48] Stepping away from a need to be important, voluntarily giving up prime working hours to be with God, and limiting the good things attempted in order to wait on God are all integral to abiding—and allow him to do more with less. Foster calls this approach to task "dependent activity." In terms of the Sabbath (which is, in effect, contiguous to daily abiding), Foster writes:

> No teaching flowing out of the Sabbath principle is more important than the centrality of our resting in God. Instead of striving to make this or that happen, we learn to trust in a heavenly

45. Westcott, *The Gospel According to St. John*, 200.
46. Foster, *Prayer*, 54.
47. Ibid., 96.
48. Nouwen, *In the Name of Jesus*, 45.

Father who loves to give. This does not promote inactivity, but it does promote dependent activity. No longer do we take things into our own hands. Rather, we place all things into divine hands and then act out of inner promptings.[49]

A spiritual theology of abiding realizes the disciple's role in ministry is not as important as most disciples think it is. As a disciple steps back and allows time and space for God to intervene, more is accomplished than what frenetic activity can produce. This does not imply that those who abide are lazy. On the contrary, resting in Jesus empowers those who abide to be the most hardworking disciples possible. "Christian mysticism in the Johannine context demands a response from the believer in the practical arena of everyday life. Doing the truth involves believing and loving, all in the framework of abiding in Christ."[50] Abiding disciples believe that God is at work, rest in him and allow space for his acts, and then join him in his labors with the guarantee of his results.

7. ABIDING IS DONE CORPORATELY.

In John 15:5, Jesus promises that the disciple who lavishes extravagant daily time will φέρει καρπὸν πολύν (he will bear much fruit). In John 15:11–12, Jesus points out that disciples who lavish extravagant time on him must love other disciples. John 15:16 reveals the reason disciples were specifically chosen is that they, in turn, produce disciples. The lavishing of extravagant daily time on Jesus is intrinsically connected to interaction with others. That interaction has an abiding component.

A spiritual theology of abiding must have both private and public praxis. Abiding corporately augments individual abiding. When disciples of Christ meet (for study, fellowship, strategizing, planning, administration, or even conflict resolution), abiding should be an integral part of their communion. Those in spiritual leadership have the responsibility to

teach and train others in the spiritual life. To do this well carries with it both the obligation and opportunity to intentionally and explicitly do the work of Spiritual Theology for the sake of personal and corporate growth—whether it is through preaching, discipleship or board meetings. God give us the grace to embrace this task for the sake of growth in the Kingdom of God.[51]

49. Foster, *Prayer*, 96.
50. Harrington, "Christian Mysticism."
51. Coe, "Spiritual Theology," 43.

Spiritual leaders cannot pass on in the public sector what they do not practice and experience privately. "Our own experience or lack of experience of the Spirit and transformation, personal and corporate, will be the limiting horizon for our teaching and life-application of the Bible, let alone our willingness and ability to do Spiritual Theology as a discipline. We all want to affect our students and disciples for Christ."[52] In order to lead corporate abiding, leaders must personally abide. Metaxas notes that Bonhoeffer advocated for this communal approach to abiding. "The restoration of the church must surely depend on a new kind of monasticism, which has nothing in common with the old, but a life of uncompromising discipleship, following Christ according to the Sermon on the Mount. I believe the time has come to gather people together to do this."[53]

Bonhoeffer's seminary community was very intentional about their communal times, but not to the exclusion of individual abiding.[54] "Each day began with a forty-five minute service before breakfast and ended with a service before bed. The services took place not in the chapel, but around the large dinner table. They began by singing a choral psalm and a hymn chosen for that day. Then there was a reading from the Old Testament. Next they sang a set verse from a hymn . . . followed by a New Testament reading."[55] At the close of the day, another corporate abiding time followed. "After dinner and recreation, around ten o'clock, there was another service of about three-quarters of an hour, as the 'last note of a day with God.' After that, silence and sleep. That was the way the day went."[56]

A spiritual theology of abiding makes room for both personal and corporate abiding.

8. ABIDING HAS REGULAR TIMES OF SOLITUDE/RETREAT.

In John 15:2, Jesus encourages the disciple who is not bearing disciples by stating that provision will be made to help. In viticulture, branches that do

---

52. Ibid., 43.

53. Metaxas, *Bonhoeffer*, 246.

54. A disciple of Bonhoeffer named Schonherr described the corporate abiding time as including a great deal of singing then Bible reading, including especially the Psalms, a chapter from the OT, a passage from the NT, and prayer by Bonhoeffer. After breakfast there was one half hour of meditation and then solitude (each to his own room—absolute quiet, no telephone, no walking around). Metaxas, *Bonhoeffer*, 268.

55. Metaxas, *Bonhoeffer*, 268.

56. Ibid., 270.

not get enough sun often drop to the ground and are incapable of producing grapes. Other branches are pressed down by rain, wind, or other unfortunate events. In such cases, the vinedresser lifts that branch and ties it in isolation to a part of the trestle where it can receive direct sunlight and recover from the trauma of unfortunate experience. This beautiful picture of care for the nonproductive branch is what is meant by αἴρει αὐτό (he lifts up) in John 15:2. In addition to the daily rhythm of abiding (concentrated times, all-day communion, corporate interaction), a spiritual theology of abiding makes room for critical periods throughout the year for retreat and solitude. "Without solitude it is virtually impossible to live a spiritual life."[57] At least quarterly, several days for spiritual renewal should be taken. Foster adds,

> In solitude, however, we die not only to others but also to ourselves. To be sure, at first we thought solitude was a way to recharge our batteries in order to enter life's many competitions with new vigor and strength. In time however, we find that solitude gives us power not to win the rat race but to ignore the rat race altogether.[58]

Annually, there should be one or two weeklong periods of personal and/or corporate retreat. Jesus often retreated to places of prayer away from the maddening crowd, "yet somehow we think we can do without what he deemed essential."[59] To neglect this component of a spiritual theology of abiding is to invite burnout.

> [W]orking feverishly with less than vital relationship with God often leaves one empty, resentful and exhausted. At the height of productivity some experience a crisis, due either to a developmental event (mid-life transition), an event that intrudes from without (career failure, divorce), a condition that arises from within (burnout, crisis of faith) or a dark night of the soul. The crisis prompts an intentional inner journey where God is fervently sought through renewing spiritual disciplines . . . After a significant layer of healing and transformation has occurred, the Spirit faithfully propels the journeyer into the active world to serve with renewed vision and purpose.[60]

57. Foster, *Prayer*, 63.

58. Ibid., 63.

59. Ibid., 101. Richard Foster references *hesychia*, the Greek word for rest, and *hesychasm*, the spirituality of the desert fathers and mothers. "They discovered *hesychia*, this perfect rest of body and soul, in the solitude of the desert" (*Prayer*, 101).

60. Demarest, "Reflections," 2008.

These periods of solitude, refreshment, and re-visioning are either judiciously planned and provided for or forced upon disciples by their inability to continue with the demands of ministry. A spiritual theology of abiding makes intentional proactive provision for retreat and solitude. Sometimes this retreat and solitude are restorative and healing. Other times, they simply bring remembrance that Jesus gives life and extravagant time with him is what brings disciples the deepest joy. Being with Jesus is the point; the point is not simply to be with him so others can be with him.

9. ABIDING TAKES DISCIPLINE AND INTENTIONALITY.

In John 15:10, Jesus says, "ἐὰν τὰς ἐντολάς μου τηρήσητε, μενεῖτε ἐν τῇ ἀγάπῃ μου, (If you keep my commandments, you will abide in my love)." This admonition follows the imperative μείνατε ἐν τῇ ἀγάπῃ τῇ ἐμῇ (abide in my love) of John 15:9. Disciples remain in Jesus' love by (τηρήσητε, you actively keep) continuing to obey or guarding his commandments. Ongoing obedience (discipline over time) guarantees abiding in the love of Jesus.

Concerns over a theology of abiding that espouses extravagant daily time with Jesus as a starting point are centered on the possibility of legalism tainting the praxis. Abiding is not antithetical to freedom nor is it undisciplined. "To come to the pleasure you have not, you must go by a way in which you enjoy not."[61] Abiding is both a freedom and a discipline. Thomas à Kempis said, "Habit overcomes habit." Abiding is a habit; it starts with discipline, which, in turn, leads to desire, and desire gives birth to delight. The process starts with habit formation. Foster teaches that Christians must "[build] new habits of prayer, and patient, kind, firm, persistence is what [we] need with [ourselves]."[62] He also reminds his readers, "Freedom is the product of discipline and commitment."[63] Bonhoeffer encouraged the formation of habit writing. "Prayer is not a free-will offering to God; it is an obligatory service, something which he requires."[64] Yet "when undertaken in the power of the Holy Spirit, acts of duty can be filled with great joy and blessing. In fact, duty is, as de Caussade teaches us, 'the sacrament of the present moment.'"[65] Foster affirms that disciples "must often begin by tackling prayer in the same way we have been taught to tackle every other

61. Foster, *Prayer*, 17.

62. Ibid., 45.

63. Ibid., 68.

64. Ibid., 68.

65. Ibid.

problem—by hard work."[66] Bonhoeffer refuted the charge of intentional abiding being legalistic when he wrote to Barth, as Metaxas recalls, "What is there legalistic in a Christian setting to work to learn what prayer is and in his spending a good deal of time in this learning?"[67] Discipline is not to be confused with austerity. In Bonhoeffer's community, there was ample time for leisurely pursuits. Metaxas writes of the seminarians living with Bonhoeffer,

> Whatever they thought of the disciplines and the daily devotions, no one at Finkenwalde could complain that there was no fun. Most afternoons and evenings a time was set aside for hiking or sports. Bonhoeffer was forever organizing games . . . There was a lot of table tennis, and anyone looking for Bonhoeffer would try the table tennis room first.[68]

Nouwen says, "To live a life that is not dominated by the desire to be relevant but is instead safely anchored in the knowledge of God's first love, we have to be mystics."[69] Mystics are both free and bound—bound to their love through discipline and freed by their discipline to be loved. In that discipline there is liberty, not legalism.

A second misunderstanding regarding abiding is that it will always mean an acute awareness of the presence of Jesus, that there will be no dry times. Ancient spiritual writers, however, talked about times when they did not feel the presence of God, even when they were disciplined in giving him extravagant daily time. These ancients termed the times they could sense the presence of God as "consolation" and the times they felt the absence of God as "desolation."

> Thus, since God is always present, the felt presence or absence of Him (consolation and desolation), at least at sometimes and perhaps in the beginning of the spiritual life, are more gifts from God than the casual result of our actions—more the result of differing ways the Spirit works in the soul at different stages of our growth.[70]

A spiritual theology of abiding recognizes the need for discipline, intentionality, and the reality that God's presence, while axiomatic, is not necessarily continually felt; neither is it earned as a byproduct of discipline—it is a

66. Ibid., 96–98.
67. *Bonhoeffer*, 271.
68. Ibid., 270.
69. Nouwen, *In the Name of Jesus*, 42.
70. Coe, "Spiritual Theology," 39.

grace. In fact, "times of seeming desertion and absence and abandonment appear to be universal among those who have walked this path of faith before us. We might just as well get used to the idea that, sooner or later, we, too, will know what it means to feel forsaken by God."[71] Abiding, then, is not a works-oriented approach to blessing or a guarantee of a constant emotional high.

> If we could make the Creator of heaven and earth instantly appear at our beck and call, we would not be in communion with the God of Abraham, Isaac, and Jacob. We do that with objects, with things, with idols. But God, the great iconoclast, is constantly smashing our false images of who he is and what he is like.[72]

A spiritual theology of abiding positions ourselves (through intentional discipline) before the God who fulfills and refreshes us, but abiding does not dictate terms and is mature enough to relish both the silence and the communication of heaven.

10. ABIDING INCLUDES SUFFERING.

In John 15:2, καθαίρει (he cleans) is a present, active, indicative, third person singular verb. The verb "involves a play on two different meanings. The one meaning involves the pruning of a plant, while the other meaning involves a cleansing process."[73] The verb καθαίρει in John 15:2 is translated "he prunes," even though its literal meaning is "he cleans." This is the only use of "he prunes" as a translation of καθαίρει in the Johannine literature. Elsewhere in John (13:10, 11; 15:3), the same root word (in adjective form) καθαρός is translated "clean." Clearly, John's intention was a "cleaning" or "purifying" process. Ernest Colewell and Eric Titus observe that it is "important to note that in verse three the idea of pruning is conveyed by the same word which is used in the story of washing the disciples feet."[74] Jesus clearly warns the disciple who bears disciples that divine allowances and intentions (painful as they must be) will assist the suffering servant to produce more fruit. This understanding is underlined in John 15:13 when Jesus reminds the disciple that the great love is a suffering love, a love that will lay down one's life for others.

71. Foster, *Prayer*, 17.
72. Ibid., 20.
73. Louw and Nida, "καθαίρει," in *Greek English Lexicon*.
74. Colewell and Titus, *The Gospel of the Spirit*, 181.

A spiritual theology of abiding embraces the cross. Abiding essentially fosters intimacy with Jesus and calls the one abiding into the full fellowship of the Son of God, a fellowship that learns obedience through suffering and participates in the agonies of Christ for redemptive ends. It is naïve and unscriptural to think that abiding is only pleasure. Intimacy with Jesus demands suffering with him. To share the heart of Christ is to weep with the things that sadden him as well as to rejoice with what gladdens him. This union of purpose, this sharing of sufferings, is what elevates the disciple from servanthood to friendship (John 15:15).

11. ABIDING IS TRANSCULTURAL.

John writes his gospel with missiological intent. The intended audience is multicultural. John pastored churches across Asia Minor and has readers from disparate cultural backgrounds. John conveys that the lavishing of extravagant daily time on Jesus is reward and recourse for every culture; that includes the Last Supper discourse intentionally centered on Jesus' teaching on abiding. In John 15:16, disciples are appointed (ὑμεῖς ὑπάγητε καὶ καρπὸν φέρητε—you should go [away] and bear fruit) to bear disciples wherever they go. Going "away, departing" implies multiple contexts and cultures, and, in the going, (making disciples of everyone, everywhere they go [Matthew 28:19–20]) the disciples made are also to lavish extravagant time on Jesus.

In order for a spiritual theology of abiding to be valid, it must be transcultural. Paradigmatically, abiding is not bound by the limitations of education, race, gender, socio-economic status, literacy, or any other geopolitical constraints.[75]

> A paradigm must be all encompassing enough to describe the Christian journey in a way that is not situationally dependent. It must be useful and valid for all believers at all times, and not just a trendy or western design. First John 2:12–14 reflects the timeless truth that Christians are to continuously grow in faith throughout their lives. The Christian is to be metamorphosed from sinner to saint, from the new birth and spiritual immaturity to full grown maturity.[76]

75. For insight from a spectrum of cultures regarding spiritual formation, Richard Foster suggests Gregory of Nyssa's *The Life of Moses*; *Revelations of Divine Love*, by Juliana of Norwich; *The Imitation of Christ*, by Thomas à Kempis; *Confessions of Saint Augustine*; *The Little Flowers of St. Francis*, by Francis of Assisi; *The Life of Anthony*; Theresa of Avila's autobiography; and Toyohiko Kagawa.

76. Willett, "A Biblical Model," 97.

Similar to the stage theory of spiritual development, which incorporates input from the Orient and Global South as well as the Occident, abiding has "formulations and insights [which] are likely not culturally bound (although culturally conditioned), but prove to be transcultural."[77] Extravagant daily time with Jesus through the word and prayer with personal and corporate implication are disciplines universally possible and applicable. There is precedent for the trans-religious nature of stage theory of spiritual development. Lillias Trotter wrote of the Sufi mystics of North Africa who seek to

> . . . be united—united, not absorbed as in Buddhist mysticism; and this union is to be brought about through a succession of seven spiritual stages of asceticism to be attained by effort and seven spiritual states to be bestowed by God. All is sought under the guidance of a director and in blind obedience to his bidding.[78]

12. ABIDING IS THE SOURCE OF DISCIPLE MAKING.

John 15:5 is the center of Jesus' teaching on abiding. "The one who abides in me, and I in that one, bears much fruit." Jesus explicitly says that the best way to make disciples is to lavish extravagant time on him. From that lavish extravagance comes the divine life that empowers disciples to introduce others to Jesus. When disciples lavish extravagant daily time on Jesus, they become like him. Disciples understand what it means to love and be loved (John 15:9–10). Disciples experience Jesus' real joy and it completes them (v. 11). Disciples learn to lay down their lives for others as Jesus did for them (v. 12). Disciples are granted friendship status (over servanthood) as a result of being conformed to Jesus' thinking and nature as a result of all the extravagant time spent with him.

A spiritual theology of abiding contends that abiding both disciples a person and empowers him to disciple others. Further, the missiological implication of abiding is the production of disciples. Abiding for personal profit alone is the "spiritual greed" warned of by the Church Fathers and antithetical to the heart and purpose of Christ.

> The very counter cultural goal in John's model of spiritual development is not some private actualization, but rather the willingness to encourage and foster the spiritual growth of others . . . John's model . . . describes growth that is both personally

77. Demarest, "Reflections," 165.

78. Rockness, *A Passion for the Impossible*, 343.

restorative and a source of encouragement and even inspiration for others.[79]

John Coe agrees. "The goal of training in Spiritual Theology is not merely understanding but actual training in prayer, obedience, and the love of God and others."[80] This love of God for others culminates in equipping them for ministry—a central function of discipleship. "In general, Spiritual Theology as defined needs to become the peculiar task of the disciple, pastor, and preacher who are given by God to the church to equip the believer for the work of the ministry."[81] Rex Andrews agrees that abiding will result in ministry and witness. "If you learn what God can teach you on [dwelling in His presence], then wherever you go you will find His Presence; you will witness to Him, you will lead others to Jesus; and He will pour out His Spirit on you and bless your work for Him."[82] He puts this result of abiding in the imperative. "It is God's will for you to witness for Jesus Christ! To people anywhere!"[83] Abiding is not intended primarily to make disciples happy, but to help them bear fruit (other disciples) in the work of the ministry. When disciples lavish extravagant daily time on Jesus, they find more effectiveness in their service of others. He encourages those abiding:

> You will use your time for others . . . redeem your time for others. And that includes, and has to do with, souls, saving souls, and seeking souls, helping souls . . . A prayer list is a wonderful thing . . . you pray for them faithfully; and you will find that God will use you that way to the salvation of souls; and in other ways for God.[84]

A spiritual theology of abiding recognizes that disciples do not abide toward selfish ends (though abiding is indeed its own reward). Disciples abide in order to make more disciples, to be conformed, and to help others be conformed into the image of Christ.

13. ABIDING IS MARKED BY JOY.

In John 15:11, Jesus affirms the result of disciples lavishing extravagant daily time on Him is joy. Jesus says, ταῦτα λελάληκα ὑμῖν ἵνα ἡ χαρὰ ἡ ἐμὴ ἐν

79. Willett, "A Biblical Model," 95.
80. John Coe, "Spiritual Theology," 8.
81. Ibid., 15.
82. Andrews, *What Are You Here For?*, 5.
83. Ibid., 12.
84. Ibid.

ὑμῖν ᾖ καὶ ἡ χαρὰ ὑμῶν πληρωθῇ (These things I have spoken to you, that my joy may abide in you, and that your joy may be full). The noun χαρὰ indicates a state of joy and gladness. Jesus has such joy in the harvest and such joy in obeying the Father who is Lord of the harvest, and he guarantees that his joy will abide (endure) in disciples as they abide in him. Joy is the sign and the reward of those who lavish extravagant daily time on Jesus. This joy is not simply the emotion of circumstantial happiness, but the deep rooted and sustained exuberance of being swept up into the dance of the God of mission. Jesus spoke these collective truths because he knew in them disciples will find great joy. The lavishing of extravagant daily time on Christ leads to making disciples. Making disciples completes the disciple's joy.

A spiritual theology of abiding is characterized by joy. "Saint Ammo-nas, a disciple of Abba Anthony, writes 'Fear produces tears, and tears joy.' Joy brings strength, through which the soul will be fruitful in everything."[85] "There is none on earth that live such a life of joy and blessedness as those that are acquainted with this heavenly conversation."[86] An indicator of the genuineness of abiding is the accompanying joy. Legalistic discipline does not lead to joy. Pretense and religiosity are exposed by their dour appear-ance. Abiding is verified by the accompanying and infectious joy of the abider. "Our Eternal Lover lures us back regularly into his presence with anticipation and delight. It is not hard to honor this regular time of meet-ing, for the language of lovers is the language of waste. We are glad to waste time with God, for we are pleased with the company."[87] As disciples learn the discipline of abiding, they become addicted to the presence of Jesus, and in that addiction there is great joy and winsome appeal. Abiding produces joyful disciples.

14. ABIDING INFORMS STRATEGY.

The shift from being δούλους (servants) to being φίλους (friends) in John 15:15 happens after Jesus has revealed all things he has heard from the Father. Days away from his crucifixion, Jesus summarizes his mission and the missionary heart of his Father by giving his disciples the basic blue-print—the plan and the means. God's plan is for them to make disciples of all nations (wider context of John's gospel). God's means for disciple bearing is through abiding—lavishing extravagant daily time on Jesus. Continuance in the word and prayer maintains this abiding, which glorifies the Father for

85. Foster, *Prayer*, 40.
86. Ibid., 77.
87. Ibid.

the relational union and the disciples that result. Continuance in the word reveals what disciples must obey, and obedience keeps disciples in God's love with the surprising benefit of complete joy. This love (of Jesus for us) and joy (of engaging in what disciples were created for) gives disciples the power to love one another at great cost. When disciples love one another at great cost, they so endear themselves to the Father that he promotes them from servants to friends because they understand his character, his means, and his ends. No longer unthinking, unknowing instruments, disciples now share a sympathetic union with the Father and ascend the heights of partnership in mission with the Lord of the harvest.[88] All this (strategic impartation) results from disciples lavishing extravagant daily time on Jesus.

A spiritual theology of abiding does not abdicate the strategic ground to the academic alone. A strategy of the Spirit of God is revealed to disciples through abiding. "For Christian leadership to be truly fruitful in the future, a movement from the moral to the mystical is required."[89] Strategic thinking that is inspired is dependent on leaders who will take the time to individually and communally abide in Christ. "It is of vital importance to reclaim the mystical aspect of theology so that every word spoken, every word of advice given, and every strategy developed can come from a heart that knows God intimately."[90] Andrews gives this advice to disciples who are seeking to learn to abide.

> We are here to dwell in the presence of the Lord. It takes time to do it . . . God is certainly preparing in this world a people on the earth who will just let the Lord have his way . . . What are you here for? It is to learn to dwell in the presence of the Lord. It becomes your life. You then come to do naturally what God plans for your life no matter where you are.[91]

Foster notes that Juliana of Norwich reminds us that "the whole reason we pray is to be united into the vision and contemplation of him to whom we pray."[92] As disciples are united with God, they share his passion. A vision of Jesus always includes his vision for the nations and his plan to reach them. A spiritual theology of abiding realizes the Holy Spirit is the executive of mission and that disciples who learn to abide in Christ (individually and corporately) will be the best positioned to hear and obey the plans of God.

88. Westcott, *The Gospel According to St. John*, 206.

89. Nouwen, *In the Name of Jesus*, 47.

90. Ibid., 44.

91. Andrews, *What Are You Here For?*, 3.

92. Foster, *Prayer*, 159.

CONCLUSION

A theory for the spiritual theology of abiding that includes the above four-teen points can be summarized through the acrostic: ABIDES.

A stands for "Always" and refers to abiding as continual communion with Jesus day and night (#1) and the journey involved in the intimacy (#2) based on lavishing daily extravagant time on Jesus.

B stands for "Blocks of Time" and refers to the daily, fixed, appoint-ments disciples make with Jesus (#1), the destination aspect of fixed mo-ments, concrete answers, definitive arrival points (#2), and the regular times of solitude and retreat (#8) that contribute to abiding.

I stands for "In the Word and Prayer" and indicates that the central disciplines for abiding are the Bible and speaking with Jesus through prayer (#5), as well as the reciprocal nature of Jesus abiding in disciples (#3) as they abide in him.

D stands for "Disciplined." Abiding includes a disciplined intentional-ity (#9) that results in joy (#13), even if the route is sometimes difficult and includes suffering (#10).

E stands for "Everyone." Abiding has corporate implications (#7), as there are times when disciples together lavish time on Jesus. At the same time, abiding is idiosyncratic (#4). Individuals communing with their Cre-ator in their own ways, informed by their current season of life. Abiding is also transcultural (#11), with contextual factors influencing how and when abiding is undertaken while retaining the common practices of the overall theory.

S stands for "Strategic." Abiding helps disciples do less that God might do more (#6), abiding is the source of disciple making (#12), and abiding informs strategy (#14).

Abiding, then, can be summed up by ABIDES: All day, Blocks of time, In the Word and prayer, Disciplined, Everyone, and Strategic.

Bibliography

Agar, Michael H. *The Professional Stranger: An Informal Introduction to Ethnography.* New York: Academic, 1980.

Anderson, Paul N. *The Riddles of the Fourth Gospel: An Introduction to John.* Minneapolis: Fortress, 2011.

Andrews, Rex B. *What Are You Here For?* Zion, IL: Zion Faith Homes, 1960.

Assemblies of God World Missions (AGWM). *Letters From Lillian.* Springfield, MO: Assemblies of God World Missions, 1983.

Athanasius. *On the Incarnation.* Translated and edited by a religious of C. S. M. V. Crestwood, NY: St. Vladimir's Seminary Press, 1996.

Baker, R. M. "Economic Rationality and Health and Lifestyle Choices for People with Diabetes." *Social Science and Medicine* 63, no. 9 (November 2006) 2341–53.

Balz, Horst, and Gerhard Schneider. *Exegetical Dictionary of the New Testament.* Grand Rapids, MI: Eerdmans, 1991.

Barclay, William. *The Gospel of John.* Vol. 2. The Daily Study Bible Series. Rev. ed. Philadelphia: Westminster, 1955.

Barrett, C. K. *The Gospel According to St. John: An Introduction with Commentary and Notes on the Greek Text.* London: SPCK, 1955.

Bauer, Martin W., and George Gaskell, eds. *Qualitative Researching with Text, Image, and Sound.* London: Sage, 2000.

Beasley-Murray, George R. *John.* World Biblical Commentary 36. Waco, TX: Word, 1999.

Beatty, James. *Nile Mother: The Story of Lillian Trasher.* Springfield, MO: The General Council of the Assemblies of God, 1939.

Bernard, H. Russell. *Research Methods in Anthropology: Qualitative and Quantitative Methods.* Oxford: Altamira, 2002.

Bernard, J. H. *A Critical and Exegetical Commentary on the Gospel According to St. John.* Vol. 2. Edited by J. A. Emerton et al. International Critical Commentary Series 29. Edinburgh: T. & T. Clark, 1928.

Billings, J. Todd. *Union with Christ.* Grand Rapids, MI: Baker Academic, 2011.

Blass, Fredrick, and A. Debrunner. *A Greek Grammar of the New Testament and Other Early Christian Literature.* Chicago: The University of Chicago Press, 1961.

Booth, Wayne C., et al. *The Craft of Research.* Chicago: The University of Chicago Press, 2003.

Brown, Raymond E. *The Gospel According to John.* Garden City, NY: Doubleday, 1970.

Bruce, Alexander Balmain. *The Training of the Twelve.* New York: Doran, 2000.

Bruce, F. F. *The Gospel and the Epistles of John*. Grand Rapids, MI: Eerdmans, 1983.

Bultmann, Rudolf. *The Gospel of John: A Commentary*. Philadelphia: Westminster, 1971.

Carson, D. A. *The Gospel According to John*. Grand Rapids, MI: Eerdmans, 1991.

Chambers, Oswald. *Prayer: A Holy Occupation*. Grand Rapids, MI: Discovery, 1992.

Charmaz, Kathy. *Handbook of Qualitative Research*. Edited by Norman K. Densin and Yvonna S. Lincoln. London: Sage, 2000.

Christie, Florence. *Called to Egypt*. Wichita Falls, TX: Western Christian Foundation, 1997.

Coe, John. "Spiritual Theology: A Theological-Experiential Methodology for Bridging the Sanctification Gap." *Journal of Spiritual Formation and Soul Care* 2, no. 1 (2009) 4–43.

Colewell, Ernest Cadman, and Eric Lane Titus. *The Gospel of the Spirit*. New York: Harper & Bros., 1953.

Cook, F. C., ed. *The Holy Bible According to the Authorized Version (AD 1611): With an Explanatory and Critical Commentary and a Revision of the Translation, by Bishops and Other Clergy of the Anglican Church*. New Testament, vol. 2, *St. John—The Acts of the Apostles*. New York: Charles Scribner's Sons, 1890.

Corbin, Juliet, and Strauss Anselm. *Basics of Qualitative Research: Grounded Theory Procedures and Techniques*. London: Sage, 1990.

Cox, Jeff. *From Vines to Wines*. New York: Harper & Row, 1985.

Daly, M. W. *Empire on the Nile: The Anglo-Egyptian Sudan 1898–1934*. Cambridge: Cambridge University Press, 1986.

Demarest, Bruce. "Reflections on Developmental Spirituality: Journey Paradigms and Stages." *Journal of Spiritual Formation and Soul Care* 1, no. 2 (2008) 149–67.

Dillow, Joseph C. "Abiding Is Remaining in Fellowship: Another Look at John 15:1–6." *Bibliotheca Sacra* 147 (January 1990) 44–53.

Dunn, James D. G., and John W. Rogerson. *Eerdmans Commentary on the Bible*. Grand Rapids, MI: Eerdmans, 2003.

Eckman, George. *Studies in the Gospel of John*. New York: The Methodist Book Concern, 1907.

Edman, V. Raymond. *The Disciplines of Life*. Wheaton, IL: Scripture, 1948.

Edwards, Mark. *John*. Oxford: Blackwell, 2004.

Elder, Earl E. *Vindicating a Vision: The Story of the American Mission in Egypt 1854–1954*. Philadelphia: The United Presbyterian Board of Foreign Missions, 1958.

Elowsky, Joel C., ed. *Ancient Christian Commentary on Scripture: New Testament*. Vol. 4b, *John 11–21*. Downers Grove, IL: InterVarsity, 2007.

Espenhain, Lorraine E. "Abiding in the Vine." http://catholic.net/index.php?option=dedestaca&id=4034.

Fanning, Buist M. *Verbal Aspect in New Testament Greek*. Oxford: Clarendon, 1990.

Flanagan, Neal M. *The Gospel According to John and the Johannine Epistles*. Collegeville, MN: Liturgical, 1982.

Foster, Richard. *Prayer: Finding the Heart's True Home*. San Francisco: HarperCollins, 1992.

Frankfort-Nachmias, Chava, and David Nachmias. *Research Methods in the Social Sciences*. New York: Worth, 2000.

Gairdner, W. H. T. *D. M. Thornton: A Study in Missionary Ideals and Methods*. London: Hodder & Stoughton, 1908.

Glenn, Lewis. *Missionary Travels in Bible Lands*. Bedford, IN: Nile Valley Mission, n.d.

Glover, Robert Hall. *The Progress of World-Wide Missions*. New York: Harper & Bros., 1939.

Grosof, Miriam Schapiro, and Hyman Sardy. *A Research Primer for the Social and Behavioral Sciences*. New York: Academic, 1985.

Guthrie, Donald. *New Testament Theology*. Downers Grove, IL: InterVarsity, 1981.

Harrington, Daniel, J. "Christian Mysticism." *America: The National Catholic Review*, May 8, 2006, http://www.americamagazine.org/content/article.cfm?article_id=4777.

Harris, Richard W. *Arboriculture: Care of Trees, Shrubs, and Vines in the L a n d s c a p e*. Englewood Cliffs, NJ: Prentice-Hall, 1983.

Hendricksen, William. *The Gospel of John*. Grand Rapids, MI: Baker, 1983.

Hensel, Robert. "καρπός." In *The New International Dictionary of New Testament Theology*, edited by Colin Brown, 721–22. Grand Rapids, MI: Zondervan, 1971.

Hoekstra, Harvey T. *The World Council of Churches and the Demise of Evangelism*. Wheaton, IL: Tyndale, 1979.

Howard, W. F. *Christianity According to St. John*. London: Duckworth, 1943.

Howell, Beth Prim. *Lady on a Donkey*. New York: Dutton & Company, 1960.

Huberman, Michael A., and Matthew B. Miles. *The Qualitative Researcher's Companion*. London: Sage, 2002.

Jessup, Henry Harris. *Kamil Abdul Messiah: A Syrian Convert from Islam to Christianity*. Philadelphia: Middle East Resources, 2008.

Kealy, Sean P. *That You May Believe: The Gospel According to St. John*. Middlegreen, UK: St. Paul, 1978.

Keener, Craig S. *The Gospel of John: A Commentary*. Peabody, MA: Hendrickson, 2003.

———. "Sent Like Jesus: Johannine Missiology (John 20:21–22)." *Asian Journal of Pentecostal Studies* 12, no. 1 (2009) 21–45.

Kittel, Gerhard, and Gerhard Friedrich. *Theological Dictionary of the New Testament*. Grand Rapids, MI: Eerdmans, 1964.

Köstenberger, Andreas J. *John*. Baker Exegetical Commentary on the New Testament. Grand Rapids: Baker Academic, 2004.

———. *The Missions of Jesus and the Disciples According to the Fourth Gospel: With Implications for the Fourth Gospel's Purpose and the Mission of the Contemporary Church*. Grand Rapids, MI: Eerdmans, 1998.

Kruse, Colin G. *John*. Tyndale New Testament Commentaries. Edited by Leon Morris. Grand Rapids, MI: Eerdmans, 2004.

Laney, J. Carl. "Abiding Is Believing: The Analogy of the Vine in John 15:1–6." *Bibliotheca Sacra* 146 (January 1989) 55–66.

Larkin, William J., Jr., and Joel F. Williams. *Mission in the New Testament: An Evangelical Approach*. Maryknoll, NY: Orbis, 1998.

Lenski, R. C. H. *The Interpretation of John's Gospel*. Minneapolis: Augsburg, 1943.

———. *The Interpretation of St. John's Revelation*. Minneapolis: Augsburg, 1961.

Lewis, E. Ridley. *Johannine Writings and Other Epistles*. Greenwood, SC: Attic, 1964.

Lexham Analytical Lexicon to the Greek New Testament, The. Lexham Bible Reference Series. Logos Research Systems, 2011. Electronic ed.

Louw, Johannes P., and Eugene A. Nida. *Greek English Lexicon of the New Testament Based on Semantic Domains*. New York: United Bible Societies, 1988.

Lozano, John Manuel. *The Spirituality of Daniel Comboni: Apostle–Prophet–Founder*. Chicago: Claret Center for Resources in Spirituality, 1989.

Lueking, F. Dean. "Abide in Me." http://www.religion-online.org/showarticle. asp?title=678.

Lussier, Ernest. *God Is Love: According to St. John.* New York: Alba, 1977.

Luther, Martin. *Commentary on Galatians.* Grand Rapids, MI: Revell, 1988.

MacArthur, John. *Abiding in Christ.* Chicago: Moody, 1986.

Maloney, Francis J. *The Gospel of John.* Collegeville, MN: Liturgical, 1988.

Mathis, David. "Missions: The Worship of Jesus and the Joy of All Peoples." In *A Holy Ambition: To Preach Where Christ Has Not Been Named,* by John Piper, 23–34. Minneapolis: Desiring God, 2011.

McCasland, David. *Oswald Chambers: Abandoned to God.* Grand Rapids, MI: Discovery, 1993.

Metaxas, Eric. *Bonhoeffer: Pastor, Martyr, Prophet, Spy.* Nashville: Nelson, 2010.

Michaels, J. Ramsey. *The Gospel of John.* Grand Rapids, MI: Eerdmans, 2010.

Miller, Keith. "The Theological Significance of John 15." http://74.125.155.132/ scholar?q=cache:c_N_qbcnfbYJ:scholar.google.com/&hl=en&as_sdt=0,26.

Mondini, A. G. *Africa or Death.* St. Paul, MN: Daughters of St. Paul, 1964.

Moore-Harell, Alice. *Egypt's African Empire: Samuel Baker, Charles Gordon & the Creation of Equatoria.* Brighton: Sussex Academic, 2010.

Morris, Leon. *New Testament Theology.* Grand Rapids, MI: Academic Books, 1986.

Moule, C. F. D. *An Idiom Book of New Testament Greek.* Cambridge: University Press, 1953.

Moulton, James Hope, and Nigel Turner. *A Grammar of New Testament Greek.* Vol. 3. Edinburgh: T. & T. Clark, 1993.

Murray, Andrew. *Abide in Christ.* Kensington, PA: Whittaker, 1979.

———. "The True Vine: Meditations for a Month on John 15:1–16," http://www.ccel. org/ccel/murray/true_vine.vii.html.

Newman, Barclay M., Jr. *A Concise Greek-English Dictionary of the New Testament.* Stuttgart: German Bible Society, 1993.

Nouwen, Henri J. M. *In the Name of Jesus.* New York: Crossroad, 1989.

Olsson, Birger. *Structure and Meaning in the Fourth Gospel: A Text-Linguistic Analysis of John 2:1–11 and 4:1–42.* Lund, Sweden: Gleerup, 1974.

Oyer, Linda L. *Continuing in Covenant: A Proposed Background of the Johannine Usage of Menein.* Columbia, SC: Columbia Graduate School of Bible and Missions, 1983.

Padwick, Constance E. *Temple Gairdner of Cairo.* London: Society for Promoting Christian Knowledge, 1930.

Patton, Michael Quinn. *Qualitative Evaluation Methods.* London: Sage, 1980.

Perkins, Harold O. *Espaliers and Vines for the Home Gardener.* Princeton, NJ: Van Nostrand, 1964.

Peters, George W. *A Biblical Theology of Missions.* Chicago: Moody, 1972.

Pigott, Blanche A. F. I. *Lilias Trotter: "Lalla Lili" (The Arabs' Name for Her), Founder of the Algiers Mission Band.* London: Marshall, Morgan & Scott, 1930.

Prescott-Erickson, Robert Davis. "The Sending Motif in the Gospel of John: Implications for Theology of Mission." PhD diss., The Southern Baptist Theological Seminary, 1986.

Rattey, B. K. *The Gospel According to Saint John in the Revised Version.* Oxford: Clarendon, 1947.

Rockness, Miriam Huffman. *A Passion for the Impossible.* Grand Rapids, MI. Discovery, 2003.

Rogers, Cleon L., Jr., and Cleon L. Rogers, III. *The New Linguistic and Exegetical Key to the Greek New Testament*. Grand Rapids, MI: Zondervan, 1998.

Rosscup, James E. *Abiding in Christ: Studies in John 15*. Grand Rapids, MI: Zondervan, 1973.

Russell, Henry. *Africa's Twelve Apostles*. Boston: St. Paul's Editions, 1981.

Scott, J. Martin C. *Sophia and the Johannine Jesus*. Sheffield: JSOT Press, 1992.

Sedra, Paul. *From Mission to Modernity: Evangelicals, Reformers and Education in Nineteenth-Century Egypt*. London: Tauris, 2011.

Segovia, Fernando F. *The Farewell of the Word: The Johannine Call to Abide*. Minneapolis: Fortress, 1991.

Senior, Donald, and Carroll Stuhlmueller. *The Biblical Foundations for Mission*. Maryknoll, NY: Orbis, 1983.

Sharkey, Heather, J. *American Evangelicals in Egypt*. Princeton, NJ: Princeton University Press, 2008.

Smith, D. Moody. *New Testament Theology: The Theology of the Gospel of John*. Cambridge: Cambridge University Press, 1995.

Sproull, Natalie L. *Handbook of Research Methods: A Guide For Practitioners and Students in the Social Sciences*. London: Scarecrow, 1988.

St. John, Patricia. *Until the Day Breaks: The Life and Work of Lilias Trotter, Pioneer Missionary to Muslim North Africa*. Bromley, UK: OM, 1990.

Steele, Francis R. *Not in Vain: The Story of the North Africa Mission*. Pasadena, CA: William Carey Library, 1981.

Stenner, Paul, et al. "Putting the Q into Quality of Life: The Identification of Subjective Constructions of Health-Related Quality of Life Using Q Methodology." *Social Science & Medicine* 57, no. 11 (2003) 2161–72.

Stenner, Paul, et al. "The Understanding of Their Illness amongst People with Irritable Bowel Syndrome: A Q Methodological Study." *Social Science & Medicine* 51, no. 3 (2000) 439–52.

Stephenson, William. *The Study of Behavior*. Chicago: University of Chicago Press, 1953.

Stevens, George Barker. *The Johannine Theology: A Study of the Doctrinal Contents of the Gospel and Epistles of the Apostle John*. New York: Charles Scribner's Sons, 1908.

Stewart, I. R. Govan. *The Love That Was Stronger: Lilias Trotter of Algiers*. London: Lutterworth, 1958.

Swanson, James. *A Dictionary of Biblical Languages: Greek New Testament*. Oak Harbor, WA: Logos Research Systems, 2001. Electronic ed.

———. "αἴρω." In *A Dictionary of Biblical Languages w/ Semantic Domains: Greek (NT)*. Oak Harbor, WA: Logos Research Systems, 1997. Electronic ed.

Thayer, Joseph. *Thayer's Greek-English Lexicon of the New Testament*. Peabody, MA: Hendrickson, 1995.

Thomas, R. L. "αἴρω." In *New American Standard Hebrew-Aramaic and Greek Dictionaries*. Anaheim, CA: Foundation, 1998.

Trask, Thomas E., and Wayde I. Goodall. *The Fruit of the Spirit: Becoming the Person God Wants You to Be*. Grand Rapids, MI: Zondervan, 2000.

Tukasi, Emmanuel O. *Determinism and Petitionary Prayer in John and the Dead Sea Scrolls*. London: T. & T. Clark, 2008.

Vander Werff, Lyle. *Christian Mission to Muslims: The Record, Anglican and Reformed Approaches in India and the Near East, 1800–1938.* Pasadena, CA: William Carey Library, 1977.

Van Exel, Job, and Gjalt de Graaf. "Q Methodology: A Sneak Preview." http://www. jobvanexel.nl.

Van Voorst, Robert E. *Building Your New Testament Greek Vocabulary.* Atlanta: Society of Biblical Literature, 2001.

Venn, Henry. *The Complete Duty of Man, or a System of Doctrinal and Practical Christianity.* New York: American Tract Society, 1838.

Vincent, Marvin R. *Word Studies in the New Testament.* Peabody, MA: Hendrickson, 1985.

Volf, Miroslav. *After Our Likeness: The Church as the Image of the Trinity.* Grand Rapids, MI: Eerdmans, 1998.

Wagner, Peter. *Frontiers in Missionary Strategy.* Chicago: Moody, 1972.

Wagner, Phillip M. *A Wine-Grower's Guide.* New York: Knopf, 1978.

Wakeman, Steven. "The Nature of Fruit as the Product of Abiding in Christ in John 15:1–17." *International Online Monthly Journal* 66, no. 5 (November 8, 2009) 58–75. http://www.christianliteratureandliving.com/nov2009/stevenjohn15.pdf.

Wallace, Daniel. *Greek Grammar Beyond the Basics—Exegetical Syntax of the New Testament.* Grand Rapids, MI: Zondervan, 1999.

Watson, Andrew D. *The American Mission in Egypt.* Pittsburgh: United Presbyterian Board of Publication, 1898.

Watson, Charles R. *Egypt and the Christian Crusade.* Philadelphia: The Board of the Foreign Missions of the Presbyterian Church of North America, 1907.

Watts, Simon, and Paul Stenner. *Doing Q Methodological Research.* London: Sage, 2012.

Weaver, Robert. *Grape Growing.* New York: Wiley & Sons, 1976.

Webster, William. *Syntax and Synonyms of the Greek New Testament.* London: Gilbert & Rivingtons, 1864.

Westcott, Brooke Foss. *The Gospel According to St. John: The Greek Text With Introduction and Notes.* Vol. 2. Ann Arbor, MI: Baker, 1980.

Whitacre, Rodney A. *John.* IVP New Testament Commentary Series 4. Downers Grove, IL: InterVarsity, 1999.

Wiersbe, Warren W. *50 People Every Christian Should Know.* Grand Rapids, MI: Baker, 2009.

Willett, Don. "A Biblical Model of Stages of Spiritual Development: The Journey According to John." *Journal of Spiritual Formation & Soul Care* 3, no. 1 (2010) 88–102.

Wilson, J. Christy. *Apostle to Islam: A Biography of Samuel M. Zwemer.* Grand Rapids, MI: Baker, 1952.

———. *Prophet: The Story of Samuel Zwemer.* New York: Friendship, 1970.

Young, Dinsdale T. Foreword to *Oswald Chambers: His Life and Work*, by Bertha Chambers. London: Oswald Chambers Publications Association and Marshall, Morgan & Scott, 1959.

Young Men's Christian Association. *Fifty Years Work amongst Young Men in All Lands.* London: The Botolph Printing Works, 1894.

Zerwick, Maxmilian, SJ. *Biblical Greek.* Rome: Editrice Pontificio Istituto Biblico, 1990.

Zwemer, Samuel M. *Taking Hold of God: Studies on the Nature, Need, and Power of Prayer.* London: Marshall, Morgan & Scott, 1937.